D0935693

VOICES IN THE PAST

ENGLISH LITERATURE AND ARCHAEOLOGY

VOICES IN THE PAST

ENGLISH LITERATURE AND ARCHAEOLOGY

John Hines

D. S. BREWER

First published 2004
D. S. Brewer, Cambridge

ISBN 0 85991 883 1

D. S. Brewer is an imprint of Boydell & Brewer Ltd
PO Box 9, Woodbridge, Suffolk IP12 3DF, UK
and of Boydell & Brewer Inc.
PO Box 41026, Rochester, NY 14604–4126, USA
website: www.boydell.co.uk

A catalogue record for this book is available
from the British Library

Library of Congress Cataloging-in-Publication Data
Hines, John, 1956–
    Voices in the past : English literature and archaeology / John Hines.
        p. cm.
Includes bibliographical references and index.
    ISBN 0–85991–883–1 (Hardback : alk. paper)
1. English literature – History and criticism – Theory, etc.   2. English
literature – History and criticism.   3. Archaeology and history – Great
Britain.   4. Literature and history – Great Britain.   5. Archaeology –
Great Britain.   6. Archaeology in literature.   I. Title.
PR25.H56 2004
820.9 – dc21   2003013807

This publication is printed on acid-free paper

Printed in Great Britain by
St Edmundsbury Press Ltd, Bury St Edmunds, Suffolk

Contents

Illustrations

Preface

I have enjoyed writing this book. It has been a long-held ambition to write an extended study which explores the scope for a thoroughly interdisciplinary approach to our human culture in the past: a book that might even offer itself as a manifesto for interdisciplinary historical and critical studies. In this, I seek to introduce archaeology to readers of serious literature, and literary criticism to all with an interest in archaeology. Beyond that, the aim is to integrate the two into a broader and deeper form of cultural history by considering a small selection of major works from English literary history within the historical, and in particular the material contexts from which they have come.

A brief *curriculum vitae* may explain how this has come about. After working as a field archaeologist, I took a first degree in English language and literature, focusing principally on medieval literatures and historical languages. As a postgraduate research student, I initially attempted to make a multidisciplinary study comparing and integrating the impact of Viking-period Scandinavian settlers in various fields of English culture: linguistic, literary, and material. But I did not then know how, conceptually, to do that, and so ended up writing a predominantly archaeological thesis on the connexions between England and Scandinavia before the Viking Period. I then spent fifteen years teaching English and Norse literature and language history at university level while continuing with research involving archaeology and making some exploratory forays into interdisciplinary work. Following a transfer to the School of History and Archaeology within Cardiff University in 1997, it is a pleasure to acknowledge the value of what seemed a much belated sabbatical year's study leave during 2001–2, which provided the opportunity to undertake the sustained research and writing, the results of which are presented here.

Not least of the pleasures of this enterprise has been the interest and encouragement of colleagues, and new acquaintances made in the course of this work. Direct and personal thanks are due to Lyn Blackmore, Julian Bowsher, Derek Brewer, Peter Coss, John R. Davis, Christopher Dyer, Catherine Gingell, Richard Ireland, Caroline Palmer, Malcolm Parkes, Elizabeth Rowe, John Schofield, Paul Stamper, Larry Trask and Alasdair Whittle for providing advice, criticisms and practical help, as a result of which many things are now put much better in the following pages than they would otherwise have been. An anonymous reader's thoughtful and constructive comments are much appreciated for helping me to express ideas and arguments with greater clarity. Ultimate responsibility for the views and the shortcomings in what follows remains, of course, with myself. What I hope above all is that the interest and pleasure that I derive from both literature and archaeology might be at least a little more widely shared as a result of this book.

John Hines
1 April 2003

The author has made every effort to trace the copyright holders for illustrative material within this book. Apologies are offered for any omission in this regard, and the publishers will be pleased to add any necessary acknowledgement in subsequent editions.

Prologue: Mere words?

This is Just to Say

I have eaten
the plums
that were in
the icebox

and which
you were probably
saving
for breakfast

Forgive me
they were delicious
so sweet
and so cold

William Carlos Williams
from *Collected Poems 1921–1931*
(New York: Objective Press, 1934)

FOR ME, the poem above succeeds as a delicate literary still-life. Like a painting of that type, it focuses on a single, immobile object: here the plums, grammatically the noun object of the first simple clause 'I have eaten the plums.' But although a visual still-life captures a moment of stasis, it does not do so without implying the continuum of time both before and after that moment, both of which are indeed essential to its effect. The edibility and the locked-in taste of the wine, fruits or game that are the most common subjects of still-life inform the imaginative response of the interested viewer, while at the same time the immanent, distasteful decay of these objects is nearly as immediately perceptible, particularly in those still-lifes (for example of the 17th-century Dutch school) where the painters habitually throw a musty sheen over the image. Likewise when we see fish, fowl or game animals depicted we are aware – often from the brightness of their sightless eyes – that these creatures are newly caught and abruptly killed. William Carlos Williams's poem subtly evokes the sensual qualities of the plums with its final epithets 'delicious' and 'sweet', appealing to both taste and sight, and 'cold' to taste and touch.

At the same time as it embodies these sensual qualities, the poem introduces a small set of characters in a vignette that differs from our typical still-life, in which the painter, besides being implicit in the existence of the painting itself, is usually represented only by an unobtrusive signature, and the viewer is anonymous: anyone or no one out of an infinitely changeable and unpredictable public. The poem is written in the first person (using 'I'), and this speaker has already eaten the plums. A direct utterance involving the pronoun *I* normally implies a *you*: the person or persons directly addressed by the subject referring to him or herself as 'I'. This anticipated readership for the poem may, of course, be as non-specific as the possible viewers of the painting; in this case, however, the implicit 'you' is individualized within the poem as the person, presumably singular, whose ownership of the plums is implied by the admission that he or she was probably saving them for breakfast.

There are then further inescapable and significant implications. This 'you' presumably also owns at least a share in the 'icebox', the other material object specified in the poem, in which the plums had been put, and therefore also of whatever house or apartment the episode would have to take place in. The relationship between the I and the you which allowed the event is left unspecified – whether they are partners sharing the living space and this appliance, or whether the I is just a visitor/guest there. The one additional clue we are given only tantalizes more, namely the elusive tone of the 'Forgive me' that opens the final stanza: a grammatical imperative that is supposed to be apologetic but is so often used as a sheer formality, and which here is neither clearly contrite nor triumphant.

This calls upon the reader to make further suppositions or guesses about the sexual-social aspects of the relationship between the two characters. It would not be mere chauvinism to construe the scene as one in which a male I has eaten a female you's plums. We know the poet to be male: the poem is from an edition of William Carlos Williams's *Collected Poems* – an author whose name emphatically consists of three masculine specifics. Whether or not one knows anything about William Carlos Williams's actual sexuality (he was in fact married to Florence [Flossie] Williams for half a century from 1912, despite having a number of extra-marital affairs), the same collection contains a number of unambiguously heterosexual poems. More subtly, and certainly most significantly in the immediate context, there is a deep conventional association of the housekeeper's role with the female, so that materially the kitchen is a classic instance of gendered space. In Frank Lloyd Wright's Usonian houses of the 1930s, for instance, the kitchen was placed at the hub of the layout, the 'command-post' of a model family living unit, significantly located immediately between the living room and the children's bedroom.[1]

Yet whatever context we consciously or subconsciously supply when reading and thinking about this poem, it is relatively unlikely to be one of typical family life in a nuclear family household. The implication of the you placing something in the icebox for her(?) own breakfast rather suggests a single household, invaded like the typist's apartment 'home' in T. S. Eliot's *The Waste Land* of 1922 (lines 215–48). Solitary people and single-person households are no peculiar feature of 20th-century and modern life, of course, although the atomization of society in this direction manifestly increased across this period, and is now

---

[1] Dell Upton, *Architecture in the United States* (Oxford University Press, 1998), 38–43.

widely and explicitly catered for architecturally by the provision of studio flats and the like. Materially, too, this is a trend that has been assisted by technological developments such as, not least, the electrically powered domestic refrigerator, allowing food storage that in turn enables the individual to shop less frequently and so frees time to make the one-person household unit more viable. This must have been a key factor in the shift from lodging houses for the single in cities, with communal eating arrangements usually presided over by a landlady, so familiar in 19th-century novels, to the private, self-contained, self-catering apartment.

It is all too easy, reading this poem now, to pass over the reference to the icebox as yet another instance of the sheer mundanity of both the language of the poem and of what it refers to. It is unlikely that many readers nowadays will suppose the icebox to be anything other than an electrical refrigerator. In the early 1930s, however, this appliance was still a novelty. It first appeared in the USA in 1913. The recorded number of sales in America in 1921 was 5,000 units; despite the Depression, between 1929 and 1931 it crossed the million mark and continued to rise towards three million by 1937.[2] Prior to the introduction of the electrical refrigerator, the American domestic icebox was simply a large insulated cabinet, kept cool by a block of ice delivered regularly by the 'ice man'. It was the early 1950s before it became more common to have a refrigerator than a simple icebox. In fact, we even have a memoir of William Carlos Williams's home and family life from his son William Eric, which locates an 'old icebox, *whence came the ice-cold plums of the poem*' (my emphasis) in an interestingly central position off the main (rear) entrance hall – paralleled by a linen closet on the upper floor. This description is thoroughly one of a traditional style of family house being steadily adapted to a growing and aging family of three generations, in relation to which the author's memories are particularly stimulated by the communal spaces of the dining and living rooms, and the unprescribed uses of the attic, which his father used for his writing during some ten years. A particularly telling comment is the declaration that the house stood 'as a buttress against the advance of commercial progress into our neighborhood'.[3]

The poem thus intersects with the material dimensions of real life through the reference to the icebox. Linguistically this is an ambiguous reference, in that the term could refer to either of two significantly different items. This ambiguity also crystallizes a tension between conservative pride in independence of, and even resistance to, the deterministic progress of a new, consumerist and commodity-dominated world, and the championing of modernism that is otherwise characteristic of William Carlos Williams's poetry. When it was written and published, outside of the poem (and the Williams family home), the ideals of the modern way of living were being strongly expressed, and quite literally

---

[2] *The Statistical History of the United States from Colonial Times to the Present* (New York: Basic Books, 1976), 695–7.
[3] William Eric Williams, 'Life with Father', in Carroll F. Terrell (ed.), *William Carlos Williams: Man and Poet* (Orono, Maine: National Poetry Foundation, 1983), 61–82, esp. pp. 65–70; first published in instalments in *The William Carlos Williams Newsletter* (later *Review*) between 1977 and 1982.

Lovely Modern Design
Super-powered "Package Unit"
Full 6-cubic foot size
About half usual price

A NEW COLDSPOT for 1935 and a
NEW Standard of Value in electric Refrig-
erators. By Value we don't mean just a
lower price. You will never appreciate the
Value offered in this COLDSPOT merely
by looking at its price. Here is all we ask:
Forget the price for the moment and consider this COLDSPOT purely in terms of
Quality. Study its Beauty. Check its features. Analyze it strictly in terms of what it
offers you. Then compare it with any other
refrigerator of similar size, selling in the
$250 to $350 class. We say that you will
find the COLDSPOT actually a *Better* refrigerator, *In spite of the Fact That It Costs Only
About Half as Much.*

USE YOUR CREDIT. You don't have to pay cash.
See Easy Payments Prices and Terms on
page at right.

All Prices for Mail Orders Only.

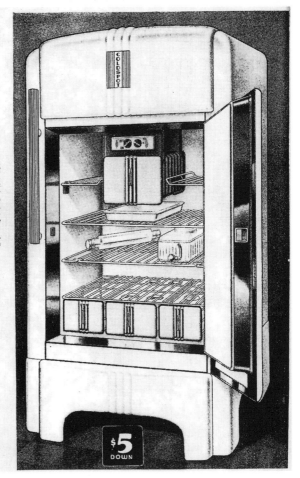

FIG. 1. Advertisement for the Sears Coldspot Super Six Refrigerator. Designed by
Raymond Loewy (1934). Sears Roebuck catalogue, Spring 1935, pages 576–7.

constructed, in material forms. This is exemplified not least in modernist architecture, a movement which became sufficiently well established to think of itself
as such at the beginning of the 1930s in Europe, although inevitably it had roots
running back several decades, particularly in North America. Technically one of
the key features of this new movement was the innovative structural use of new
technologies within buildings and new materials in construction, such as steel
frames and concrete. Socially, many modernist architects consciously sought to
harness the momentum of the sort of social changes referred to just above, and
to take control of their direction through the careful design and construction of
both domestic and public spaces in accordance with their own, usually more or
less broadly socialist, ideals.

Aesthetically, these trends were accompanied by an extreme preference for
plainness and simplicity, leaving surfaces and spaces open rather than (percep-
tibly at least) imposed upon. Amongst the values that influenced this attitude

was a desire for hygienic purity that infused far more of the work and ideas of architects and designers of the time than they ever seem to have realized. In an almost absurd way, the classic domestic refrigerator became central to this new, easier, happier, ideal way of living; and in the same year as William Carlos Williams published 'This Is Just To Say', the designer Raymond Loewy produced the classic design of his Sears Coldspot Super Six model, with its rounded corners in white or cream, and looking like something new and different from the standard box or store cupboard (Fig. 1). Thus, according to one historically realistic reading, William Carlos Williams's poem, implicitly embracing the potential of new technologies and showing indifference to conservative social anxieties, and in its assertive plainness and simplicity, really is a *thoroughly* modernist poem. It is all the more telling as an insight into lifestyle and writing in the early 1930s if, when we compare the specific history of the Williams household with the general history of the period, we may conclude instead (or as well) that Williams's poem actually recast his own domestic experience in this ideal modernist mode.

This particular poem has been a *cause célèbre* in arguments over the understanding and appreciation of self-consciously modernist English poetry of the inter-war period, and in the mid-1970s appeared as a significant example (albeit rather briefly discussed) in two influential books on modern critical theory, which at that time was on the verge of achieving the dominance it has held in British and American academic English studies through the 1980s and 1990s.[4] One of the essential views of literature in this self-consciously 'modern' school of literary and critical theory represents the culmination of a desire for and belief in the autonomy of literature (and with that of language, and of 'text') that has been handed down through many generations and in many different permutations. In simple terms, this view is that literature is a self-contained system, to be understood and discussed on the basis *only* of intelligent literary reading and an understanding of what literature is. Both Culler and Hawkes therefore focussed crucially on the 'disturbing' unconventionality, in literary tradition, of Williams's poem: formally it looks like a poem, not least by being published in an anthology entitled *Collected Poems*; but actually it consists of 28 words that could just as well, with the addition of punctuation, have been written out as prose. Even in their own terms, however, we may query the suggestion that the words are therefore intrinsically prosaic rather than poetic, and somehow *ought* to appear in prose – particularly, indeed, when we look at the many ways we might punctuate the final stanza as prose. More than anything else, though, the discussion of the poem offered above implies that it is anything but 'otherwise . . . a banal domestic piece', to use Hawkes's words. Domestic, yes; but absolutely invoking and embedding itself in a context in which domestic life was an issue not only of serious intellectual and moral reflection, but also of both conscious and unconscious material engineering.

Culler and Hawkes do not entirely miss this. Culler recognizes the importance of the personal relations between the I and the you, but goes on to deny that the world of notes and breakfast can be assimilated to language, as well as to assert that the eating of the plums 'cannot be captured by the poem except negatively'; while Hawkes insists even more strongly that the poem makes us think about the nature of the social conventions and processes of interpretation – although again he restricts the application of this thinking to language and poetry. What is most certainly not being claimed here by way of alternative is that, by being fully alert to the material and social implications of the text, we discover its true, hidden meaning, which had eluded these critics. At one level, the meaning of the text is no more than the meaning of the words, which (*icebox* notwithstanding) is clear and straightforward. Indeterminacy of meaning – a reluctance to impose or convey clearly defined messages – is very much a characteristic of 20th-century art in various media. It is undeniable, too, that the title Williams gave to the poem, 'This Is Just To Say', encourages and colludes with a reading of it as principally a reflection upon the conventions of language and

---

[4]   Jonathan Culler, *Structuralist Poetics: Structuralism, Linguistics and the Study of Literature* (London: Routledge & Kegan Paul, 1975), 175–6; Terence Hawkes, *Structuralism and Semiotics* (London: Methuen, 1977), 138–40. More generally, see C. Doyle, *William Carlos Williams: The Critical Heritage* (London: Routledge & Kegan Paul, 1980).

communication, and thus as an epitome of self-contained literariness. Williams himself rejected as 'just nonsense' one imaginative published reading, which claimed that 'the plums' death . . . is symbolically anticipated in the icy charm of their living flesh', and appears personally to have participated in a parodic transformation of a note or reply by his wife into a poem.[5] However Williams can no more control or deny the implications of his writings than he could create the world around him. His own *Collected Poems* published in 1934, in which this poem first appeared, abundantly confirms his deep thematic concern with architecture, furnishing, lifestyle and experience.[6]

A fully contextualized approach to Williams's poetry is consistent with the explicit attitude of the time that anything could be made into art (and thus into poetry). An important, if negative, aspect of this attitude was a desire to subvert the authoritarianism implicit in conventional 'high' art. Artistic movements such as Dadaism embodied this powerfully. One cannot be other than nervously aware that in discussing this poem in such sententious terms, one is making a great deal of a set of stanzas that are perilously close to the ironically vacuous parodies of E. Jarvis Thribb from *Private Eye*. There can, nevertheless, be an artistically mature tension between the everyday and its artistic transformation, as in the Cubist style of William Carlos Williams's day, that does not simply problematize art out of serious existence but gives it a special impact.[7] My own reading, offered here, in no way excludes or is incompatible with those of Culler and Hawkes, who approached the poem from a quite different, a *purely* literary, perspective. What we can claim is that the contextually informed reading, in this case depending crucially upon an awareness of the implications of the material world reflected in the poem, opens up many more, and significant, layers of meaning within and around it. These may not be the meanings of its words, but they are their conditions and show us just how much the poem represents. With that they bring us to a broader and deeper understanding of what is, for me, the generation of my parents' childhood. It is the intention of this book to make an extensive exploration of how the study of the material culture and the literature of various ages may profitably be integrated.

---

5   A. Walton Litz and C. MacGowan (eds.), *William Carlos Williams Collected Poems I: 1909–1939* (Manchester: Carcanet Press, 2000), 536.
6   See, for instance, 'This Florida: 1924'; 'New England'; 'The Attic Which Is Desire'; '8 Rain'; and above all '6 The House'.
7   Peter Halter, *The Revolution in the Visual Arts and the Poetry of William Carlos Williams* (Cambridge University Press, 1994), 80.

1

Text and Context

Material Culture and Archaeology

THE material remains of the past are a huge source of information. The academic discipline of archaeology is the study of these. The past, moreover, is the whole of time up to the present moment. A popular misconception is that archaeology is really only about the distant past, such as a prehistory inhabited by Stone-age hunters, or exotic, long-dead civilizations like those of Pharaonic Egypt or the Central American Maya. Archaeology inevitably does have a special role to play in providing us with knowledge of past contexts from which we simply have no written sources: circumstances which thus, in terms of how we define our academic disciplines, have produced no *historical* record. In the same practical way, the presence, absence or character of existing documentary evidence automatically affects the development and scope of what archaeology attempts to do in relation to different periods and places. But the breadth of archaeology is clearly shown by the fact that the archaeology of the Second World War has recently emerged as a significant field of study: reflected, for instance, by a TV programme in the popular *Time Team* series in 1999 devoted to the excavation of the wreck of an RAF Spitfire in Normandy.

There is a subtle but important difference between two otherwise straightforward ways of describing archaeology: that archaeology is the study of the past *through* its material remains, and that archaeology is the specialist study *of* the material remains of the past. In the former case, the material evidence, although essential, is treated as transitional: it is the route by which the scholar proceeds to a reconstruction or understanding of the past which itself transcends the window that has made that view possible. Used in this way, archaeology becomes a means of writing more, and even new, history. In the other case it is rather the intrinsic nature of what we frequently refer to as the 'material culture' itself that is the principal focus of scrutiny – asking why, for instance (if for any significant reason at all), physical products such as buildings, tombs, tools and utensils should have taken a particular form in particular contexts. This latter perspective is inherently more likely to direct the archaeologist towards comparative studies of different periods and places: to assess, for instance, the different scope for human activity with the technological capacities of the prehistoric Stone, Bronze and Iron Ages. Both of these are valid approaches to the evidence, and there is no reason to regard such uses of archaeology as anything but complementary.

As a complete academic discipline, archaeology, like history, seeks to combine knowledge of the past with an understanding of it. Understanding without knowledge is an absurd impossibility. Equally, understanding based on imperfect knowledge can only be flawed, so that no archaeologist (or historian) can afford to take a cavalier attitude to the factual details of the evidence upon which the subject is founded. Correspondingly, knowledge without under-standing, a sheer accumulation of facts placed in no sort of bigger picture, is sterile. Understanding therefore involves the production of more general, even abstract, propositions about the past, which will on the one hand subsume, but at the same time explain, the evidence upon which they are based.[1]

Reconstructions of the past of a general kind are often called 'models', and can take a variety of different forms and levels of complexity: from, for instance, the inference of a specific historical event, such as a Viking raid on a Scottish coastal monastery that was apparently deliberately destroyed during the 9th century, to elaborate systems such as comprehensive structures of economic and social relations. Without seriously oversimplifying the situation, however, we can point to the concept of *culture* as something that is crucial to the general-izing ambitions of archaeology. This particular aspect of the concept of culture – otherwise a truly multifaceted term[2] – has its origins in the empirical recogni-tion that groups of people may do certain things in habitual, even regular, ways. Vital to the recognition of these habits as cultural is the premise that the partic-ular action is variable – it *could* be done in a different way. Biology determines that we must eat and drink in order to live. But what we consume, where we do it, when and with whom, are all culturally specific. Archaeologically, the constituent elements of a culture-group will be definable types or ranges of types within the material record from a coherent area and period: such as specific artefact-types, building-types or burial-types.

There is a small set of further ideas fundamental to the theory of culture. These are applied in seeking to interpret the bundles of consistent cultural prac-tice that may thus be observed, but not without themselves being put to the test as premises at the same time. The first and foremost of these is the notion that superficially distinct features of habitual practice are in some way inter-related, and so do not occur merely as random selections from the whole range of possi-bilities. If this is true, it means that manifestations of the culture are determined by deeper constraints, and that what is observable on the surface is representa-tive of a deeper cultural structure or pattern. We may take as an example a prop-osition for which the present author is responsible, namely that the appearance of new and distinctive dress-fasteners in a certain area of northern Germany along with a gradual shift from the cremation of the dead to the inhumation of

[1] The term 'hermeneutic circle' or 'spiral' refers to the potentially paradoxical process of trying to differentiate between some object of particular study and its general historical context in order to use the latter to understand the former better, when the object itself is part of that general context and contributes to our perception of it.
[2] See Terry Eagleton, *The Idea of Culture* (Oxford: Blackwell, 2000).

unburnt bodies in the 4th and 5th centuries AD represents an intense stage in group (ethnic) redefinition, in relation to which controllable aspects of the body – how it was clothed *and* its manipulation as a dead and decaying object – were assertively used as the principal modes of expression.[3] Whether or not this specific hypothesis is correct does not, just at the moment, matter: it is an example of how the evidence of artefact history on the one hand and funerary practice on the other may be integrated within a broader culture-historical inter-pretation.

This example also serves to illustrate a second key supposition about archae-ological culture, namely that elements of material culture and actions involving the production and use of physical objects are *meaningful*: not just in the sense of transmitting information about the past to the present-day archaeologist who observes them, but also meaningful to people within their original contexts. It is a special case when we can talk about the straightforward symbolism of material objects which denote group-association or identity in the manner of either a 5th-century Saxon woman's brooches, or the crucifix, rosary and habit of a Roman Catholic nun; although we must not, conversely, underestimate the importance of sheer convention in material practice in reinforcing group soli-darity, even if it takes no more articulate form than habitually drinking tea at a certain time of day rather than coffee. A particularly rich seam of meaning that has been identified and explored in recent archaeology resides in the way in which people, as groups or as individuals, may interact with their material culture and with one another through their material culture. These interactions incorporate the material world into a series of dynamic negotiations.

Let me try to give a familiar example. If I were to place a pair of my shoes in front of you and ask you 'What do these shoes *mean*?', I should not be surprised if you were to regard the question as incomprehensible, and even to show some impatience at the sort of academic dottiness that imagines there is something to be gained by wasting the time of people of robust good sense in such a way. Shoes do not make statements in the way that, say, a wedding ring or a regi-mental tie do. The shoes would be useless to me if they did not serve a purely utilitarian function, keeping my feet relatively clean and dry, and enabling me to move around, especially out of doors, in comfort. The type of shoes, however – men's lace-ups with leather uppers and synthetic soles, as opposed, say, to moccasins, sandals or sealskin boots – at least implies something about my place in the world, demographically and geographically, while a closer, forensic study might reveal that they are of British make, or bought at a British shop, or repaired with replacement heels and soles of British manufacture.

None of that would make me, their owner and wearer, necessarily British. But the fact that my well-worn shoes are of this type rather than, say, suede slip-ons, fashionable trainers or some jazzy bichrome numbers, is a semi-conscious expression of my character, and of the image I wish to present, as indeed is the fact that I keep a very small number of pairs of shoes repaired rather than having

---

[3]   John Hines, 'Culture groups and ethnic groups in northern Germany in and around the Migration Period', *Studien zur Sachsenforschung*, 13 (1999), 219–32.

a wide selection, worn less frequently, or simply buy a new pair whenever the old ones start to leak. It is thus not just the intrinsic character and qualities of my particular shoes that are meaningful rather than purely functional; it is also a matter of what I do with them. If I intermittently appear with them smartly polished but more often wear them slightly dull and scruffy, this may be either because I am extremely busy or because I take only limited care of my appearance in this respect – perhaps both of these. If they are unfailingly gleaming, or constantly dirty, the implications are different. Also significant of my character and attitudes, and an intrinsic part of the organization of my domestic life, is whether I put the shoes regularly and neatly away in a specific place when I come home, or leave them lying haphazardly around in the hallway, kitchen or bedroom.

The point is not so much that the objects accidentally betray information about what part of the world I live in and what income group I probably belong to, as that I have a series of choices about how I treat these objects; moreover these choices literally *matter*, and mean something to me and to those around me. These meanings are not so much contained within the actual artefact, as would be the case with the symbolism of a pendant cross, but are generated through the inter-relationship between object and context: a context made up of people (the wearer, and an observant society, habituated to making assessments of individuals on the basis of their self-presentation through dress) and of other material circumstances: the home, public open spaces and the office; alternative forms of footwear; even other garments of hues that may or may not 'go' with the shoes. This illustrative example is deliberately trite. But if we can recognize such a diversity of facets of meaning in such a mundane case, it should be easier for us to appreciate that more complex artefacts, in more serious economic, social and ritual contexts, are likely to bear much more important meanings.

The past century has seen extensive scholarly discussion of the phenomenon of meaning. This arose particularly in the study of language, emerging in the form of what are known as semantics and semiotics. Both terms derive ultimately from the Greek root σῆμα (*sēma*), 'sign': in practice what they represent overlaps considerably, although in general *semantics* focuses principally on the structures and forces operative within the range of meanings, the 'signified', while *semiotics* concentrates more on the structures and forces within the range of signs, the 'signifiers'. Even though these analyses were developed in the context of linguistics, descriptive textbooks of the subject almost invariably introduce and illustrate the various types of sign and signification using familiar examples from the material and active world rather than from language itself.[4] One may argue from this that the material world is not only being used to provide concrete and easily recognizable analogies to linguistic sign-systems, appropriate for use at a nursery stage of learning the science, like the pictures supposed to educate the illiterate in a medieval church. There may rather be an unconscious recognition that the sign-system of the material world embodies

---

4   Thus even Umberto Eco, *A Theory of Semiotics* (London: Macmillan, 1977). See, for instance, pp. 22–9.

some sort of fundamental, real, and universal essence of sign-use in human culture; something that may even, in an absolute sense, be pre-linguistic.

In practice, the study of meanings in material culture has concentrated on a certain range of themes. Categories of information, or 'semantic fields', of particular importance in social relations have had the lion's share of attention. There are many studies examining the expression of identity or association with a social group through material forms – groups that may be ethnic, social classes, gender-specific, age-related, occupational, and more. Assertions of status and power may similarly be embodied in material culture. In their simplest form, these social statements are open signals, broadcast generally to the world at large. Statements made in a material form may, however, reflect quite different social configurations. Gift transactions are more likely to be directed, one-to-one statements. And at the personal level, the intransitive state-ment, the use of material culture for self-definition, directed at one's own subjective satisfaction at self-government and control, should not be discounted simply because it is of individual rather than social concern. Association with an individual can indeed be a meaningful attribute that imparts a special value to the object, as well as the other way around – witness the public interest in 'mem-orabilia' associated with public figures. At a more private level, souvenirs and associations with loved ones can be highly cherished.

An important dimension of the study of meaning for a discipline like archae-ology, which looks back across time, must be the way in which meaning can change. We have seen how meaning can be different in different contexts; from period to period variation of meaning can crystallize into absolute historical change. There are particularly interesting examples of this that we can catego-rize as examples of *appropriation*: the taking over of a specific set of material objects from one context and using them to different effect in another. A clear though intrinsically transitory example of this is the way the high-fashion industry exploits elements of the dress- and body-styles of many different groups – such as the exotically ethnic; the military; drug-ruined 'subcultures' etc. A more substantial and long-term example that has been recognized in recent years rather more fully by traditional social historians than by archaeolo-gists is the development of sports such as football and boxing, which have followed a course of development from demotic festivities and shows located almost entirely within the working material environment, with little or no special equipment or dedicated spaces, to elite pastimes, refined, codified and cultivated in public school gymnasia and playing fields, and on to popular spec-tacles, staged in monumental stadia and serving as a route to wealth and fame for a lucky talented few irrespective of their social background. Meanwhile sportswear is having its own enormous impact on the clothing and fashion industries.

In the end, though, perhaps the most inescapable aspect of meaning residing in material culture is the way in which culture as a whole serves to embody or promote (although it can equally well defy) a dominant ideology. Thus our sports stadia, whether showing live action or broadcasts played on giant televi-sion screens, inculcate and enforce a value-system comprising competition, winning, ranking and league tables, high technology, globalization, playing by

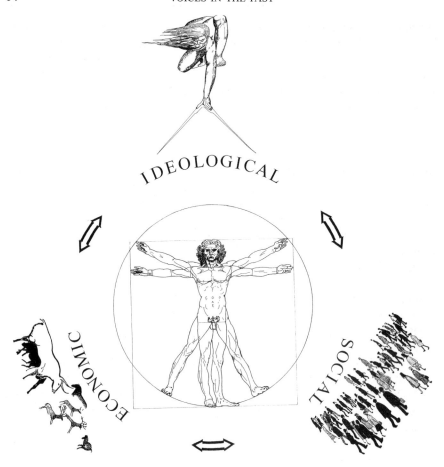

FIG. 2. A functional model of human culture: three inter-connected zones of
ideological, economic/technical, and social culture mediating between Man
and the enviroment. After the Lascaux palaeolithic cave paintings, Leonardo da
Vinci, William Blake and L. S. Lowry.

rules (albeit rules that can be changed by the authorities), refereeing, youth,
outstanding physique, public acclaim, and so on and so on. It is only typical of a
dominant ethical myth-system that this ideology of sport should ambiguously
balance conflicting values such as individual excellence and team-spirit.

  Throughout all of the above, it is implicit that human culture is not just a
curious foible of human nature but rather is essentially *functional*. To many
cultural anthropologists and archaeologists, indeed, function has appeared to be
the key to an overall understanding of culture. Culture has been defined, for
instance, as 'an extrasomatic [external to the body] means of adaptation for the
human organism'.[5] A diagrammatic model of culture that may be a little more
lucid can be achieved by dividing the culture that mediates between Man as

5   Lewis R. Binford, *An Archaeological Perspective* (New York: Seminar Press, 1972), 22.

species and as individual and the exteriority to which he must adapt into three basic zones: the economic or technical, for the relations between Man and the natural environment; the social, for relations between Man and fellow Man; and the ideological, as the relationship between humanity and its world of ideas and visions – its real or imagined spirit world (Fig. 2). Any one zone of culture can thus impinge upon, influence and be influenced by any other; and variation and change may arise either from changes in external circumstances or from the human centre.

As archaeology is essentially the study of the past, it inevitably has a deep interest in the passage of time. From this perspective, it becomes clear that cultural solutions to human needs or desires are not endlessly created afresh but rather are passed on, in cultural traditions: indeed the inertia of cultural tradition can prevent people from making the most effective response at certain points of need. Other definitions of culture accordingly stress the *learnt* nature of the distinctive and consistent configurations of practice of the type referred to above as culture-groups. Archaeologists still commonly simplify the task of discussing the past in such terms by talking about *the [N] Culture*, incorporating the term 'culture' within a proper noun. Inevitably this begs the questions of precisely how unitary and consistent a particular culture-group, or Culture, is within itself, in relation to its population, and in its geographical and chronological extent. In most cases, however, such terms are now used circumspectly enough to serve their purpose as a valid shorthand way of referring to distinct configurations of practice traceable in the material record.

Archaeology may thus be identified as itself a feature of contemporary culture: it is an intellectual way in which we engage with the existence and substance of physical evidence of the past. It too bears the imprint of its own tradition, which can either constrain what we do or provoke (but still thereby influence) reactions in the practice of archaeology. As an intellectual pursuit, moreover, archaeology can hardly be exempt from the influence of current ideology, or ideologies competing for dominance, from the conservative to the determinedly radical. We should not, however, underestimate the degree to which archaeology has developed as a passive or 'objective' response to the presence of remains of the past rather than as a purposeful extension of some wider ideological agenda. Looking back practically throughout human cultural history, we can not only detect a constant awareness of physical remains of the past but also responses to those which are essentially creative.

Archaeology is consequently no new invention. We can trace the development of the subject as we know it in its modern guise over at least the past three centuries, for instance from 1707, when the Society of Antiquaries of London began meeting. The systematic excavation of archaeological remains also began in the 18th century, at that time directed by gentleman scholars, often clergymen. A particularly significant formative stage for modern archaeology in Britain was the 19th century, which saw the foundation of many local (often county-based) societies, often with revealing names such as the *Loamshire Natural History and Archaeology Society*. These societies saw their goal as the systematic and thorough investigation and understanding of what materially constituted their own part of the world. It was widely assumed that common sense and experience were sufficient to identify and interpret archaeological finds and their original contexts, and in this way the archaeology of the time was inescapably a reflection of its own age. Prominent monuments like Stonehenge have an understandably prominent place in early archaeological (alias antiquarian) scholarship, while stray finds unearthed in digging or by accident tended to make their way into collections of 'curiosities'. But the antiquarians and early archaeologists were considerably less inclined to prescribe what, within the archaeological record, counted as being of interest or not than is sometimes suggested.

In responding to the material and thus deciding where to focus further investigative efforts, certain value-systems were nevertheless influential. One of these was an evaluative scale from high to low, between civilization and barbarity or primitiveness. It is easy, and justifiable, to associate this in the 17th to 19th centuries with the dominance of the Classical languages and literatures in the educational system, inculcating a powerful sense of superlative standards of material achievement in what we call the Ancient World, reinforced by massive monumental constructions from that date still visible over large parts of Europe. We should note, however, that this classicism was itself a symptom of its historical circumstances, and thus as much a parallel product as a cause of this intellectual attitude. To the Ancient Greek and Roman kernel other civilizations – Egyptian, Persian, Oriental, for instance – could be added, or contrasted. A predictable concomitant of such a keen appreciation of the extraordinary feats of the ancient past was a sense of loss of capacity, a falling off from those heights of achievement. As a framework in which human history was viewed at that time, this had a powerful, non-Classical counterpart in the Biblical concept of the Fall.

A sense that human culture could progress up a scale of quality and capability, albeit in a quite contrary direction of evolutionary advancement through time, was also very much in the minds of people of the 17th and later centuries who were conscious of the advances in mechanics and industrial processes in their own time. Such a model was most clearly generalized for human development with the delineation of the Three Age system, identifying Stone, Bronze and Iron Ages in human prehistory, by a Danish archaeologist, Christian Jürgen Thomsen, in the early 19th century. The three Ages were ostensibly defined by the predominant and technically most demanding material worked by the populations of each epoch to produce their tools. We should not see the lapsarian and evolutionary models of human history as intrinsically contradictory though. Having fallen, one can rise. The Three Age system was introduced in a context in which public ideology fully endorsed the Biblical creation story and with it that of the Fall. Not until these were displaced could there be any concept of *pre*-history. The term *prehistoric* is not, in fact, recorded in English until 1851.

The prehistoric and historical story of the ascent and descent of Man was dramatically expanded and rewritten from around the mid-19th century. Yet the belief that a relatively secure chronological framework, together with general human experience and intuition, were the best foundation for identifying and interpreting archaeological material, were to remain firmly in control for a good century more. It was eventually to give way to radical questioning, challenges and changes that have marked the rise of 'theoretical archaeology' since the 1950s. This movement has seen two quite contrastive schools of thought successively enjoy periods of dominance. The first of these, which particularly flourished in the late 1960s and 1970s, enshrined a doctrine that we have already noted as adopted in its own way by literary studies: that archaeology was an autonomous science – no mere ancillary to an as yet unreformed discipline of history. This school of thought is known principally as New Archaeology (already now an ironic misnomer) or 'processualism'. It postulated and then sought to verify the existence of laws peculiar to the phenomenon of material culture. It spoke of 'process', which in its simplest sense meant a recognition that the material remains were likely to be incomplete and only superficial reflections of deeper currents which caused and produced them. Thus it tilted the balance from a careful dependency on the particular archaeological evidence from which one might attempt to infer historical explanations, to extensive patterns of archaeological circumstances that could be claimed to form the whole that can be the only object of a full explanation. A processual cycle is closed in the materialist way this school preferred when it is seen that the material products emerging from these processes themselves modify the initial situation and so condition further action in a form of potentially perpetual motion.

The merits of this phase of theory were both constructive and destructive. It introduced a refreshing diversity of explanation, largely inspired by recent anthropological analogies, to the examination of the archaeological record; at the same time it expelled easy assumptions, for instance about ethnic and cultural links, that belonged to an increasingly anachronistic set of ideological values. Unfortunately and inevitably, however, it was not long before one set of dogmata was simply replaced by another, and on the whole this period of transition in archaeological theory undermined considerably more than it could put back in the space created.

But a period of transition it proved to be; particularly unsustainable was its intensely impersonal materialism, and a hostility to intuitive common sense that all too readily moved beyond critical scepticism to a preposterous contrariness according to which nothing could ever be allowed to be as it seemed. The major subsequent theoretical shift was to what is generally known as 'symbolic' or 'post-processual' archaeology. For some archaeologists this has meant little more than a covert reintroduction of humanist interpretations of the material; for others it represents logical progress in the theoretical transformation of the discipline to one in which explanation is a more sophisticated matter. Symbolism as a perspective prefers to relate 'action to its sense rather than behavior to its determinants',[6] thus making a further shift in emphasis from cause to impact. As has already been noted here, though, the deepest problem is the practicality of how we can actually unlock, and then express, the meanings or 'sense' of the past. It seems impossible to steer an effective course between the Scylla of intuition on the one hand and the Charybdis of analogy on the

---

6   Clifford Geertz, *Local Knowledge: Further Essays in Interpretive Anthropology* (New York: Basic Books, 1983), 34. For a comprehensive introduction to Geertz's influential and seminal work in cultural anthropology, see also *idem, The Interpretation of Cultures: Selected Essays* (New York: Basic Books, 1973).

other. The first of these constrains past contexts to be like what we imagine
them to have been, and the other to be the same as something we know separately (or imagine we know separately). Symbolic archaeology has proved
stronger in identifying systems of signification than in explaining what these
signs mean.

This does not mean that archaeology has become stuck in an insoluble theoretical fix, in which archaeologists can at best revert to talking knowledgeably
about specific sites and finds, hoping to interest themselves, one another, and
the general public in them, whilst helplessly out of their depth in trying to relate
these to any sort of coherent bigger picture. That archaeology is a fluid and challenging subject, with parameters and horizons that may not be fully mapped but
can at least be identified with good sense, makes it a field of study that is
exciting and full of potential. Besides its developing theoretical and methodological dimensions, archaeology is virtually unique amongst disciplines
concerned with the past in that its basic source of information is constantly
changing and growing: new finds are made at a faster rate than most archaeologists can cope with, while it is very rare indeed for hitherto unknown historical
or literary documents to be discovered. There are abundant possibilities to be
explored and real progress to be made within archaeology, even if the ultimate
end of the enterprise is not fully foreseen in terms of both what one should
discover and how one should discover it – truly a Doomsday scenario.

In this book, we shall look at aspects of the material cultural history of
England from the earliest times in which one can refer to an area as England, the
Anglo-Saxon Period, to, in archaeological terms, the quite recent period of the
mid-19th century. In doing so, we shall encounter a range of topics within
archaeology, from broad landscape archaeology to the archaeology of human
settlements and architecture and the necessarily smaller scale of focus on
portable artefacts. At the same time it should become clear that in many practical respects archaeology operates as a sort of coalition of different branches of
specialist knowledge, reflecting the diversity of the material record. Nevertheless, under the definitive formula first suggested to describe archaeology, a
knowledge and understanding of the past concerned with its material culture,
these skills have to be deployed so that they produce a sharable general understanding of the context they are applied to. What is more, this must apply to the
relations between archaeology and the adjacent cultural/historical disciplines as
much as to those between archaeological subdisciplines. It remains true that one
can only properly 'do' archaeology by knowing and understanding its own
domain: the material evidence, and archaeological methodology and aims. But
archaeology can still – *easily* – communicate with other disciplines, and it is on
this basis that this interdisciplinary study is undertaken.[7]

---

[7]   Recommended further reading on the topics discussed here is Bruce L. Trigger, *A History of Archaeological Thought* (Cambridge University Press, 1989); on symbolic archaeology, Ian Hodder, *Reading the Past:
Current Approaches to Interpretation in Archaeology* (Cambridge University Press, 1991); for an up-to-date
introduction to archaeological theory, Matthew Johnson, *Archaeological Theory: An Introduction* (Oxford:
Blackwell, 1999).

Literature and Criticism

Literature is a sophisticated human product, and thus a distinctive part of the cultural whole. Literature may be defined as art in the medium of language. Like culture, language is a universal attribute of the human population; the mere possession of the language faculty – an ability to use and understand natural, vocal language – cannot by itself be counted a cultural trait. But the particular language(s) one speaks, the range of registers one can use within them, and the purposes to which they are put: all these are cultural variables in the sense just explained.

The inter-relationship between material culture and language has been the focus of much interesting research and discussion. Amongst the topics considered in the process of trying to give an account of the evolution of human language – *evolution* being a contentious choice of term in itself, although generally used in the sense of the emergence of language as opposed to its creation or improvement – is that of at what point activities materially attested to in the archaeological record must imply a language faculty equivalent to that of known natural languages.[8] By the latter is usually meant a mental ability to classify phenomena into categories, and then to refer to these symbolically through the use of verbal signs. What can be talked about must include actions and relations as well as objects. Examples of activities that have been proposed to presuppose language include the appearance of regular styles of design for early stone tools; the establishment of trading relationships; and the ability to organize migratory movement, especially when involving boat-construction and lengthy voyages over open sea. At a much later stage, there is at least a case to be made that the crystallization of language in material form – through writing – may itself modify the actual grammatical structures of languages, for instance by promoting the syntactical patterns known as relativization (clauses like 'the book, *which you are reading now* . . .').[9] An important implication of all this is that there is no reason why literature in its most basic character – an artistic use of language – should develop any later than a socially shared material culture.

Literature may exist in both oral and written forms. In absolute terms, the latter is the later invention. The oldest scripts that are written representations of natural language (as opposed to non-linguistic graphic symbols) appeared about 5,000 years ago; in the case of many communities and languages for which the introduction of literacy is historically observable, we can find in the earliest literary writings formal features characteristic of a preceding oral literature. Writing has a considerable range of possible functions, of course, and it is apparently seldom the case that the production of a written literature in the language concerned is the first purpose and result of the creation of a written

---

[8]   Steven J. Mithen, *The Prehistory of the Mind: A Search for the Origins of Art, Religion and Science* (London: Phoenix, 1998).
[9]   Suzanne Romaine, *Socio-Historical Linguistics: Its Status and Methodology* (Cambridge University Press, 1982).

form of the language. One can make that claim better for the establishment of durable bureaucratic records and instruments of administrative control.

Without endorsing any crude notion of the evolution of literature from a single point of origin of such a politically self-interested kind, it is easy to understand that even in those circumstances the force of rhetoric is inherently likely to be deployed in various ways in the written texts – to threaten, to cajole, to deceive, to inspire – with the result that both between and within the several functions of writing a diversity of literary types, or genres, comes into being. These genres are categories of text whose defining characteristics must include both a contextual dimension – records of rent or tribute payments are kept to be consulted at certain times, and places, and in predictable circumstances; monumental inscriptions are intended to be read in other circumstances – together with certain textual peculiarities that distinguish one category of writing from another purely by literary form. In creative, especially modernist writing, these categories can be deliberately disrupted – not least in the poetry of William Carlos Williams, as we have seen – but on the whole we would rightly feel there was something odd (or a special point being made) if someone's epitaph were laid out like a summary of their tax accounts.

The shift from orality to literacy as the dominant mode of art in discourse meant a shift from performance to reading as the way in which literature was encountered. It is not, of course, a simple either/or matter. In the case of England, we know that written literary texts were commonly read out loud, by one person to a group or even one person to him or herself, as the dominant method of their enactment and experiencing throughout the Middle Ages and well into modern times. There are certain forms of literature, such as song and drama, that are, although written, intended primarily for performance rather than for silent, private reading and contemplation. Nonetheless, the development of written literature – the preservation of literary art in forms in which its future readers cannot be entirely foreseen or controlled – introduced a separation between the ostensible source of the literature and its recipients that was of crucial importance for the development of literary criticism. While we cannot confidently assert that the concept of authorship was born with that of readership – oral tradition is perfectly capable of quoting the words of specific individuals – it is easy to see how authorship could take on a new importance as a category associated with a literary text when the performer-audience relationship became less normative.

It is the new, or extra, space around literature created for the reader by literacy that promotes literary criticism. Pausing briefly to dismiss the unfortunate and pejorative connotations of the word 'criticism' that suggest it principally involves earnest discontentedness and supercilious fault-finding, let us first put in that place a more favourable characterization of criticism as a form of reading aloud. The literary critic who does not read entirely privately reads literature publicly; not simply in the way that different performances can re-interpret, vary the emphases within, or even absolutely modify nominally single texts, but in sharing with others thoughts and ideas dependent upon the reading of literature. While criticism has its own oral forms – not least in school and university lectures and seminars, and in radio and television broadcasts –

literary criticism has for a long time been predominantly a body of writing about writing. With less licence than the director of a stage play, however, the role of the critic remains generally that of the reader rather than that of one trying to supplant the writer. The critic is an essential assistant, perhaps, but not one who is trying to do the writer's job better for him or her.

Literature can serve a wide range of functions – to entertain, to inform, to edify, or to move. In some cases, the purposes for which the literature was originally produced are readily identifiable. They may even be explicitly stated along with or as part of the text. In other cases they are less so. Likewise we have texts whose intrinsic meaning ranges from the clear and unambiguous to the obscure and difficult. Linguistic semantics recognizes a number of different, concurrent categories of meaning. Most basic is the *conceptual*, e.g.:

man = [MALE/NOT FEMALE; ADULT/NOT CHILD; HUMAN/NOT ANY OTHER SPECIES]
woman = [NOT MALE/FEMALE; ADULT/NOT CHILD; HUMAN/NOT ANY OTHER SPECIES]

Another major category is the *associative* or *connotative*. A simple case of this is the association of the word *bird* with wings and flight, a set of connotations that is strong enough for a surprisingly large number of respondents to tests to identify a bat as a more typical example of a bird than a penguin or an ostrich. This is the range of meaning where the specific cultural context can be most obtrusive, and even controversial, as for instance if terms such as *woman* or *womanly* are taken to imply conventional stereotypes of feminity like wearing a skirt or dress, or having maternal instincts. A further significant category is the *collocative*, whereby phrases such as 'a handsome woman' and 'a pretty woman' differ in respectively implying a conventionally masculine form of attractiveness (smart, with non-ostentatious dress and grooming) and conventional femininity (colourful, expressive, delicate). There is also the *emotive* or *affective* range, whereby to different individuals and in different circumstances to actually refer to a woman as either handsome or pretty could be either a welcome compliment or a serious impertinence. In a similar way, William Carlos Williams's poem is, according to the reading suggested at the beginning of this chapter, conceptually transparent but more complex in what it connotes and represents. It is within such areas of uncertainty, and above all in the face of complexity, that the critic becomes involved.

Three principal and complementary exercises that constitute critical activity are interpretation, analysis and evaluation. Interpretation means the exploration and explication of details and complexities of meaning, like those alluded to just above. With the passage of time, the semantics of the text tend to become obscure as the meanings of words change – even the word *icebox* from a poem published in the 1930s – and allusions and implications of the words and sentences become less obvious without access to a secure frame of reference. Some literature – James Joyce's *Finnegans Wake*, to take an extreme example – is deliberately written in a disconcertingly difficult style. In such circumstances it is hardly likely to constitute valuable criticism for a critic to produce explications of the kind 'What Joyce really meant was . . .': to supplant the author, and re-word the text for him, as it were. But it is obvious that informed, specialist guides and commentaries can be an aid to reading. Interpretation need not always involve scholarly learning. But interpretation comes first amongst the critical exercises for the simple reason that we need to know what the text is and contains before we can do anything more with it.

Analytical procedures are, of course, involved in the interpretation of literature. But an important and further area of analysis as a critical procedure is that which moves to a much wider range of investigation and explanation of the role of the text relative to its external circumstances. This can involve contextualizing it historically (*historicism*), to account for its production: an exercise that is likely to be able to lead in many different directions through the range of economic, social and ideological history as well as through the more specialized sequence of literary tradition and influence. It is an approach that can involve further information about the author, either in the form of non-literary biographical records or of that author's other writings; this may very well reveal cultural or psychological forces operating upon the author of which the author him or herself was apparently quite unconscious. But analysis can also and equally be concerned with the post-production reception and impact of the text. With a shift of emphasis from cause to effect parallel to that in symbolic archaeology, recent critical approaches have sought to focus upon reading as much as writing, showing that reading cannot simply be construed as a passive, neutral exercise, merely receiving the text as a fixed and unalterable object. As reading and criticism are essentially one and the same, every reader is an interpretative critic, construing the text (consciously or not) as seems right or best to him or her.

If one looks the term *criticism* up in a standard English dictionary, one will find 'judgment' and 'evaluation' usually given as its primary sense. Another aspect of the recent triumph of self-consciously 'modern' critical theories has been the large-scale rejection of evaluative literary criticism of an older fashion, which assessed literature primarily against scales of value running from 'major' to 'minor' or even 'beneath serious notice', and 'good' to 'bad'. Only to a relatively limited degree have alternative evaluative scales been promoted in place of what can be dismissed as such conservative conventions, for instance in the case of Marxist or feminist critics' preference for and praise of texts that they read as furthering their political ideology and aims. It can be argued, however, that this resistant reaction to what has all too often been a series of ideological elites' imposition of their own, self-interested, aesthetic standards has gone too far in dismissing evaluation altogether; and that in particular it loses sight of the point that a sense of quality may be an intrinsic feature of art itself. While the relevant criteria of judgment may never be absolute, and will certainly vary hugely, it does always matter in the end whether the artwork in question is any good by at least *some* applicable criterion or not. It would be a truly worthwhile challenge for critical theory to try to understand this persistent idea of quality scientifically; and to do so should not reinstate only 'great' literature as worthy of critical study.

The criteria by which a work of literary art is evaluated are necessarily reflexes of the culture that produces them. As critical reading is an intrinsic feature of the existence of literature, and continuing critical reading is a continuation of the history of literature and criticism, the history of criticism is also part of the history of culture which archaeology seeks to uncover and understand from the material record. The specific values that art embodies in its own special way in cultural history can therefore be found both implicitly in the history of art, and explicitly in historical critical writings (reminding ourselves once more that 'historical' means the whole of the past up to the present moment). The most basic issues assessed in critical evaluation are, however, actually both simple and largely constant: they comprise the aims or role of the text, which may non-judgmentally be allowed to be decided by the author, or contrastively themselves be evaluated in ideological/political terms; the methods or style by means of which the text works towards this purpose; and finally its success in meeting those aims, which can be measured by critical comparisons with other texts that appear to attempt to fulfil equivalent functions. To put it succinctly: What does the text try to do? How does it go about this? How successful is it? Of course, none of these aspects is necessarily an obvious and unambiguous feature of every work of literature; many critics both in the past and the present would unhesitatingly praise complexity and subtlety over direct and simple transparency of purpose and technique.

The place of evaluation in criticism draws attention to an important cultural role of literature – and at the same time reinforces the functionalist concept of culture by indicating that literature is not just phenomenologically *there*, whether we want it or not, but that it has a purpose to serve. This function is to enhance the totality of cultural life – noting again that 'cultural life' means much more than the rarefied, esoteric experience of aesthetic indulgence: rather the whole of the way the human population lives, economically, socially and ideologically. This can be achieved both by maintaining the accessibility of literature produced in the past, which may involve substantial investment in education, not least where long obsolete languages are concerned, and by creatively producing new literature. An obsession with quality judgments, battling over exact positions in some sort of league table of literary merit, is not the spirit of good criticism; but an acceptance of the sense of value in the whole literary process, and beyond that a recognition of the cultural value of literary value, most certainly is.

Although it is literary criticism with which this book will be concerned, criticism as described here need not be limited to literature any more than it is applicable only to 'high' art. By defining literature initially as art in the medium of language, we might be accused of producing the deferral of meaning typical of any attempt to describe what something substantially and essentially *is*: we have simply displaced the problem of definition on to another term. Just what, then, is art? The modern conceptualization, or 'sense', of art sees it all too often as a category of the superfluous, the redundant, and the decorative: something that really isn't needed in any practical, functional sense. But the terms *art*, *artifice* and *artefact* have a common root. Historically in the English language (up to the late 18th century, in practice), *art* was actually the term for practical skills and *science* that for purely speculative, intrinsically inapplicable ideas and knowledge.

Art, therefore, is hardly distinguishable from culture *per se*, in so far as it comprises all action and interventions that shape and change the raw material of that which surrounds us, be that in turn from nature or the gift of cultural tradition. It is far from difficult for an archaeologist to comprehend all technical artefacts – from stone hand-axes to bridges and massive shipyard cranes – as essentially works of art at the same time as they are highly utilitarian tools or structures, irrespective of whether or not there was any idea of art in existence at all, let alone consciously applied, when they were made. It is not a great step from here to a realization that all linguistic discourse could be regarded as literature – with the possible exception only of some totally invariable, spontaneous utterance such as, perhaps, a cry of pain or delight.

It is nevertheless implicit in all that has just been said, that we recognize a spectrum of categories for cultural products, running from the predominantly utilitarian at one end to the primarily artistic at the other. That the two characters can co-exist, as in the form of some artistic embellishment of a thoroughly practical tool, in no way subverts the conceptual distinction. This distinction need not be universal in human cognition, although it is, and probably always has been, common. It has consequently been declared in literary theory that, while of course there would be no category of literature without literature in some concrete form, i.e. art in the medium of language, equally essential to the existence of a category of literature is the *idea* of literature. From this, it follows that it is an act of criticism itself to determine where the boundaries between literature and the remaining whole of linguistic discourse lie.

Especially in a book like this, which deliberately discusses a broad range of types of literature from diverse historical contexts, the question of how closely our modern categorization of the literary coincides with that of the past becomes quite an urgent one. This is, however, truly more of a theoretical than an actual difficulty. Many types of literature are clearly marked by formal devices such as rhythmical metricality, grammatically distinctive syntax and diction, or topics and compositional structures that recur non-randomly to characterize genres. Literature, as a result, simply is not difficult to identify. What would, however, be unjustifiable would be to assume that other periods would break up the discursive spectrum in the same way as we would – for instance that in the Anglo-Saxon Period, Old English manuscript poetry, vernacular sermons, and the letter King Alfred of Wessex prefaced to the English translation of Gregory the Great's *Cura Pastoralis*, would all have been assigned to any single category other than that of mere writing (*englisc gewrit*) along with records of property transactions. The most distinct artistic category in this historical context appears in fact to have been poetry, recorded in Old English as *scop-gereord* or *lēoþweorc*, literally 'poet-voice' and 'songwork' respectively: terms that interestingly reveal the continuing influence of a prototypically oral conception of literature.[10]

---

[10] It is important, however, to note that the first known instance of one of these terms in Old English uses the phrase *in scop-gereorde* as a result of a need to translate the Latin *verbis poeticis* ('in poetic words'), in the 10th-century English version of Bede's *Historia Ecclesiastica Gentis Anglorum* (Ecclesiastical History of the English People), Book IV, chapter 24. *lēoþweorc* likewise occurs only as a gloss for Latin *poesis*, in Ælfric's *Glossary*.

Actually, there is no practical difficulty even in this case in tracing a clear chain of associations between all of these examples of Old English writing, which justifies our grouping them into a corpus of Old English *literature*. Alfred's letter is linked to a number of translations into English of explicitly educational and homiletic purpose which bridge the period from Alfred's reign in the late 9th century to the flowering of vernacular sermon composition under Ælfric and Wulfstan in the late 10th/early 11th centuries. Many of those homilies, in turn, are written in such a highly rhythmic and metrical prose that it has been a serious matter of discussion whether they should not properly be regarded as a species of free and loose verse. What do form an awkwardly marginal range between between the literary and non-literary categories are certain ostensibly utilitarian texts, such as recipes, charms, charters and chronicles. The key distinction appears to be one of the relative functional importance of the contents and the form of the text respectively. Non-literary is the category of text whose information context is primary while the form does not matter as long as it is legible. For the literary category, the form in which the text is presented is indispensable to its cultural impact. Style and structure may vary within certain parameters for literary works, but cannot do so freely and open-endedly. A Modern English prose translation of *Beowulf* can never substitute artistically for the Old English poem itself, but a paraphrase of culinary recipe can practically do just as well.

We shall see, in the course of this book, how in the modern world our sense of a real opposition between creativity and utility, between art and implement, are subject to the influence of a radical dissociation of what was recognized as most meaningful in intellectual and spiritual terms from the material world at the birth of what we call the modern era. These are challenging ideas, with profound implications, and a reader could now be forgiven for feeling that much of what has just been said makes a mockery of the previous assertion that literary criticism should not be feared to be synonymous with high-brow solemnity. We have claimed that criticism is, at heart, no more than the act of reading; but an act of reading that can be made more valuable, and above all more enjoyable, by being thoughtful and informed, and shared through open discussion. The position adopted in this book is fundamentally opposed to any notion that there is only one way to read literature properly. The more innovative critical approaches which it embodies are, first and foremost, to read literature in light of the material circumstances of its production and transmission, and secondly to re-instate evaluation as an essential and explicit feature of critical practice. In relation to conventional literary criticism, then, the purpose of this study – and its justification, if it is successful – is to open up a wider range of critical possibilities. With that, it should enhance the contribution of literature to our own cultural life.[11]

---

[11] As further reading on the topics discussed in this section, Terry Eagleton, *Literary Theory: An Introduction*, 2nd ed. (Oxford: Blackwell, 1996) can be recommended, particularly as a *critical* review of development of literary theory and criticism over the past century.

Interdisciplinary Cultural History

We have now seen that there is a close and deep affinity between material artefacts and literature as products of human cultural activity. There is an equally close affinity between the scholarly disciplines dedicated to the study of this pair of fields. Archaeology involves the same exercises of interpretation, analysis and evaluation as literary criticism, although the terms are normally understood differently within the two disciplines, so that conventional archaeology would usually invert the sequence at the beginning, and insist that analysis is the primary exercise, and must precede interpretation.

The difference is in fact scarcely even a terminological one: rather a matter of emphasis. For the archaeologist, faced with 'mute' material remains, consciously structured analytical procedures are vital to establish the basic facts of the object of study; although it subsumes its own forms of analysis, this process is more appropriately called interpretation when dealing with semantic layers and complexities of meaning in an ostensibly directly communicative text. What in archaeology is 'interpretation', meanwhile, is what we have also called 'understanding' (as supplementary to 'knowledge') or, simply, building the bigger picture: contextualizing the basic material in the same way as the expansive analytical stage of literary criticism does. Yet perhaps even more than in modern literary criticism, archaeology in its post- (even anti-) Great Civilizations mood is intensely disinclined to evaluate cultures of the past. In so far as it is deeply concerned to evaluate itself – a highly pragmatic exercise, since practical archaeology is a much more expensive pursuit than practical criticism – as well as to explore value-systems in the past, however, archaeology is directly involved in precisely what literary criticism at least *could*, and in the present author's view *should*, be doing.

Literature and material culture have been linked in cross-disciplinary perspectives by a number of scholars in the past. Regrettably, these initiatives have overwhelmingly been highly selective in relation to cultural history: in some cases because they are reasonably specially focused; in others, though, because the linkage of the two subjects really is superficial and brief, not a deep and lasting partnership. A further restricting factor has been an understandable tendency to turn consciously to the historical context for help only in reading literature from the relatively distant past.

The most widely developed schools of interdisciplinary cultural history of recent times have emerged in France, with, understandably, a particular interest in topics from the Francophone world. The most accessible and probably the most familiar of these scholars has been Jacques Le Goff. Le Goff's work represents a culmination of several generations of interest in the mundane daily life of the past (*l'homme quotidien*) which – less paradoxically than might initially seem – constitutes a *longue durée*: a steady, only slowly developing, set of conditions that have too often been regarded as too banal to be worthy of attention, either in contemporary records or by later historians concerned with major events in the history of the world. The demotic, the unspectacular, even the inconsequential in the human past are valued nonetheless for being substantial, real, and representative of the mass of people who have lived.[12]

Le Goff's studies are a fine advertisement for what can be achieved in interdisciplinary historical studies without either imposing daunting doses of philosophy on the reader or demanding equally daunting levels of expertise in more than one academic field of the practitioner. At the same time they thoroughly reinforce certain limitations of perspective that this book will try to push beyond. Despite what he claims, Le Goff never really gets involved in archaeology: he is interested in the material phenomena and conditions of life in the past he studies, but draws his information about them overwhelmingly from textual sources rather than from the material remains themselves. And although his work includes outstanding discussions of relationships between what appear as the outer points of a triangular set of profoundly different forces, comprising the court (high culture), the outside (a natural world) and the phenomenon of urbanization, he persistently finds the positive associations between different manifestations of culture largely in the refined and esoteric contexts of court and ecclesiastical life. His own implicit defence against this criticism is to argue that the life of the Church was socially comprehensive, not exclusive, and so can be taken as representative of medieval life.

At first glance utterly different in character from the accessible and conservative Le Goff is Michel Foucault. As a propounder of cultural and historical theory that has stimulated scholars in many different academic disciplines to consider and respond to his work, he has been one of the most challenging and influential cultural historians of recent times. Part of the attraction has been the radical and innovatory character of his writings, although they are a clear example of the forceful narrowing of perspective on past culture. While Foucault's reflections upon this field defy easy summary, they are at least clear and consistent in ultimately prioritizing the human mentality associated with what he sees as a series of phases of the post-medieval past, and in relation to which 'power' is the topic that principally attracts his attention. For Foucault, culture lies between a set of inherited fixed forms – material facts, words of a language – and a realm of pure science or absolute truth, a set of ideas that purports, in Olympian detachment, to account for the essence and order of all things. Culture is of especially intellectual interest because it becomes, or just *is*, conscious of those intrinsically inert parameters, and so of how they can be appropriated and modified. An 'archaeological', as opposed to 'epistemological', approach to history emphasizes the vital role of unconscious habits of thought, presumed knowledge and an acceptance of the supposedly given form of the world in maintaining coherency in cultural life. Foucault's *archéologie du savoir* ('archaeology of knowing') is a study meant to account for the conditions that underlie such thought and knowledge in specific contexts.

Although he works with a similar concept of culture, as a network of

---

[12] Recommended reading for a substantial introduction to Jacques Le Goff's work are two volumes of collected essays, both translated into English: *Time, Work and Culture in the Middle Ages* (trans. A. Goldhammer; University of Chicago Press, 1980) and *The Medieval Imagination* (trans. A. Goldhammer; University of Chicago Press, 1988).

inter-relationships between material culture, language and text, Foucault's archaeology is quite different from our concept of archaeology. His archaeology is focused upon phenomena that have already been made abstractions, not a discipline indissolubly tied to its own material domain. And an irreconcilable difference between these two models of culture is that in Foucault's idea-oriented and -dominated system, Man is only of interest as a concept and thus as a product of culture rather than as a form and, in absolute terms, the producer of culture. 'It is a reassurance, however,' writes Foucault, to conclude the Preface to *Les Mots et les choses*, 'and a deeply soothing thing, to think that Man is merely a recent invention, a figure less than two centuries old, a particular twist in our knowledge, and that he will vanish as soon as the latter has found a new form.'[13] Now it is not a revolutionary idea that the *perception* of humanity, and in particular the relationship between Man and science both as a subject (i.e. as scientist) seeking to order the world, and as an object in reflexive studies (i.e. the 'humanities': not least anthropology, archaeology and history), has had a distinct and historically specific form since Enlightenment rational philosophy was superseded by scientific modernism in the mid-19th century. Yet this rhetorical assertion is deliberately provocative rather than comforting; and the main reason for that is the frustrating indifference to historical sequence characteristic of Foucault's approach. Whence science, and where, if not produced from and in Man, irrespective of what Man thinks of himself?

So idiosyncratic is Foucault's cultural history that the very notion of a Foucauldian school strikes one immediately as impossible. Yet Foucault remains intriguing and stimulating. The effective aspects of his writings are not so much the theory, which in so far as it is credible is not distinctly Foucauldian, and where it is distinctly Foucauldian is not in the least bit plausible, but his empirical studies, exploring the cultural ramifications and significance of, for instance, 18th- and 19th-century clinics and prisons.[14] However, to dismiss Foucault's theorizations of his historical readings in this way is not the prelude to a general rejection of theory *per se*; rather the first stage in a theoretical reassessment. Indeed one of the most hamstrung manifestations of the integrated study of archaeology and literature has been the virtually theory-free illustrative

---

[13] 'Réconfort cependant, et profond apaisement de penser que l'homme n'est qu'une invention récente, une figure qui n'a pas deux siècles, un simple pli dans notre savoir, et qu'il disparaîtra dès que celui-ci aura trouvé une forme nouvelle': Michel Foucault, *Les Mots et les choses: une archéologie des sciences humaines* (Paris: Gallimard, 1966), Préface, 15.

[14] Recommended reading for a fuller encounter with Foucault of relevance to the discussion and context here is M. Foucault, op. cit. in note 13: English trans. A. Sheridan, *The Order of Things: An Archaeology of the Human Sciences* (London: Tavistock, 1970); *Archéologie du savoir* (Paris: Gallimard, 1969): English trans. A. Sheridan, *The Archaeology of Knowledge* (London: Tavistock, 1972); *Surveiller et punir: naissance de la prison* (Paris: Gallimard, 1975): English trans. A. Sheridan, *Discipline and Punish: The Birth of the Prison* (New York: Vintage, 1977); *Power/Knowledge*, ed. and trans. C. Gordon *et al.* (Hassocks: Harvester, 1980). Referring to the original French text and titles is not a mere affectation, even though, as Chris Tilley effectively observes, Foucault is known in the Anglophone world very largely in English translations, and 'Foucault, then, is the proper name we ascribe to a series of texts . . .': C. Tilley, 'Michel Foucault: towards an archaeology of archaeology', in *idem* (ed.), *Reading Material Culture* (Oxford: Blackwell, 1990), 281–347, on p. 287. It is crucial for as full as possible a comprehension of the Foucault phenomenon to realize how difficult it is to translate his writings, which in French are linguistically playful, and difficult enough to pin down, into English. Even the term *archéologie* had quite different connotations in the Francophone world of the 1960s than English *archaeology* at that time, let alone nowadays.

mode, depending upon connexions that are immediately obvious where the literature refers to something that archaeology happens to have found, or vice versa.

A disappointingly clear and familiar example of this within the field of English studies is the '*Beowulf* and Sutton Hoo' syndrome. The striking and extensive coincidences between the material world in which the action of the Old English epic *Beowulf* is set and the material-cultural phase brought emphatically to the forefront of Anglo-Saxon archaeology by the excavation of the Sutton Hoo mound 1 ship burial in 1939 have given rise to a number of authoritative, descriptive accounts of the parallels, that only draw ever greater attention to the absence of any real idea of what one might actually make of them. By default, the archaeology and literature link here is assigned a role – not one to which it is particularly well suited – in the controversy over the date of the poem.[15] Ironically, the importance of this date (if there ever were such a thing) would lie precisely in its ability to contextualize the poem, not only in relation to other Old English literature, which is the limit of interest of most specialists in Old English literature, but historically and archaeologically as well. More regrettable still is the fact that this focus on dating surreptitiously reinforces the misconception that archaeology is only really useful when one is dealing with remote, and usually ancient, contexts, which leave the date and provenance of works of literature in doubt. We don't need archaeology to date Chaucer's works, therefore we don't need to consult archaeology in reading Chaucer.

While this particular problem is created by dependency upon direct correlations between literary references and archaeological finds, there is an effectively similar range of work that refers to the one field precisely and only to fill the gaps in the other. Thus *Beowulf* and its manuscript do not give us an indisputable date for the poem; archaeology might remedy this deficiency. (It doesn't, in fact.) This approach has most recently seen its richest developments in a Scandinavian school of multidisciplinary cultural history, using archaeology and medieval Germanic literature as its principal components. Scholars have turned to Old Norse and other early literatures to supply a well-defined and explicit body of ideology, comprising religious beliefs and practices, social ideals and rituals, to explain, explore and vivify the relevant archaeology and art history of what in the Scandinavian chronological scheme is the later Iron Age and Viking Period.[16] While in a general way these approaches are more constructive than simply describing direct correspondences between the material record and the literary, it is far from the case that archaeology and literary sources will always be able to complement one another in the ways or to the extent one might wish.

---

[15] For a general critique of these issues, see J. Hines, '*Beowulf* and archaeology – revisited', forthcoming in C. E. Karkov and H. Damico (eds.), *Constructions of Wood, Stone, and Ink: Studies in Honor of Rosemary J. Cramp* (Kalamazoo: American Medieval Assoc.).

[16] Lotte Hedeager, *Skygger af en Anden Virkelighed: Oldnordiske Myter* (Denmark: Samleren, 1997); *eadem*, 'Myth and art: a passport to political authority in Scandinavia during the Migration Period', in T. Dickinson and D. Griffiths (eds.), *The Making of Kingdoms*, Anglo-Saxon Stud. Archaeol. Hist., 10 (Oxford University Committee for Archaeology: 1999), 151–6, and 'Sacred topography: depositions of wealth in the cultural landscape', in A. Gustafsson and H. Karlsson (eds.), *Glyfer och Arkeologiska Rum – en Vänbok till Jarl Nordbladh* (Stockholm, 1999), 229–52; Frands Herschend, *Livet i Hallen* (Uppsala: Institutionen för arkeologi och antik historia, 1997); *idem*, *The Idea of the Good* (Uppsala: Institutionen för arkeologi och antik historia, 1998).

Indeed, as far as the pre-Christian Germanic religion goes, there are severe problems concerning the evidential value of mythological texts that may virtually all be substantially distorted by Christianity. This can be an effective approach to the study of specific historical issues, but as a general model for interdisciplinarity it carries us no closer to a situation in which archaeology and literary criticism will always and necessarily complement one another. Moreover the specific topics that have been explored again tend to marginalize the useful interface between the two ranges of cultural activity, by linking them to esoteric zones of human behaviour: iconographic art, religious ritual, and exclusive social contexts.

The implicit surrender to the view that archaeology and literary studies are really good for quite separate things is neither unreasonable nor difficult to understand in light of the fact that, as we shall repeatedly see in this book, the relationship between the literary and material cultures is often one of opposition. What is meant by this is that literature tends to be idealistic, and so to distort or even to deny material and economic facts of life, however important these were in reality. The idea that literature forms part of a 'superstructure' which, in bourgeois/non-socialist cultures and societies, consistently seeks to avoid the truth of material power relations in the economic and social 'base' is a classic tenet of traditional Marxism: a model of cultural relations which, although falling rapidly from favour over the last decade, has been one of the most distinctive and influential theoretical positions of the 20th century. One might have expected, therefore, that the critical correlation of literary production and its material circumstances would be a field that Marxism has already fully explored.

However, to judge by one very recent general summary of Marxism as applied to the study of literature and culture, one could justifiably doubt that Marxism exists any more.[17] This presentation of Marxism is so careful to divest it of its now discredited materialist dogma, together with most of the at best clumsy, at worst barbaric, totalitarian political consequences that it had, that Marxism is left with nothing much more than a general interest in the social and economic conditions in which literature has been produced and which it may directly or indirectly reflect, plus a rather vague and certainly now thoroughly passive left-wing allegiance: producing little more than sloganizing and verbal sniping at such hot political issues as the *Daily Telegraph*'s portrayal of striking coalminers in the 1980s. There may still be people who call themselves Marxists, but they seem now to be the equivalent of regular churchgoers devoid of any belief in God or the tenets of the Christian faith. The terms of the current study might be quasi-Marxist, then, but if so, that reveals how far Marxism has loosened its definitive boundaries and characteristics, not some accidental or covert embrace of Marxism.

There is, moreover, at least one core feature of classic Marxism that has survived unscathed, and which does stand as a significant difference between that school and the standpoint of the present study. This concerns the issue of

---

[17] Moyra Haslett, *Marxist Literary and Cultural Theory* (Basingstoke: Macmillan, 2000).

materialism. The disagreement in approach is not, however, simply a matter of an – actually needless – rejection of what Marxist apologists disingenuously call the 'vulgar Marxist' myth of blanket material determinism, whereby everything finds its explanation as a virtually automatic outcome of economic forces and Man is reduced to an automaton. On the contrary, it is the criticism that, despite its much vaunted 'materialist dialectic', Marxism has actually proved pretty poor at comprehending the material world. It is overwhelmingly interested in structure and system instead – in production rather than in products. Marxist archaeologists have made some excellent analyses and interpretations of past economic and social systems. But they are no better on the actual artefacts than any other school of archaeological thought – indeed are rarely very interested in or expert on specific categories of artefact. A comcomitant of this position is that Marxism tends to create 'material' categories to remedy the deficiency, hence claiming materiality for essentially immaterial categories such as language and culture.

The paradigm of the base-superstructure 'dialectic', meanwhile, remains an over-determinative dogma within Marxism. In literary and cultural study this manifests itself particularly in a constant suspicion, indeed a presupposition, that ideology, which is promulgated through literature and art as well as other forms of ritual, takes the pernicious form of distortion, and so serves to maintain social control by generally distracting, confusing or repressing the lower classes to the benefit of the higher. As the comments on the role of public sport above should show, I am far from unsympathetic to such a critical stance. What is a particular problem when this is built into a Marxist literary criticism is the sort of axiom formulated by Haslett, discussing the criticism of French Marxists Louis Althusser and Pierre Macherey, that 'What is significant in a text is . . . what it does *not* say or is unable to say . . .'.[18] Can this historicist approach to literature therefore have no interest in, or nothing positive to say about, harmonies and consistencies between text and context? If this really is as far as it can aim, the prospect is unappealingly formulaic, reductive and pessimistic.

Realism is an artistic style that has been strongly associated with Marxism – in both its theoretical-critical and its political manifestations – but this is an appropriation. Versions of realism were around long before Marxism, and while realism – and the sort of modernism of William Carlos Williams's poem – are of particular interest to Marxist criticism, it does not have a monopoly on such interest. From our point of view, realism is just one optional style – or rather a range of optional styles, for there is certainly more than one form of realism. As in the case of 'socialist realist' art, realism and idealism can co-exist, ironically or not, just as a utensil can also be a work of art. We shall find some aspects of the realist-idealist relationship to be of considerable interest within a broad cultural history of English literature. But the interdisciplinary approach is not restricted to a special interest in realist literature. The mid-19th-century resurgence of realism was a response to Romantic idealism. However Romanticism was itself a radical response to reality; a reality which remains, therefore, just as

---

18 *Op. cit.* in note 17, p. 67.

pertinent to an understanding of either form of artistic expression.[19] Far more important, from our perspective, than whether literature is realist or idealist is the simple fact that all literature is *real*, and became so within a particular context.

This tangible presence of literature – or, more generally, of texts – has emerged at the focus of interest in a recent wave of deeper thought about the practices of 'historical archaeology'. The latter is defined here quite simply as archaeology relating to contexts for which there is also a substantial documentary record. These reflexive initiatives have come from archaeologists working primarily in two fields: western and northern Europe of the later Middle Ages and early post-medieval times; and European colonial settlements in Africa, America and Australasia. While historical archaeology can comprise much earlier contexts, such as Ancient Egypt, Greece and Roman Italy, there has thus been a particular concern to establish effective ideas about what archaeology can do in relation to relatively recent periods, and familiar places.

An important article by David Austin from 1990 emphasized the point that a central concern for both medieval history and archaeology had to be the transformative power of the text in its original context; we should therefore not innocently regard the historical document as merely a window through which we gain an image of past reality, but rather as part of that reality itself.[20] Such too is a prominent theme of John Moreland, who is particularly concerned with the materialization of text through the post-medieval introduction of printing, and the intense Protestant emphasis on the Book and the Word – which, as he notes, coincides intriguingly with a general proliferation of artefacts and commodities.[21] Reflecting the primacy of identity amongst the semantic fields of cultural symbolism noted above, he focuses particularly on how 'people in the past wove their identities from the threads provided by written, spoken and material discourses'.

In concluding a more broad-ranging book on historical archaeology, Anders Andrén suggested a general division of artefactual-textual relationships into three basic categories, which can be described as object-centred, text-centred, and balanced.[22] The former category is a feature of contexts where orality is still, or has recently been, the dominant mode. Its characteristics are that texts are considered very much as material objects, with concrete effects in the world, and textual commentaries on material culture are prominent. This model fits the case of *Beowulf* remarkably well. Unfortunately, the other two categories, which should reflect the majority of situations in which we can correlate material culture and literature, offer rather fewer substantial or significant links between the two. In respect of the balanced or 'integrated' context, Andrén notes exam-

19 Cf. Eagleton, *op. cit.* in note 11, 139–40.
20 David Austin, 'The "proper study" of medieval archaeology', in David Austin and Leslie Alcock (eds.), *From the Baltic to the Black Sea: Studies in Medieval Archaeology* (London: Unwin Hyman, 1990), 9–42.
21 John Moreland, *Archaeology and Text* (London: Duckworth, 2001).
22 Anders Andrén, *Between Artifacts and Texts: Historical Archaeology in Global Perspective* (New York: Plenum, 1998), esp. 150–3.

ples of texts replacing artefacts, for instance in legally binding social exchanges, or interassociations between text and artefact in the form of monumental epigraphy. In a text-centred culture, our attention is drawn to material culture being created from writing, as in the form of visual iconographic symbolism.

Once again, then, we end up somewhat boxed into a corner. The situation is fundamentally no different with Moreland and Austin's discussions, however, which are more concerned with what we have assigned to a category of non-literary texts and documents than with literature *per se*. Moreland directly challenges what he calls the relegation of archaeology to a place among the 'bottom feeders', concerned principally with the technology and subsistence of the demotic mass, but his outlined solution to the challenge of combining texts and material culture into a whole cultural history again tends to the art-historical, for instance discussing the fate of 'images of cult' under the Reformation. He dislikes the historical and modern academic hierarchy that contrasts the elite, the historical and the elaborate with the peasant, the archaeological and the gross, but his answer is to claim a higher place up the ladder for archaeology, not to seek to collapse the hierarchy.

At the same time as archaeology has been reaching out to literary theories and materials in such ways, literary criticism has shown some willingness to re-embrace historicism. At heart, literary historicism is a concern to understand how a text may have functioned in the specific historical milieux from which it has derived or through which it has passed; and how, concomitantly, it may add to our understanding of those circumstances. Simultaneously it explores how such contextual information may affect our critical reading of the text. Rather than being pursued in a naively trusting way, a keen historicist reading will seek to understand who claims to be speaking for whom in a given text, and how they may (mis?)represent their situation. One might have thought that these reciprocal developments in historical archaeology and literary historicism could have resulted in a real meeting of the disciplines, but regrettably they have missed each other by a long way.

At the heart of what has called itself 'New' Historicism lies a concept of the 'textuality' of the past. This is based upon the premises that the past is only knowable to us through texts, and that therefore the theories and methods of textual analysis (literary criticism) are all one needs (as well as being what one essentially needs) to study and write history. Any idea of distinct material, archaeological evidence for the past is swept up into this all-embracing perspective by the doctrine that there is no reality that is not mediated through language and thus textualized: a position that is often presented as an *a priori* truth with the stark assertion that 'language constructs reality'.

This position is an unfortunate recrudescence of propositions concerning the nature and importance of language that characterize several strands of 20th-century scholarship and philosophy. These include linguistic structuralism, and the linguistic anthropology of Edward Sapir and Benjamin Lee Whorf, together with the logical positivism of Ludwig Wittgenstein and other philosophers. The proposition that language constructs reality is, however, a myth – although not least mythical in being a rhetorical approximation to an important truth. Language constructs only an image of reality, and has only a marginal

conditioning effect on thought.[23] Most people are perfectly well able to distinguish reality – especially material reality – from the linguistic image and its
structuration when it matters, and languages indeed constantly adapt to
changing material circumstances. In fact all languages appear to be equally
usable in any circumstances, although this is perhaps not true for all speakers,
some of whom may be handicapped by being able to express themselves only
through restricted codes or *paroles*. Culture creates a far more tangible and
determinative reality than language, while language, which is itself a cultural
variable, will encode cultural rules and values. It is consequently not a harmless
metonymy but a seriously misleading fallacy to assert that culture and history
are textual, rather than that textuality is just one manifestation of culture.
Culture remains the abstract but unifying whole behind the tangible and familiar
media in which it subsists, language and material life. It has no existence separate from its manifestations in these forms, but is equally implicit in both.

The work of the medieval literary scholar Lee Patterson can be held up as an
example of good recent historicism.[24] He recognizes that the past almost
certainly is far less securely known, and was far less consistent, than modern
historians may think, although still too real to be broken down into the subjective selection-box that extreme New Historicism would make of it. While
rejecting that form of reader-centredness, however, he does emphasize the role
of the modern historian-critic as a participant observer in the (re-)creation of the
past. For reasons that are not entirely clear – or at least not obviously necessary
– he insists upon the contemporary *political* (rather than cultural) significance
of this critical activity. This is an approach that marries history and criticism
without seriously swerving from sound, and conventional, historical practice. As
in the case of Jacques Le Goff, literary historicism of this kind continues to
restrict itself to documentary sources, and so to consult history rather than
archaeology as a means of contextualizing the literature. This partially explains,
although it is also a consequence of, a predominant interest in relating past literature to social history, just one aspect of the culture-historical whole.[25] A newer
development in the area of Renaissance studies linking historicism to
psychoanalytical criticism has differed only in narrowing the focus of attention
even further, to a preoccupation with anxiety, sexuality and peculiarity.[26]

It is the ambition of this book to see how much wider the bounds might be
set. Presumptuous though it may be, this is undertaken in the firm belief that the
potential of such interdisciplinary studies remains enormously under-realized.
Archaeology and literary criticism can be regarded as fundamentally compat-

---

[23] John A. Lucy, *Language Diversity and Thought: A Reformulation of the Linguistic Relativity Hypothesis*
(Cambridge University Press, 1992); *idem, Grammatical Categories and Cognition* (Cambridge University
Press, 1992).
[24] Lee Patterson, *Negotiating the Past: The Historical Understanding of Medieval Literature* (Madison:
University of Wisconsin Press, 1987).
[25] E.g. Gabrielle Spiegel, 'History, historicism, and the social logic of the text in the Middle Ages',
Speculum, 65 (1990), 59–86; Helen Barr, *Socioliterary Practice in Late Medieval England* (Oxford University
Press, 2001). Barr does, however, make substantial use of the evidence of art and objects associated with the
court of Richard II: see esp. pp. 63–105; also this volume, 109–10.
[26] See Carla Mazzo and Douglas Trevor (eds.), *Historicism, Psychoanalysis, and Early Modern Culture*
(London: Routledge, 2000).

ible, both in their domains and in their methodologies. That might, indeed, create a danger of their being too similar for anything to be gained from conjoining them. They have to be more than alternative routes to the same destination – the direct and scenic options, if you like. They have to take us somewhere new: but that does not have to be to a situation in which we feel alien and ill-at-ease.

Even with a whole book at one's disposal, the approach to demonstrating what may be done has to be to try to select a small number of strongly illustrative examples. To avoid any implication that archaeology and literature are only mutually illuminating in special cases, the following chapters offer discussions of texts and topics drawn from across the history of English literature. These form a series of stepping stones from the foundations of England, past the Norman Conquest and the High Middle Ages, to the turbulent and drawn-out transition between what we now recognize as the medieval and modern eras, ending up closer to home in the industrialized Victorian Period. With this it is also possible to cover a broad spectrum of literary types from narrative poetry to the lyric, theatrical drama and the novel. The facets of material culture discussed cover the colonization and moulding of the landscape, places of habitation both rural and urban, and the production and exchange of artefacts.[27] A consideration that is essential to the archaeologist, namely the way in which the survival of material evidence is shaped by the way past societies used their inventory of material culture, runs throughout these discussions.

What this seeks to constitute is a comprehensive cultural history of a hitherto undeveloped kind. By reading archaeology and literature together it is possible both to understand and to appreciate the complexity, and what is often the coherency, of a past that is made more open and more richly available to us than if approached in a more selective manner. The conjuction of these two perspectives can be shown to shed particular light on what things meant in the past. The material context can be argued to be genuinely fundamental to linguistic and thus literary semantics, while the literature can reveal much about the value and meanings of objects. The material world does not only impinge on the meaning of literature in the form of what is referred to, however; it also constitutes a context in which literature is performed. Performance in this sense includes private reading, but can be most readily appreciated when imagined in the form of vocal performance or acting.

With an extended historical perspective, it becomes especially apparent how literature and material culture become directly involved in processes of change over time. As with their relation to the abstraction that is culture, they do not just represent historical processes in a detached way, but are amongst the very media in which those changes take place. Most excitingly, their participation in the course of history extends to their use for critical and active responses to what was happening: at times endorsing and encouraging changes; in other cases opposing and even redirecting them.

---

[27] As in the present chapter, no prior specialist knowledge of the periods of history, archaeological topics, or works of literature discussed is assumed on the reader's part. Selected further reading is suggested in every case.

There is an optimism at the heart of this enterprise which, if realised, will itself be positive outcome and novelty enough. The aim is to do more than to see the text simply as an object, or to treat everything as merely textual. The past should not be represented as virtually *only* a series of struggles for power or prestige between social groups and classes, or as an endlessly gloomy tale of repression and crisis, any more than the interdisciplinary study of fields such as material culture and archaeology should be thought only to be useful in respect of the more arcane aspects of human experience such as art and religion. It has, however, been a common response from literary scholars to readings of the kind collected here to have expected them to be more dramatically innovative – to deliver more surprises. Quite pragmatically, it is better to err on the side of caution than to alienate specialists within a particular field by making extreme claims that long-held and reasonably based understandings are seriously deficient. What this approach offers is not a replacement, but a substantial reinforcement and extension of monodisciplinary literary criticism. The reinforcement falls largely in the stages of interpretation and analysis, affecting the meaning of texts, while encouraging new and wider explorations of the impact of literature in its historical contexts, as of the significance of material practices. The greatest extension, meanwhile, may be held to be in the area where both archaeology and literary criticism as we know them today are shyest: in respect of evaluation. This is where the two forms of expression are truly unified, as both can be assessed together for the quality and strength of their roles within a past culture seen as a whole.

If our subject is cultural history, then the philosophy and method of this enterprise might reasonably be called cultural historicism. Cultural historicism does not entomb the text in the past, like an artefact waiting to be excavated by an archaeologist; rather it re-locates it in the full context of both that re-opened past and current intellectual concerns, only in relation to which can it fully be understood and without which its cultural meaning and force are inevitably truncated. Just as an archaeologist recognizes material culture as a medium of adaptation between people and external circumstances that have always included the products of the past, the archaeologist, cultural historian and literary critic seeking to read and interpret what the past has produced and left to us are ultimately involved in the same continuing process as they are describing. We write our accounts from within the experiences of cultural history, not standing outside and apart from them. This may not make our task any easier, but it is not a paradox that subverts all pretences to historical factuality and objectivity. Properly understood, this situation will strengthen our hand, not least by reassuring us of the wholeness and integrity of the cultural record, and of the importance of thoughtful participation in the reproduction and transmission of that huge entity through commentary and creativity. It seems worth a try.

2

Knowledge and Vision in Old English Poetry

The Earliest English Literature

HISTORY is rarely a neat and straightforward narrative. One of the more convenient facts of the history of Britain is, however, that the creation of Englishness took place in relatively clear circumstances. From soon after the beginning of the Christian Era (AD 43) until the early 5th century, the area of southern and eastern Britain that was to become England formed the heart of the Roman province (later provinces) of Britannia. This northernmost projection of the Empire was considered relatively remote, but while aspects of life in Roman Britain were peculiar to the island, in general the Roman Period saw the introduction of a typically Roman provincial culture. Many in the population could have regarded themselves as both Roman and Briton simultaneously. Linguistically, both Latin and the British language from which Welsh has descended must have been in widespread use in the Roman provinces, although we cannot now be sure precisely which social, geographical and practical domains were occupied by each.

In the 5th century, however, the Roman Empire in the West collapsed in a few dramatic stages. Internal stress and external pressure from 'barbarian' masses outside the Empire were the principal factors: historians debate whether one or the other of these can be considered primary, but either problem can only have exacerbated the other. One of the earliest signs that the Western Empire had entered into a new severity of crisis and what was to prove its terminal decline was the withdrawal of imperial military protection and political government from Britain. While no one at the time may have thought of these as more than temporary measures, the removal of large numbers of troops during the usurpation of an imperial pretender from Britain, Constantine III, between 407 and 409, and a 'rescript' of the Emperor Honorius dated AD 411 telling the cities of Britain to look to their own defence, represent the concluding events of Roman rule.

A striking change then took place in the southern and eastern parts of the island. It involved the ingress and colonization of Germanic peoples and their culture from across the Channel and the North Sea. For centuries beforehand, 'free' Germanic barbarians had been the northern neighbours of the Roman Empire on the Continent, living in a symbiotic relationship that, in the last centuries of the Roman Period, had seen ever growing Germanic involvement in the affairs of the Empire, and a more diverse and frequent presence of Germanic folk within its territories. Increasing numbers of Germanic men were recruited as troops for Roman armies, and such nominally barbarian individuals could rise to the highest ranks of command. Only marginal areas of the Germanic-speaking world had been incorporated within the Empire by conquest, but the Germanic population of the Empire grew as border areas were ceded to Germanic communities settled with military obligations to the Empire. There had been Germanic troops in Britain across much of the period of Roman rule there, and the imperfect and in some cases semi-legendary sources we have concerning immediately post-Roman Britain suggest that 'sub-Roman' British leaders of the 5th century continued to recruit Germanic forces for military assistance.[1]

Two recorded visits to Britain by a Gallic bishop, St Germanus of Auxerre, dated to 429 and the 440s, to provide a combination of civil, military and spiritual leadership, especially in combating the Pelagian heresy that had arisen there, testify to the continuation of a romanized life after the formal demise of Roman rule. Archaeology, however, paints a more drastic picture of the demise of Roman material culture. There are at best exiguous signs of the continuation of activity at the leading sites of civilized Roman culture, the towns and the villas, and even here such evidence as we have often points to the breakdown of previous rules and orders, such as the use of the baths basilica as some sort of workshop and market area at Viroconium (Wroxeter, Shropshire). Industries such as that of mass-produced and widely distributed pottery simply came to an end, and very little new coin seems to have arrived or circulated in Britain after the first decade of the 5th century.[2]

Concomitant with this decline is a transition in the archaeological record to a Germanic material culture with its sources on the Continent and in Scandinavia, which we appropriately label Anglo-Saxon. It is not unusual to find early Anglo-Saxon artefact-types, such as pottery or metalwork, or structural types, such as the characteristic *Grubenhaus* or sunken hut, in the uppermost, final layers of late-Roman sites of virtually all types – towns, villas, forts and even temples. Curiously, though, such deposits do not mark a simple transformation of the site from Romano-British to Anglo-Saxon. Activity on these sites tends not to continue without a break; rather, the Anglo-Saxon elements represent final activity or influence there at the same time as a different range of Anglo-Saxon sites, particularly small villages and burial places, were appearing at new locations within the landscape. It is at present impossible to date this

[1] Reams have been written on the end of Roman Britain. For an introduction see Peter Salway, *Roman Britain* (Oxford University Press, 1981), 348–501; Simon Esmonde Cleary, *The Ending of Roman Britain* (London: Batsford, 1989).
[2] John Wacher, *The Towns of Roman Britain*, 2nd ed. (London: Batsford, 1995); Roger Wright and Philip Barker, *Wroxeter: Life and Death of a Roman City* (Stroud: Tempus, 1998); Sally White *et al.*, 'A mid-fifth-century hoard of Roman and pseudo-Roman material from Patching, West Sussex', *Britannia*, 30 (1999), 301–15.

primary Anglo-Saxon stratum as closely as we would like, but we can be confident that it was established by the middle of the 5th century.[3]

Over the following 200 to 250 years, we see a persistent multiplication and geographical expansion of characteristically Anglo-Saxon sites and material culture over what we can now refer to as England. According to a British Christian polemicist, Gildas, writing in the 6th century and offering an account of recent calamitous events in the history of his nation in order to blame them on the sins of the Britons and especially their rulers, Germanic ('Saxon') forces invited as allies rebelled against the Britons, encouraged more of their own people to invade, and conquered a large part of the island. As a historical narrative this is unlikely to be the whole truth and nothing but the truth, but as a part of what happened, perhaps in a specific area, it is perfectly plausible.[4]

There has been great controversy, particularly during the last two decades, over whether we should attribute the massive, extensive and thorough establishment of Englishness and Anglo-Saxon material culture in England during the 5th to 7th centuries to a huge influx of settlers over the sea from the east, or to a total cultural and ethnic shift whereby the descendants of the Roman-period native population became English, adopting the culture and identity allowed them and provided for them by a new, immigrant, ruling elite. Rather than choosing between these as mutually exclusive alternatives, the sensible view is probably to presuppose variety, and combinations of these processes. Complete demographic replacement, or anything close to that, is not plausible for England as a whole, while at present the strongest argument for high levels of migration comes not as the only conceivable explanation of anything we can observe in England, but rather from the consistent evidence of the widespread abandonment of settlement sites and farmed landscapes in northern Germany at this time.[5]

Whatever the underlying genetic and demographic factors, through this initial Early Anglo-Saxon Period we can trace the establishment of the earliest English communities and examine how their culture was developing. A primary source from this phase is the burial evidence, conspicuous and well-recorded as an archaeological source owing to the widespread practice of interring durable

[3]   On the archaeology of the Anglo-Saxon settlements, see Martin Welch, *Early Anglo-Saxon England*, English Heritage (London: Batsford, 1992), and David A. Hinton, *Archaeology, Economy and Society: England from the Fifth to the Fifteenth Century* (London: Routledge, 1990), esp. 1–20. With particular reference to the dating problem, John Hines, 'Philology, archaeology and the *adventus Saxonum vel Anglorum*', in A. Bammesberger and A. Wollmann (eds.), *Britain 400–600: Language and History* (Heidelberg: Carl Winter, 1990), 17–36.
[4]   *Gildas: The Ruin of Britain and Other Documents*, trans. M. Winterbottom (Chichester: Philimore, 1978). See also Michael Lapidge and David Dumville, *Gildas: New Approaches* (Woodbridge: Boydell, 1984) and Nicholas J. Higham, *The English Conquest: Gildas and Britain in the Fifth Century* (Manchester University Press, 1994).
[5]   On the settlement controversy, see Christopher J. Arnold, *An Archaeology of the Anglo-Saxon Kingdoms*, 2nd ed. (London: Routledge, 1997), esp. 19–32; Welch, op. cit. in note 3, 97–107; Nicholas J. Higham, *Rome, Britain and the Anglo-Saxons* (London: Seaby, 1992), reviewed by John Hines, 'The Anglo-Saxons reviewed', *Medieval Archaeol.*, 37 (1993), 314–18. Also John Hines, 'The Anglian migration in British historical research', *Stud. zur Sachsenforschung*, 11 (1998), 155–65; Helena Hamerow, *Early Medieval Settlements: The Archaeology of Rural Communities in North-West Europe 400–900* (Oxford University Press, 2002), esp. 106–14.

grave goods with the deceased. This itself undergoes changes in detail, according, for instance, to varying social and economic circumstances, and from place to place; and not least as a result of the gradual assimilation of the newly introduced Christian religion over the century of what has been called the Conversion Period, from the late 6th century onwards. Although the Christian attitude to burial practices and traditions, and especially to the provision of grave goods, was neither clear nor consistent, it cannot seriously be disputed that it was in accordance with a preferred Christian practice that the furnishing of graves with artefacts dwindled to the point of effectively disappearing around the beginning of the 8th century. We have to recognize with this that while Anglo-Saxon culture developed, or evolved, in its own autonomous way during this period, it was also under steady, and substantial, influence from outside – from every direction, in fact, west, north, south and east; Christian and non-Christian alike.

Politically, Anglo-Saxon society came to be organized and administered through a series of kingdoms. There is a clear trend, over the period from the 6th century to the 10th, from a number of relatively small kingdoms in England, such as Kent, Essex and East Anglia, towards the dominance of a smaller number of large kingdoms (Northumbria, Mercia and Wessex), and eventually to a single English monarchy in a unified kingdom of England.[6] The under-standably tempting idea that this process started with an atomized society, orga-nized only in small local communities that progressively merged is perhaps a little naïve: it seems we can allow for extensive if unstable overkingship from a very early stage, and some of the local subdivisions that we know of – for instance Middlesex between Essex and Wessex – may well have been created within larger units for local administration rather than preceding them.[7] Particu-larly important concomitants of the political situation for us were that with the political consolidation of kingdoms in the late 6th century came Christianity, Latin literacy, documentary records, and thus history itself, to England.

The Anglo-Saxon culture that became established in Britain has its own linguistic character, attested from a very early stage indeed through a different form of literacy, runic writing. The runic script had emerged in Germanic Europe by the 2nd century AD and provides our earliest written (inscribed) records of Germanic language. It has to be admitted that, so obscure are the earliest runic texts from England, it is only a minority of them that we can even certainly identify as being in some Germanic language, let alone translate. Nonetheless we do have such inscriptions from the 5th century onwards with details of form that reflect the grammatically reconstructable development of the Old English language out of ancestral Germanic.[8] Literacy, however, became a much more significant feature of English cultural life with the introduction of

[6]   For an up-to-date and broad-based account, see Edward James, *Britain in the First Millennium* (London: Arnold, 2001).
[7]   Stephen Bassett (ed.), *The Origins of Anglo-Saxon Kingdoms* (London: Leicester University Press, 1988).
[8]   Raymond I. Page, *An Introduction to English Runes*, 2nd ed. (Woodbridge: Boydell, 1999); John Hines, 'Some observations on the runic inscriptions of early Anglo-Saxon England', in A. Bammesberger (ed.), *Old English Runes and their Continental Background* (Heidelberg: Carl Winter, 1991), 61–83;

the Church and the adoption of the roman script (using the alphabet we are familiar with now) together with the technology of writing with pen and ink on prepared animal-skin parchment. The conversion of the Anglo-Saxons did not, in fact, proceed through a single channel, and for a period in the 7th century there was serious rivalry between a southern-influenced Roman party, looking largely to Canterbury, and a more northerly, Irish-orientated Church, looking largely to the great monastic centre of Iona.[9] Certain adaptations were eventually made in roman script to accommodate the peculiarities of the English language, such as the use of a runic letter þ (*thorn*) to represent the sounds now spelled *th* (as in *this* and *thin*), for which a crossed *d*, ð (*eth*), adopted from Irish roman script, could also be used.

The productivity of vernacular literacy, in a wide range of texts and literature, proved to be unusually high in Anglo-Saxon England; rivalled in the early-medieval centuries only by Old Irish texts. In areas where Romance languages descended from Latin became the norm, the lack of a conceptual distinction between the spoken, 'vulgar' language and sub-Classical written Latin delayed the emergence of French, Spanish and Italian literatures, while far less has survived – or apparently was written – in any other variety of Germanic at this date. The earliest extended texts either partly or wholly in Old English, normally using the roman script and datable from the 7th century onwards, are generally non-literary as defined in the previous chapter: charters recording transactions and ownership of property (usually land) and rights; law codes; and glosses of lists of Latin words. In their known forms, the earliest written vernacular texts of definitely literary character take the form of poetic quotations that have been used as part of some larger artistic artefact or literary work: the inscription on a carved stone cross at Ruthwell (Dumfries and Galloway); the verses on the Franks Casket (now in the British Museum); and 'Cædmon's Hymn', added peripherally to manuscripts of Bede's Latin *Ecclesiastical History of the English People*. None of these need be dated earlier, or later, than the first half of the 8th century. The former two, which are carved in stone and whalebone respectively, use runic script: on the Ruthwell cross contrasting with roman used for Latin texts; on the Franks Casket also used to write some Latin words. The Bede manuscripts are all on parchment and use only roman script.[10]

There was a significant step forward in English literary history from the later 9th century, starting in the kingdom of Wessex, which then had its capital in Winchester (Hants). Wessex was the only independent English kingdom to survive relatively intact at the end of the first century of the Viking Period, which had seen intense and devastating attacks on England by piratical Vikings from Scandinavia. The first of these attacks were in the late 8th century; from the middle of the 9th century largely Danish hosts mounted a series of

David N. Parsons, *Recasting the Runes: The Reform of the Anglo-Saxon* futhorc (Institutionen för nordiska språk, Uppsala Universitet, 1999).

[9] Henry Mayr-Harting, *The Coming of Christianity to Anglo-Saxon England*, 3rd ed. (London: Batsford, 1991).

[10] For a general introduction to and survey of Old English literature, see Malcolm Godden and Michael Lapidge (eds.), *The Cambridge Companion to Old English Literature* (Cambridge University Press, 1991).

successful campaigns to conquer and occupy English territory, reflected in the establishment of what became known as the Danelaw. The King of Wessex in this crucial period was Alfred (the Great: ruled 871–899). Alfred and his counsellors developed a thoughtful and constructive strategy for consolidating and extending the power of the English monarchy which included a deliberate renaissance of English and Christian culture. The policy was announced in a prefatory letter to Alfred's 'own' translation of Pope Gregory the Great's *Cura Pastoralis* (a handbook on the pastoral duties and organization of the Church), and involved programmes of translating 'essential' texts of this kind into English and educating young people of a certain social rank to be able to read them. An interesting detail in this letter is that Alfred declares that he recalls how in former times *monige cūðon englisc gewrit ārǣdan* ('many were able to read English writing'), implying not only extensive vernacular literacy by the 9th century but also that written English was relatively common.[11]

The re-establishment of a secure English state and its Late Anglo-Saxon culture proceeded relatively steadily for much of the 10th century. The reconquest of the Danelaw south of the Humber was efficiently effected by Alfred's son Edward (the Elder: 899–924), and by the time of his death in 939, Edward's successor Athelstan could not only claim kingship over all of England but supremacy over Welsh and Scottish rulers too. There were vicissitudes through the middle of the 10th century, especially in Northumbria, but by the end of the reign of Edgar (959–975) the establishment of a single English kingdom was a concluded fact. And it was under Edgar's rule particularly that a powerful movement of ecclesiastical renovation and re-organization was imposed upon the English Church, known as the Benedictine Reform from the crucial role played by the establishment of monasteries strictly following the monastic rule of St Benet. Before long, this produced its own rich vernacular literature in the prose writings of Ælfric, who moved from Cerne Abbas (Dorset) to become Abbot of Eynsham (Oxon.) in 1005 and died c. 1010, and Wulfstan, variously and sometimes plurally Bishop of London and Worcester and Archbishop of York, flourishing in the first quarter of the 11th century.[12] The later 10th and first half of the 11th centuries produced a fascinating range of other serious and learned English prose writing, some by known authors such as Æthelwold, Bishop of Winchester, and Byrhtferth, a monk of Ramsey (Cambs.); but mostly anonymous, ranging from homilies through catechisms and herbals to curious translations such as the *Wonders of the East* or the story of *Apollonius of Tyre*.

The later 10th and earlier 11th centuries were a turbulent time, politically, in England. Edgar's reign was followed by the long and infamous reign of Ethelred the Unready, which saw a resurgence of ruthless warfare between the English and a new generation of Scandinavian Vikings, and eventually a Dane, Cnut, as King of England and Denmark from 1016 to 1035. A son of Ethelred, Edward (the Confessor: 1042–1066), was subsequently to regain the throne, but, porten-

---

[11] For a collection and discussion of the sources concerning Alfred, see Simon Keynes and Michael Lapidge, *Alfred the Great* (Harmondsworth: Penguin, 1983). Highly controversial is Alfred P. Smyth's massive critical assault on these sources, *King Alfred the Great* (Oxford University Press, 1995).

[12] James, *op. cit.* in note 6, 252–60.

tously, he had spent a significant part of his early life in exile in Normandy, and was to be the last of the line of secure Anglo-Saxon kings. Yet besides the flourishing of late Old English prose writing, this period saw the copying and illumination of many fine manuscripts, and all of the four major manuscript books containing significant collections of Old English poetry can be dated between the mid-10th and early 11th centuries.[13] Old English poetry is marked by a distinctive and consistent form of verse: an alliterative line involving a fixed number of stressed syllables, at least two of which must alliterate, and also paying attention to the length of the syllables in these stressed positions. Rhyme appears only as an occasional embellishment of Old English verse, and is just one of several stylistically heightening devices that may be employed. It has long been recognized that there are aspects of the composition of Old English poetry that point to the continuing influence of an originally oral form of composition and performance.[14] As we have already seen, though, we have extant written Old English poetry from the first half of the 8th century, and an intimate co-relationship between oral and written practices is already implicit in Bishop Asser's contemporary story of Alfred the Great, as a boy, learning to recite the poems contained in a book by heart so that he could gain the book from his mother.[15] Essentially written in form is also the poetry of one Cynewulf, who encrypted a signature of his name in runes into the conclusion of four known poems. Cynewulf's compositions date to some time within the period from the mid-9th century to the early 10th century.[16]

The surviving corpus of Old English poetry includes poems of quite diverse character. But readers who come to this earliest English literature with a romantic taste for the sort of folksy myths and heroic legends associated with the highly popular fiction of a distinguished Old English scholar, J. R. R. Tolkien, tend to be disappointed by the way conventional Christianity dominates this poetry. There is indeed no small number of devotional poems and uninspired exemplary allegories that fail to be anything more than slight and predictable verses, although other poems within the same categories – for instance *The Dream of the Rood* and *The Phoenix* – are richly crafted and offer powerful reading experiences. The range of religious (i.e. Christian) verse in Old English is certainly wide: from the raw cry of acknowledgement and praise in 'Cædmon's Hymn' – according to Bede, the first Christian poem in the vernacular language and traditional metre of English – to scriptural narratives and tales of saints showing the influence of secular, heroic ideals; proverbial or 'gnomic' verse; and elegiac poetry, focusing intensely on individual experience.[17]

---

[13] Janet Backhouse *et al.*, *The Golden Age of Anglo-Saxon Art 966–1066* (London: British Museum, 1984).

[14] Andy Orchard, 'Oral tradition', in Katherine O'Brien O'Keeffe (ed.), *Reading Old English Texts* (Cambridge University Press, 1997), 101–23.

[15] Asser's *Life of Alfred*, chapters 22–3. Keynes and Lapidge, *op. cit.* in note 11, 74–5.

[16] Pamela O. E. Gradon, *Cynewulf's 'Elene'*, rev. ed. (Exeter University Press, 1977), 9–15 and 22–3; Patrick W. Conner, 'On dating Cynewulf', in Robert Bjork (ed.), *The Cynewulf Reader* (London: Routledge, 2001), 23–56.

[17] The entire Old English poetic corpus is edited in George P. Krapp and Elliott V. K. Dobbie, *The Anglo-Saxon Poetic Records*, 6 vols. (New York: Columbia University Press, 1931–53). The most thorough and informative studies of many poems are provided by individual scholarly editions (cf. Gradon,

The principal category of secular rather than religious poetry, however, is that of the heroic tradition. Contrary, again, to what is largely wishful thinking, it is doubtful that the known Germanic heroic cycles can really be identified as a pre-Christian heritage as far as England and the Continent are concerned. A number of characters emerging in related sequences of heroic legend recorded in Old English, Old and Middle High German and Old Norse can be identified with real, and datable, historical figures: for instance Hygelac (in *Beowulf*), Siegfried, Brunhilde, Gunther, Hagen, Attila, Ermanaric . . . And it is striking with what consistency these historical individuals pertain to the period from the late 4th century to the beginning of the 7th, around the time of the fall of the Roman Empire in the West and great migrations of Germanic peoples. The inference then has to be that, if it was out of this period that these legends arose, it was somehow at the end of that period that the heroic tradition became defined, and effectively closed to possible newcomers. This should then have been co-ordinated with the social and political developments that saw the consolidation of the major kingdoms, and the Conversion to Christianity, in Anglo-Saxon England.

Beowulf, an outstanding Old English heroic epic of more than 3,000 lines, is no explicit Christian tract, and makes an unconvincing allegory although some have tried to read it so; but it is no surprise, nor an inappropriate overlay, to find that it enunciates a firm religious and moral stance, and that this is essentially monotheistic and salvational. If anything, it takes a Christian faith for granted. The ethical position it reflects and propounds most especially, however, involves the virtues of a warrior society, a society that we call 'heroic'. That physical strength and military prowess should be highly prized in this code can hardly be a surprise, nor courage and loyalty to one's duty, even to death. Rather more distinctive in the heroic mode – in comparison, for instance, with chivalric romance – is the value attached to prudence and even cunning on the hero's part: something that tends to be replaced with Christian virtue as the vital ingredient for Arthurian knights. *Beowulf* is the supreme example of genuinely traditional heroic poetry in Old English; otherwise we have only fragments of poems such as *Waldere* (on the tale of Walter of Aquitaine) and *The Fight at Finnsburh*. From the 10th century we have examples of the military narrative style of the heroic being adapted, panegyrically and elegiacally, to mark major contemporary events such as the battle of Brunanburh (937), a reconquest of the Five Boroughs (942), and most notably the tragic defeat of Byrhtnoth, ealdorman of East Anglia, at the battle of Maldon (Essex) in 991. It is a matter of contention whether or not these compositions mark a new and later stage of heroic poetry from that which produced *Beowulf*. In my opinion that is the case, but this is not an issue that we need argue out here.

The decline in both the quality and quantity of Old English literature produced after the early 11th century was severe, and is difficult to explain. The Danish conquests of Sweyn Forkbeard and his son Cnut, and subsequently the

---

op. cit. in note 16). Modern English translations of a large proportion of the Old English poetic corpus are conveniently available in Sidney A. J. Bradley, *Anglo-Saxon Poetry*, Everyman's Library (London: Dent, 1982).

Norman Conquest of 1066, certainly did not encourage vernacular literature, but there is no clear reason why they should have been the cause of such a collapse. The English language also underwent a relatively intense period of change in the 11th and 12th centuries, to appear eventually with the markedly different phonological and grammatical structures of Middle English, together with a considerable influx of Scandinavian and French vocabulary. Yet even though we have a comparable period of low literary output at the next period of similar linguistic transition, from Middle to early Modern English in the 15th century, there is again no obvious reason why such developments should virtually put a stop to literary production. Whatever the explanation, Old English literature, and the Anglo-Saxon Period and state, came to just about as clear and decisive an end as they had a beginning. By the late 12th century Old English literary culture was decidedly a thing of the past, and we see the first stirrings of something new in Plantagenet England.

An Englishman's Home

By the end of the Anglo-Saxon period, the processes of settlement, cultural colonization, and political unification just outlined had created an entity known as *Engla-land*: our word *England*, and etymologically meaning 'land of the English'. The geographical extent and gradual expansion of this territory is traceable first through archaeological remains, later through historical sources. This vital dimension of the creation of Englishness thus involved not only the physical imposition of an Anglo-Saxon presence, cultural and demographic, upon the landscape, but also a mental mapping and claiming of the territory. In such ways, the Anglo-Saxon English lived between horizons that were simultaneously material and ideological.

The transition from Late Roman Britain to early Anglo-Saxon England saw a great simplification of the economic system. This was directly reflected in contrasts in the range of occupation and activity sites that we tend to refer to collectively as 'settlement archaeology'. Principally because the state (i.e. the Empire) required surpluses and payments in the form of both goods and money, the Roman system had encouraged specialization of activity at particular sites, and with that a system of interdependencies that was inevitably hierarchical. In the civilian sphere, rural settlement and economy thus comprised villages and farmsteads of an essentially peasant character at one level, manifestly lower in status than the romanized country house complexes known as villas, with their characteristically rectangular layouts, and where one might expect to encounter amenities and luxuries such as hypocaust heating, mosaic floors and painted plaster walls. While the economic basis of most villas appears to have been farming, it is not unusual for such sites to have specialized in other productive activities such as tile-making or iron-extraction. These rural sites were linked into a system of urban centres of greater diversity of function and larger size, amongst which a useful distinction is drawn between 'small towns', which might be found just a few miles apart, and 'towns', a category to which about two dozen sites in Britain can be assigned. Using the same road system, but distinct

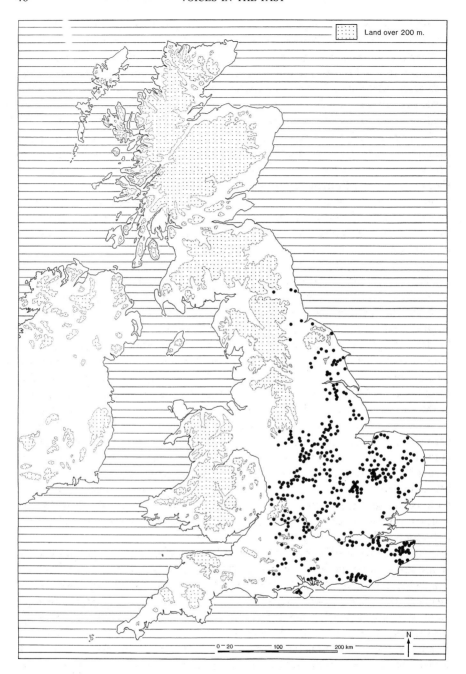

FIG. 3. Early Anglo-Saxon furnished burial sites of the Migration Period (to c. AD 570).

in form and usually in location, was a series of military sites, ranging in size from small depots and communication stations to the large legionary fortresses at Caerleon, Chester and York. In the later Roman period, changes in practical strategy saw a greater reliance on a mobile field army than on massed frontier troops, and with this came a closer interface between civilian and military sites, reflected, for instance, in the fortification of towns with walls and towers. The landscape also included special temple sites.[18]

A re-organization of practical life in Roman Britain going far beyond these military developments is apparent in the 4th century. This included a decline in urban institutions and life so widespread that it has been suggested – somewhat rhetorically – that Roman Britain had culturally come to an end long before the formal end of Roman rule in the years 407–411.[19] While the 4th-century changes were both substantial and significant, however, they were nothing like the wholesale disappearance of characteristically Roman sites and artefact-types of the first few decades of the 5th century.

The positive development of the 5th century in the area of England was the gradual replacement of the Roman-period settlement pattern with the early Anglo-Saxon one. At the most general level, we can best map the distribution of early Anglo-Saxon settlements by inference from the distribution map of Early Anglo-Saxon burial sites, which are considerably easier to find and a bit easier to date closely. These show us, for instance, an overall territorial range of Anglo-Saxon material culture up to the late 6th century in a clearly bounded area of southern and eastern England (Fig. 3), revealing also an understandable paucity of settlement in inhospitable areas such as the Weald in the south-east, or the forested Chilterns and Essex clay plateau on the other side of the Thames. At a more local level, we are justified in assuming that cemeteries and settlements were close together, which allows us to identify the topographical contexts favoured for settlement. An important exception is a few very large cremation cemeteries in eastern England that appear to have served as central burial places for several communities over a larger district. Not surprisingly, though, the general pattern shows a preference for relatively light, easily worked, productive agricultural soils, especially over well-drained gravels, often to be found in riverine contexts.

Although they were common, furnished burial sites were not ubiquitous and so are not an unfailing guide to the presence of 5th- and 6th-century communities using the Anglo-Saxon material culture in their daily lives. A marked increase over the past two decades in the number of early Anglo-Saxon settlement sites identified by the structural and artefact-types referred to above (p. 38) has shown that one can find several such settlements in areas from which no signs of furnished cemeteries have come. In the great majority of cases, such settlement sites can only be excavated in part, and there have been few extensive investigations that have revealed anything like a whole settlement site. All the

---

[18] For a general view of Roman Britain, see Salway, *op. cit.* in note 1; Martin Millett, *The Romanization of Britain* (Cambridge University Press, 1990); Simon James and Martin Millett (eds.), *Britons and Romans: Advancing the Archaeological Agenda* (York: Council for British Archaeol., 2001).
[19] Richard Reece, 'Town and country: the end of Roman Britain', *World Archaeol.*, 12 (1980), 77–92.

same, the typical early Anglo-Saxon settlement-types that we know of were what we can call small villages: grouped communities of more than one household unit rather than individual and solitary farmsteads. The best-known examples to date are West Stow (Suffolk) and Mucking (Essex).[20] The number of farmsteads at West Stow need have been no more than three or four. Mucking appears to have been – or to have grown – considerably larger, with perhaps a dozen or more contemporary houses occupied by a community of up to a hundred. The range of buildings on the early settlement sites is limited and consistent. Besides the sunken huts, whose structural character has been much argued over but which are widely agreed to have served as utilitarian working and storage sheds, we find rectangular post-built timber houses, unfortunately often called 'halls', and in the normal run of things providing an internal space of around 40 to 80 square metres. Fireplaces, a feature that we usually regard as essential to a dwelling house, can be identified in at least some of these buildings.

In a famous theoretical paper of the early 1950s, reflecting on what archaeologists can properly infer about the past from material remains, Christopher Hawkes stated that the easiest and securest matter was to recognize economic and technical facts.[21] If we find a quantity of charred barley grain in a corner on the sealed floor level of an Anglo-Saxon building, we can safely conclude that the local economy included barley cultivation. But the fact is that the survival of such evidence from this period is haphazard, and its retrieval a painstaking business. We are gradually accumulating a detailed picture of Anglo-Saxon farming and other economic practices, but are still a long way from a full picture. On the evidence of surviving grains in distinct deposits (= 'stratified'), or as grain impressions in pottery and even from stratified pollen rather than grain, we know of cereal cultivation, predominantly of types of barley, rye and wheat, and rather less evidence of oats. Beans and peas are regularly in evidence, and the cultivation of flax, presumably both for linen fibres and linseed oil, is widely attested.[22] A striking contrast between buildings on early Anglo-Saxon settlement sites and those in northern Germany of the preceding Roman Period – a type that continued to be used in Scandinavia throughout this time – is the absence of identifiable animal byres in England, typically found conjoined with the dwelling area in the Germanic longhouse. A milder winter climate will have been a factor in this, although another would appear to be a reduction in the importance and the proportion of cattle amongst the livestock kept – as reflected by bone counts from the sites – towards a more equal representation of the

20 Stanley E. West, *West Stow: The Anglo-Saxon Village*, 2 vols., East Anglian Archaeol., 24 (Bury St Edmunds, 1985); Helena Hamerow, *Excavations at Mucking. Vol. 2: The Anglo-Saxon Settlement* (London: English Heritage, 1993); *eadem, op. cit.* in note 5; Dominic Powlesland, 'Early Anglo-Saxon settlements, structures, form and layout', in John Hines (ed.), *The Anglo-Saxons from the Migration Period to the Eighth Century: An Ethnographic Perspective* (Woodbridge: Boydell, 1997), 101–24.
21 C. F. C. Hawkes, 'Archaeological theory and method: some suggestions from the Old World', *American Anthrop.*, 56 (1954), 155–68.
22 Peter J. Fowler, 'Farming in early medieval England: some fields for thought', in J. Hines (ed.), *op. cit.* in note 20, 245–68; James Rackham (ed.), *Environment and Economy in Anglo-Saxon England* (York: Council for British Archaeol., 1994), *passim*.

caproids, sheep and goat.[23] While caution has to be exercised in interpreting such figures as we have, this does suggest a shift away from what was familiar in the Germanic homelands and assimilation of farming practices to what had been typical in Roman Britain.

The transition from Roman Britain to Anglo-Saxon England saw a clear decline in the technical capacities of material life. This is manifest, for instance, in the demise of good-quality wheel-thrown pottery industries, tile-making, and building in stone. Anglo-Saxon culture nonetheless involved a wide range of crafts throughout its history, and the systemic shift from a relatively high level of specialization and interdependency to a greater local range of skills and self-sufficiency should be regarded as one that redistributed complexity rather than a mere reversion to a simpler way of life. Amongst the crafts most essential to sustain the material culture in a practical way will have been wood- and ironworking: both crucial for producing the tools required for agriculture, as well as the weaponry that a high proportion of men in the early Anglo-Saxon period were equipped with. Special skills are needed both for the procurement and the working of these commodities. As yet, our best evidence for regular woodland management, such as coppicing, in the form of documentary refer-ences and a predominantly westerly distribution of the specific place-name element *grāf(e)* or *grǣfe* (Modern English *grove*), relates to later in the Anglo-Saxon period, and careful analysis suggests that the wood used for char-coal at a 6th- to 7th-century saltmaking site at Droitwich (Worcs.) was freely collected from underwoods and scrubland.[24] This does not, of course, mean that more carefully nurtured wood was not used elsewhere – for instance ash for spearshafts – but does indicate how freely people of this time could gather the resources of the areas they found themselves in.

Iron ore, in the form of either rock or bog-ore, is quite widely available in England, and evidence from rural settlement sites, mostly in the form of charac-teristic smelting slag, indicates widespread local extraction where ores were available. A charter of the year 689 refers to an iron mine in a Wealden clearing, and a site specializing in iron-production from the end of the 8th century onwards has been excavated at Ramsbury (Wilts.).[25] Anglo-Saxon charters of the 7th and 8th centuries nicely illustrate the range of resources wanted to main-tain a working agrarian landscape, and, for the benefit of the new ecclesiastical

[23] W. Haio Zimmermann, 'Why was cattle-stalling introduced in prehistory? The significance of byre and stable and of outwintering', in Charlotte Fabech and Jytte Ringtved (eds.), *Settlement and Landscape* (Aarhus: Jutland Archaeol. Soc., 1999), 301–18.

[24] Oliver Rackham, 'Trees and woodland in the Anglo-Saxon period: the documentary evidence', in J. Rackham (ed.), *op. cit.* in note 22, 7–11; Della Hooke, *The Landscape of Anglo-Saxon England* (London: Leicester University Press, 1998), esp. 164–7; Margaret Gelling and Ann Coles, *The Landscape of Place-Names* (Stamford: Shaun Tyas, 2000), 226–30; John D. Hurst *et al.*, *A Multi-Period Salt Produc-tion Site at Droitwich: Excavations at Upwich* (York: Council for British Archaeol., 1997).

[25] R. F. Tylecote, *The Prehistory of Metallurgy in the British Isles* (London: Institute of Metals, 1986), esp. 179–201; Jeremy Haslam, 'A Middle Saxon iron smelting site at Ramsbury, Wiltshire', *Medieval Archaeol.*, 24 (1980), 1–68; Glenn Foard, 'Medieval woodland, agriculture and industry in Rockingham Forest, Northamptonshire', *Medieval Archaeol.*, 45 (2001), 41–95. The charter referred to is no. 12 in Peter H. Sawyer, *Anglo-Saxon Charters: An Annotated List and Bibliography* (London: Royal Hist. Soc., 1968); for the text see Walter de Gray Birch, *Cartularium Saxonicum*, 3 vols. (London, 1885), vol. I, no. 74, at pp. 107–8.

centres, the building up of extensive holdings comprising a range of natural resources and ecological and agricultural niches. Some degree of communal organization for the production and distribution of resources must always have existed in Anglo-Saxon England. However, it remains a matter of contention whether these 'multiple estates' were constructed and expanded as the Anglo-Saxon communities settled into more stable, hierarchically organized kingdoms in the 6th and 7th centuries, or could have been taken over as going concerns from a Roman and sub-Roman native past.[26]

Whatever its background, increasing specialization of activity and site-function was a marked feature of Anglo-Saxon settlements and economy in the 7th century. One of the most potent expressions of this change was the re-introduction of towns in England, at Southampton (Hants), London, Ipswich (Suffolk) and York in this century. From Ipswich was subsequently to come the re-introduction of mass-produced, wheel-thrown and widely distributed pottery: an 'Ipswich Ware', found widely in eastern England, especially in East Anglia, and currently dated from c. AD 700 onwards. These new urban sites are commonly referred to as *wics* (pronounced *week*, from Old English *wīc*), reflecting the place-name element that is common to their Old English forms: *Hamwīc, Lundenewīc, Gypeswīc, Eoforwīc* – as well as Sandwich and Fordwich in Kent, and maybe others besides. Each site has its own history, not least in respect of the influence over its development from the preceding but apparently long defunct Roman towns either at or near most of these sites. Yet certain recurrent characteristics can be discerned: for instance the presence of 6th-century communities in the area, with no obvious signs that a special trading site is already developing; a rather hectic development from the mid-7th century onwards, at least as far as the *ad hoc* use of sites for human burial, later built over, is concerned; and eventually the introduction of a regular street layout. These settlements were obviously sited to serve as ports, and clearly attracted productive craftsmen too. It has been noted that they would provide a principal port for each of the kingdoms of Wessex, Kent, Essex/Mercia, East Anglia and Northumbria. Their appearance in England is part of a wider northern European phenomenon, extending across the Channel and the North Sea to the littoral from northern France to Ribe in western Jutland, and even into the Baltic. Both in terms of distribution, and the evidence for careful planning in some cases, the international perspective reinforces the belief that royal powers stood behind the development of such sites, as secure havens to nurture production and trade, from which the kings could profit.[27]

Many other changes were taking place in Anglo-Saxon society at this time besides incipient (and still very limited) urbanization. A growth not just in the stability but also in the depth and extent of social hierarchy is evident from

[26] Hooke, *op. cit.* in note 24, esp. 62–83.

[27] Christopher Scull, 'Urban centres in pre-Viking England?', in J. Hines (ed.), *op. cit.* in note 20, 269–310; *idem*, 'Burials at emporia in England', in David Hill and Robert Cowie (eds.), *Wics: The Early Medieval Trading Centres of Northern Europe* (Sheffield Academic Press, 2001), 67–74. For the wider European context see Helen Clarke and Björn Ambrosiani, *Towns in the Viking Age*, rev. ed. (London: Leicester University Press, 1995), esp. 5–45.

burial sites, amongst which a few exceptionally rich, princely or royal barrows of the 7th century are known, as at Sutton Hoo (Suffolk), Broomfield (Essex) and Taplow (Bucks.), at the same time as the famous royal palace site of Yeavering (Northumberland) adds a new tier to the occupation-site range. A number of settlement sites that, largely from the later 7th or the 8th century onwards, stand out for both the quality and the quantity of artefacts found there have been the subject of much debate lately. A combination of recent developments including changing agricultural practices (deeper ploughing), the popularity of metal-detecting, and the implementation of an effective Portable Antiquities Scheme by the government, have led to the recognition of a large number of find-rich sites, particularly in eastern England, for which the term 'productive site' has come into use. This blanket categorization must embrace sites that were originally of quite different characters, not all of one type or function. In some cases at least, though, there is clear topographical and/or later historical evidence to identify these sites as the locations of fairs or markets.[28]

A complicating factor in the organization of the settled and economic landscape at this time is the presence of the Church. As indicated already, the early charter evidence is dominated by ecclesiastical institutions gaining territorial property and economic rights. In contrast to the medieval parochial system of ubiquitous churches in the countryside – a product of the late Anglo-Saxon and post-Conquest periods – for much of the Anglo-Saxon period we must think of a more centralized Church, residing in and providing pastoral services from communal houses, of different types according to their ecclesiastical foundation but consisting principally of cathedral churches at the episcopal sees; monasteries; and collegiate minster churches which would have had primary responsibility for general pastoral care. Besides this, it is clear that monastic and minster centres became focal points of economic activity. In some cases, indeed, historical evidence clearly associates 'productive' sites with what were, later at least, to be the sites of religious houses, and it is a matter of some controversy how many of the productive sites might be explained as minster sites from the beginning.[29]

Both historically and archaeologically, the identification of an Anglo-Saxon monastery in the 8th century is a problematic issue. From the year 734, a letter of Bede to Egbert, Archbishop of York, denounces the practice of noblemen turning their properties and homes into nominal monastic houses and estates for the privileges and exemptions that brought,[30] so that a distinction between what was materially a typical secular household and what was formally a monastery might be non-existent. In archaeology, there has correspondingly been much

[28] Katharina Ulmschneider, *Markets, Minsters and Metal-Detectors: The Archaeology of Middle Saxon Lincolnshire and Hampshire Compared*, British Archaeol. Reports British Ser., 307 (Oxford, 2000); *eadem* and Tim Pestell (eds.), *Markets, Fairs and Productive Sites* (Windgather, forthcoming).
[29] Peter H. Sawyer, 'Early fairs and markets in England and Scandinavia', in B. L. Anderson and A. J. H. Latham (eds.), *The Market in History* (London: Croom Helm, 1986), 59–77; John Blair, 'Minster churches in the landscape', in Della Hooke (ed.), *Anglo-Saxon Settlements* (Oxford: Blackwell, 1988), 35–58; *idem*, 'Palaces or minsters? Northampton and Cheddar reconsidered', *Anglo-Saxon England*, 25 (1996), 97–121.
[30] Dorothy Whitelock (ed. and trans.), *English Historical Documents I: c. 500–1042*, 2nd ed. (London: Eyre & Spottiswood, 1979), 799–810.

debate over whether, not just 'productive sites', but some richly endowed excavated sites – particularly ones that have what appear to be church buildings
acting as foci for burial, evidence for literacy on site in the form of writing
implements (*styli*), and explicitly Christian artefacts, apparently book or shrine
mounts – should be regarded as specifically ecclesiastical or could be the homes
of ostensibly pious layfolk living in an already essentially literate culture.[31]
Whichever position we take on the classificational problem (i.e. ecclesiastical or
secular), the whole situation is clear testimony to the deep penetration of the
Church into the English settlement and economic systems by the 8th century.

While these processes undoubtedly saw the development of the Anglo-Saxon
settlement pattern with the addition of layers above the simplest working
agricultural communities, that basic rural settlement pattern itself did not simply
provide a static foundation over which this superstructure rose. On the contrary,
none of the known settlement sites representing the earliest part of the
Anglo-Saxon period to archaeology continues beyond the 8th century, as far as
we can tell, and sites representing occupation in the 8th century show at the
earliest some signs of activity there in the 6th. This discontinuity in settlement
location has come to be termed the 'Middle Saxon shuffle', but the term itself
may be misleading in suggesting a more unitary, and chronologically more
sharply defined process than was probably the case. In some instances, such as
at Raunds (Northants) and Walton (Bucks.), settlement relocation appears to
have involved a straightforward move to an adjacent site.[32] In other cases, such
as in the Rockingham Forest area of Northamptonshire and around the Fens, especially in southern Lincolnshire, extensive survey work, involving identifying
settlement locations from surface scatters of pottery, firmly indicates an early
pattern of small, dispersed settlements nucleating into a series of fewer but
larger village sites through the Middle Saxon Period. Here, however, it has been
noted that the change in one district may pre-date that in a neighbouring one by
up to two centuries, clearly implying that that we cannot seek to explain this as a
response to some ubiquitous economic or social imperative.[33]

It is also likely that some overall growth in the size of the population was
involved in these changes. This is impossible to quantify, not least because we
cannot judge the reliability of an apparently sharp drop in population levels in
the 5th and 6th centuries in southern and eastern England without making
doubtful assumptions about the possible size of an archaeologically invisible
population, either English or sub-Romano-British, at that time. A comparison of
Domesday Book figures with the population levels implied by early Anglo-
Saxon cemeteries nonetheless suggests a considerable increase in numbers

[31] Tim Pestell, 'An Analysis of Monastic Foundation in East Anglia, c. 650–1200' (Univ. of East Anglia,
Ph.D. thesis, 1999), 57–68. I am grateful to Dr Pestell for the opportunity to consult his thesis in advance
of publication of a revised version (Woodbridge: Boydell, forthcoming).
[32] Helena F. Hamerow, 'Settlement mobility and the "Middle Saxon Shift": rural settlements and settlement patterns in Anglo-Saxon England', *Anglo-Saxon England*, 20 (1991), 1–17.
[33] Foard, *op. cit.* in note 25; David Hall and John Coles, *Fenland Survey: An Essay in Landscape and
Persistence* (London: English Heritage, 1994), 122–31; P. P. Hayes, 'Roman to Saxon in the South
Lincolnshire Fens', *Antiquity*, 62 (1988), 321–6.

between one end of the Anglo-Saxon period and the other.[34] It would be equally impossible to determine whether such growth was absolutely the cause of economic re-organization – demanding higher production and efficiency – or its result, allowing a larger population to be sustained. What we do see clearly in the 8th century and throughout the following age of Viking incursion, however, is an extension of settlement into what had hitherto been marginal land. This includes both upland settlements, as at Simy Folds (Co. Durham) and Ribblehead in the Yorkshire Pennines, and coastal wetland colonization, for instance in the Fens, and in Somerset and Lancashire in the west.[35] The immediate explanation of these examples of effective land reclamation is not, however, crude population pressure, forcing some people out into the margins; rather, both an ability and a desire to exploit special resources that were available in such places. Considerable amounts of slag implying iron-extraction have been noted at sites around Simy Folds.[36]

This gradual rural re-organization, which in the main arable lowlands saw a steady trend towards substantial nucleated villages, was the precondition for the creation of the open- and strip-field systems that still corrugate the English landscape so extensively. This too was no quick and blanket change. Precisely when it began, and even why, we do not know, but both archaeological and historical evidence show it to have been underway by the 10th century, although in some places not introduced until the Norman period. In a general way, like the establishment of the earliest towns, greater efficiency and productivity, as well as active social control, seem to be essential factors of the change; however the element of lordly direction involved may only have been at a local level, which would neatly explain the gradual and even rather leisurely progress it made.[37] The strip-field system became intimately linked to the later medieval common-field system of intermingled strips cultivated by different farmers, but neither system is absolutely a precondition for the essential elements of the other. Altogether, though, these changes constitute the emergence of the familiar medieval manorial system, consisting largely of compact, local estates administratively headed by a manor house and its home ('demesne') farm, which had to compensate for the lack of diversity and quantity of resources characteristic of the earlier large 'multiple' estates by higher productivity and trade.

The ramifications of such developments are nicely represented in post-Viking-settlement, Anglo-Scandinavian Yorkshire. At the intensely studied medieval village site of Wharram Percy, for instance, it remains impossible to be sure whether the open fields around the village were established in the 10th century or the 12th. However a comparison of pottery distributions in the area between the Middle- and Late Saxon periods and a judgment of historical prob-

34 Tim Malim and John Hines, *An Anglo-Saxon Cemetery at Edix Hill, Cambridgeshire (Barrington A)* (York: Council for British Archaeol., 1998), 326–7.
35 Hooke, *op. cit.* in note 24, 170–95.
36 Dennis Coggins, 'Simy Folds: twenty years on', in John Hines *et al.* (eds.), *Land, Sea and Home: Proceedings of a Conference on Viking-period Settlement* (Society for Medieval Archaeol. Monograph Ser., forthcoming).
37 Trevor Rowley (ed.), *The Origins of Open-Field Agriculture* (London: Croom Helm, 1981); Hooke, *op. cit.* in note 24, 114–30.

ability point towards the earlier date for the emergence of the nucleated village with which the new field system was eventually to be associated.[38] Meanwhile the growth in the importance or the pretensions of rural estate centres in 10th-century Yorkshire is preserved for us in the distribution of Anglo-Scandinavian sculpture of this date, presumably representing the patronage, and the desire to leave a permanent memorial, of the local landlords, as a well-ordered Christian society was rebuilt there following the 9th-century Viking disruptions.[39]

Throughout the Anglo-Saxon Period, control and use of land thus remained the foundation stones of social position and power. But while of course environmental facts imposed constraints upon the exploitation of the landscape, there was scope for considerable variation and creativity in the manipulation of the land to achieve those goals. This overview has outlined how the land of the English was defined and exploited in terms of the economic and social zones of the cultural circle. By the end of the 10th century, Ælfric, in his homily on St Oswald, a 7th-century King of Northumbria, could use the term *Engla land* for the first time that we know of to refer unambiguously to 'England', and Byrhtnoth, in *The Battle of Maldon*, could be made to state his determination to defend:

>   . . . ēþel þysne
> Æþelredes eard,   ealdres mīnes
> folc and foldan.   (lines 52–4)

>   . . . this land:
> Ethelred's territory; my lord's
> people and ground.

Further consideration of Old English poetry shows the ideological dimensions of the Anglo-Saxon cultural relationship with the landscape to have been every bit as complex and as significant as the socio-economic factors.

Everything in its Place

According to the model of culture represented in Figure 2 (above, p. 14), the human place in the natural and cultural world is not just a matter of geographical location, but rather at an intersection of environmental, social and ideological spheres of experience. For the literate Anglo-Saxons who sought to enrich their

---

[38] John G. Hurst, 'The Wharram research project: results to 1983', *Medieval Archaeol.*, 28 (1984), 77–111, esp. 81–8; Julian D. Richards, 'The Anglo-Saxon and Anglo-Scandinavian evidence', in Paul Stamper and R. A. Croft *et al.*, *Wharram: A Study of Settlement on the Yorkshire Wolds. Vol. 8: The South Manor Area* (University of York, 2000), 195–200; Dawn M. Hadley, *The Northern Danelaw: Its Social Structure*, c. *800–1100* (London: Leicester University Press, 2000), 207–10.

[39] James Lang, *Corpus of Anglo-Saxon Stone Sculpture. Vol. 3: York and Eastern Yorkshire* (British Academy and Oxford University Press, 1991), 26–7; cf. David Stocker, 'Monuments and merchants: irregularities in the distribution of stone sculpture in Lincolnshire and Yorkshire in the tenth century', in Dawn M. Hadley and Julian D. Richards (eds.), *Cultures in Contact: Scandinavian Settlement in England in the Ninth and Tenth Centuries* (Turnhout: Brepols, 2000), 179–212.

lives and their world through poetry, the ideological sphere was dominated by the tenets of early-medieval Christianity. Those doctrines proved to be capable of comfortable assimilation to separate martial and secular ideals embodied within heroic poetry. The merger of the two codes manifests itself most clearly in the form of Christian dramas (Biblical, apocryphal and hagiographical) presented in the mode of heroic warfare and social relationships. It is equally consistent for an intrinsically non-Christian legend, such as *Beowulf*, to be adapted to Christianity by making a belief in and deference to a single, all-powerful and just God a significant feature of the hero's wisdom.

There is one aspect of the topic of place that has been thoroughly explored in Old English literary studies. This represents the centrality of the human subject, but at the cost of being essentially negative in respect of normal conditions of life, in that it concerns the separation of the individual from his (and sometimes her) home, in the state of exile.[40] The exile, *wrǣcca* in Old English (giving us our word *wretch*), is a familiar and potent image in this poetry. Exile is repeatedly alluded to as an abject state in *Beowulf*, and the lamentable experiences of exiles are directly portrayed in several of the elegies. The apocryphally expanded stories of the rebellion of Lucifer-Satan and the fallen angels, and Adam and Eve's loss of Paradise, are made familiar through the use of exile imagery in the connected poems *Genesis A* and *Genesis B*. The salience of the concept of exile in Old English poetry cannot be disputed, but it should not be overlooked that there is also a reciprocal, positive representation of 'home' within this body of literature. Thus in both *Beowulf* and *The Battle of Maldon* – the latter with a more explicit merger of secular and religious ideals than the former – home emerges as the place where the individual is most secure, and where the hero can expect to be remembered.[41]

Old English poetry as a whole is persistently idealistic rather than realistic. With the generically quite distinct exception of the Riddles of the Exeter Book, this poetry reveals a minimal concern to describe, let alone to endorse or delight in, the realities of its own context: even the fragments of *The Ruin* form a moralizing, elegiac, cliché-ridden meditation upon the physical ruins of a Roman city, devoid of any reference to Anglo-Saxon towns or other habitations. The Christian and heroic idealism of the poetry is scarcely even surreptitiously buried in dramatic or descriptive portrayals of the contemporary context in the way that, say, Dickens would do in Victorian times. Thus, when we approach the extant corpus of Old English poetry with a clear knowledge of the practical and actual realities of Anglo-Saxon life, such as those that were outlined in the preceding section, we search nearly in vain for even accidental reflections of contemporary circumstances.

---

[40] E.g. Stanley B. Greenfield, 'The formulaic expression of the theme of "exile" in Anglo-Saxon poetry', *Speculum*, 30 (1955), 200–6; Marti Rissanen, 'The theme of "exile" in *The Wife's Lament*', *Neuphilologische Mitteilungen*, 70 (1969), 90–104; Marilyn Desmond, 'The voice of exile: feminist literary history and the anonymous Anglo-Saxon elegy', *Critical Inquiry*, 16 (1990), 572–90.

[41] See, e.g., *Beowulf*, 518–23, and the speeches of Ælfric and Leofsunu in *The Battle of Maldon*, 212–24 and 246–53; cf. Anita R. Riedinger, ' "Home" in Old English poetry', *Neuphilologische Mitteilungen*, 96 (1995), 51–9.

A rare – I believe, in fact, unique – extended simile in *The Phoenix* does assume familiarity not only with the details and demands of agricultural production but also with their importance. *The Phoenix* is a paraphrase and expansion of a 4th-century Latin Christian poem by Lactantius, *Carmen de Ave Phoenix*, an allegorical poem seeing in the phoenix reborn in fire an image of the redemption, resurrection and immortality offered for the Christian soul by Christ:

> Sumes onlīce
> swā mon tō ondleofne   eorðan wæsmas
> on hærfeste   hām gelædeð,
> wiste wynsume,   ær wintres cyme,
> on rypes tīman,   þȳ læs hī rēnes scūr
> āwyrde under wolcnum;   þær hī wraðe mētað,
> fōdorþege gefēon,   þonne forst ond snāw
> mid ofermægne   eorþan þeccað
> wintergewædum.   Of þām wæstmum sceal
> eorla ēadwela   eft ālædan
> þurh cornes gecynd,   þe ær clæne bið
> sæd onsāwen.   Þonne sunnan glæm
> on lenctenne,   līfes tācen,
> weceð woruldgestrēon,   þæt þā wæstmas bēoð
> þurh āgne gecynd   eft ācende,
> foldan frætwe.   Swā se fugel weorþeð,
> gomel æfter gēarum,   geong ednīwe,
> flæsce bifongen.   Nō hē fōddor þigeð,
> mete on moldan,   nemne meledēawes
> dæl gebyrge,   sē drēoseð oft
> æt middre nihte;   bī þon se mōdga his
> feorh āfēdeð,   oþþæt fyrngesetu,
> āgenne eard   eft gesēceð.   (242–64)

> Partly the same way
> as people carry home for sustenance
> the fruits of the earth at harvest-time,
> pleasing provisions, before the coming of winter
> at the reaping season, lest the falling rain
> should destroy them beneath the clouds; there they find sustenance,
> the enjoyment of eating, while frost and snow
> with their irresistible force cover the earth
> in her winter clothing. From these fruits shall
> the happy well-being of Men be born again
> through the nature of the grain, which is first sown
> as pure seed. Then the brightness of the sun
> in the Lententide, a symbol of life,
> awakens the world's treasure hoard, so that the fruits,
> in their natural way, will be brought back to life,
> the adornment of the land. Thus this bird –
> old in years – becomes young once more,
> [re-]clothed in flesh. He eats not a thing,
> no food upon the earth, other than a taste
> of honey-dew, which often falls

in the middle of the night; by which, lofty-minded, he
feeds his own life, until he returns once more
to his ancient dwelling-place, his own land.

Nothing in the Latin source convincingly explains the extent of this passage, although the conceit is congruent with, and so may have been inspired by, a favourite patristic simile.[42] And even in this passage, the intrinsic realism of the simile is turned to make the point that the blessed phoenix lives on the dews that fall, like manna from Heaven, not on the fruits of the necessary toil of sinful Man.

It is, indeed, more common for the fruits of the earth to be presented as effectively self-generated rather than systematically cultivated; as in *The Seafarer*, when:

> Bearwas blōstmum nimað,   byrig fægriað,
> wongas wlitigað,   woruld ōnetteð . . .   (48–9)[43]

> The woods invest themselves in blossoms, habitations grow fair,
> the landscape becomes lovely, the world quickens . . .

In fact, the word *wongas* here, normally translated as 'plains', is one of the words most frequently used to denote the landscape in Old English poetry. It is a word with no semantic connotations involving the cultural modification or use of the land. There are no certain examples of its use to form place-names in Anglo-Saxon England, although names in Viking-period and later Scandinavian-influenced areas may include the Norse cognate element *vangr*, which came to mean 'field'.[44] Old English poetry emphatically presented a raw wasteland, an *uncūþ gelād* or *wēsten* ('unknown expanse', 'waste'), as its typical rural setting: an uncultivated and open stage on which its heroes, be they Beowulf, the fleeing Israelites, or holy characters facing their temptations, could be tested and proved.

There are, in consequence, certain generic characteristics that both affect and inform our reading of Old English poetry. We must still beware of assuming that Old English poetry is always indifferent to realism; but the acknowledgement that this is typical of the poetry makes variations from the norm potentially all the more significant. This premiss proves to be particularly productive when applied to the two poems now to be discussed in closer detail. The historical validity of isolating individual poems for close reading might be challenged on the grounds that an Anglo-Saxon audience and readership may have conceived of Old English poetry primarily as a mass rather than in an individualized form.[45] The great majority of our known Old English poetry is preserved for us

---

[42] Text quoted from Bernard J. Muir, *The Exeter Anthology of Old English Poetry*, 2 vols. (Exeter University Press, 1994), vol. I, 175–6. Cf. also Norman F. Blake, *The Phoenix*, 2nd ed. (Exeter University Press, 1990). Blake's edition quotes Lactantius' poem and cites the patristic sources in the note to lines 242ff.

[43] Muir (ed.), *op. cit.* in note 42, 233.

[44] Kenneth Cameron, *English Place Names* (London: Batsford, 1961), 206.

[45] Peter S. Blake, 'Textual boundaries in Anglo-Saxon works on time (and in some Old English

in four large manuscript books (*codices*) written between the mid-10th and early
11th centuries. None of these contains just one poem, and in certain cases where
one poem ends and another begins is a matter of justifiable doubt. But this does
not render the concept of the discrete poem in Old English an improper anachro-
nism: many poems have quite clear starting or ending formulae. We are not,
therefore, obliged to submerge what appear to be special cases of material allusion within the general idealism and detachment of Old English poetry.

The first poem to be considered is *Andreas*, a relatively long account (1,722
lines) of St Andrew, one of Christ's disciples and apostles, coming to the rescue
of his fellow apostle Matthew from the hands of the cannibal population of
Mermedonia, whom he converts to Christianity for good measure. This poem is
preserved in a codex called the Vercelli Book from the Italian cathedral in the
library of which it has lain, perhaps since the Anglo-Saxon period itself. This
codex is suspected to be the earliest of the four poetic codices, dated to within
the third quarter of the 10th century, and it contains four Christian poems
(*Andreas*, *The Fates of the Apostles*, *The Dream of the Rood* and *Elene*), interspersed with a collection of Old English prose homilies.[46]

Andreas is a clear example of how the selective literary reflection of reality
in such poetry is to be interpreted and understood within a Christian emblematic
scheme. Surrounding the city of Mermedonia, for instance, there is predictably
no more than an open, unregulated land: the ideal *herefeld* (lines 10 and 18),
meotudwang (11) or *wælwang* (1226) – all terms we can translate as 'battlefield'
– for the apostles' spiritual warfare:

> Eal wæs þæt mearcland   morðre bewunden,
> fēondes fācne,   folcstede gumena,
> hæleða ēþel.   (19–21)

> All of the territory was engulfed in wickedness,
> in devilish crime, the country of those people,
> the homeland of those men.

In the noun *folcstede* (line 20), the element *folc* ('folk') can have a military
sense – the term *folc-toga* (lines 8 and 1458) means 'troop-leader' – but it is
associated especially with the Mermedonians in *Andreas* and seems to be
imbued with connotations of an uncivilized population and economy. At one
point, the chief priest in Jerusalem is quoted (ironically) as referring contemptu-
ously to Jesus' background with Mary and Joseph in Nazareth as lying in the
folc-scearu: 'out in the countryside' (684).

In the absence of the proper development of the land on the island of
Mermedonia, the use of the conventional terms *burh* and *ceastre* to describe the
city (our words *borough* and *chester*: e.g. lines 40–1) is ironic: not so much
scornfully inappropriate as awaiting a real fulfilment, when Mermedonia can

poems)', in Mary J. Toswell and Elizabeth M. Tyler (eds.), *Studies in English Language and Literature*
(London: Routledge, 1996), 445–56.
[46] All quotations here are from the edition of Kenneth R. Brooks, *Andreas and The Fates of the Apostles*
(Oxford: Clarendon Press, 1961).

take its place amongst the properly civilized, Christian cities of the world. Similarly premature is the use of the term *ēþel* in line 21, translated above as 'homeland', to describe the land. This *ēþel* is immediately revealed to be an unexploited *wong*:

> Næs þǣr hlāfes wist
> werum on þǣm wonge,   ne wæteres drynce
> tō brūconne,   ah hīe blōd ond fel,
> fīra flǣschōman   feorrancumenra,
> ðēgon geond þā þēode.   (21–5)

> There was no provision of bread there
> for the men in that land, nor drinking water
> to consume, but they fed on the blood and flesh,
> the bodies of men who had come from afar,
> throughout that nation.

In line 74, the captured Matthew refers to himself as *ēþel-lēas* ('*ēþel*-less'), a term with a double implication: in one sense, he is without a homeland, an exile from his own people; at the same time, he is without any formal claim to property in the land of Mermedonia, for no such organization yet exists. One of Andreas' key achievements therefore is to establish a Christian state there, a devout and claimed (*getihhad*) land and people, as lines 1320–1 express it. Throughout the poem, the human condition within *middangeard*, literally the middle zone, between Heaven and Hell in the Christian scheme, is contrasted with God's domain. The latter is persistently referred to using the normal, mundane terminology for defined and organized, occupied lands and places, but with a special, distinguishing adjective – *þæt ūplice ēþelrīce* ('the upper kingdom': lines 119–20); *se mǣra hām, se clǣna hām, se hālga hām* ('the glorious home'; 'the pure home'; 'the sacred home': 227, 978 and 1683).[47]

Complementary to this contrast between divine and savagely human domains, and thematically even more central to the poem, is a set of contrasts drawn between the Mermedonians' cannibalism and spiritual nourishment, with normal human food and drink in an intermediary position. Not long after we are told that the Mermedonians eat and drink neither bread nor water in the lines quoted above (21–2), we hear that they are so under the spell of pagan sorcerers (*drȳas*: 34) that:

> hīe hīg ond gærs
> for metelēaste   mēðe gedrehte.   (38–9)

> weary for want of food
> they suffered [to eat] hay and grass.

– truly, just like beasts. The term *wist* ('food', 'provisions'), introduced in line 21 where the Mermedonians lack provision of bread, reappears in lines 302 and 312, where Andreas sets out on his sea-journey to the island as directed by God:

---

[47] Phrases cited in this way are all put into the nominative case.

he does so precipitantly, unprepared and without supplies, trusting faithfully in God's provision. In the latter, of course, he is not disappointed (lines 365–6) and, again with an irony that is spiritually positive rather than satirical, Andreas, who has not yet recognized it is God Himself who is his ferryman, invokes a *heofonlic hlāf* ('heavenly bread') for Him as a reward (389). There may be a fleeting reference to the normality of pastoral food production when Matthew, in prayer, declares himself ready to face slaughter like the unspeaking cattle (*swā þā dumban nēat*: 67), but upon conversion the Mermedonians are not portrayed as becoming regular farmers as well as regular Christians, but rather seem destined to live by a form of passive spiritual vegetarianism. After Andreas has been tortured by them for several days, his drops of blood fall into the ground as seeds for fruitful plants:

> Þā on lāst besēah   lēoflic cempa
> æfter wordcwidum   wuldorcyninges;
> gesēh hē geblōwene   bearwas standan
> blǣdum gehrodene,   swā hē ǣr his blōd āgēat.   (1446–9)

> Then the beloved warrior looked behind him
> in accordance with the words of the King of Glory;
> he saw full-grown woodlands standing there
> adorned with blossoms where he had formerly poured out his blood.

The final act by which Andreas achieves the conversion of the Mermedonians is to unleash a mighty baptismal flood of water from an ancient marble pillar that he orders to split apart (1489–1521). The impact of this flood is denoted by a series of cruelly ironic consumption metaphors, famous, unfortunately, more for the fact that they appear to have been appropriated from *Beowulf* than for their thematic importance:

> Næs þā wordlatu   wihte þon māre
> þæt se stān tōgān.   Strēam ūt āwēoll,
> flēow ofer foldan;   fāmige walcan
> mid ǣrdæge   eorðan þehton,
> myclede mereflōd.   Meoduscerwen wearð
> æfter symbeldæge;   slǣpe tōbrugdon
> searuhæb[b]ende.   Sund grunde onfēng,
> dēope gedrēfed;   duguð wearð āfyrhted
> þurh þæs flōdes fǣr.   Fǣge swulton
> geonge on geofone,   gūðrǣs fornām
> þurh sealtes swelg;   þæt wæs sorgbyrþen,
> biter bēorþegu.   Byrlas ne gǣldon,
> ombehtþegnas;   þǣr wæs ǣlcum genōg
> fram dæges orde   drync sōna gearu.   (1522–35)

> Then there was not a moment's further speech before
> the stone split apart. A great torrent welled out
> and flooded the ground; foaming waves,
> as dawn broke, engulfed the soil:
> the sea-flood grew mightier. It was the serving of mead
> after the day of feasting; the warriors

> started from their sleep. A sea seized the land,
> boiling deep within; the veterans were terrified
> by the onrush of the flood. Doomed, they died,
> young men in the water; its charge destroyed them,
> swallowed in the salt. That was a brewing of grief,
> a bitter draught of ale. Cupbearers were not waiting,
> serving-men: there was plenty for everyone
> from the break of day, drink immediately to hand.[48]

In a very obvious way, this is the converse of God's gift in the form of the feeding of the five thousand, recalled by Andreas on his voyage (lines 573–600). And yet, as a revelation of God's power, and ultimately as a benevolent intervention releasing the Mermedonians from their innate sin, those two acts are properly consistent.

How far might we claim, then, that an archaeologically informed perspective assists a reader's recognition of this thematically contrastive structure throughout *Andreas*? Could we even claim that a full understanding of the poem depends upon an awareness of external realities? It is certainly an important consideration, that imagery of cultivation and consumption is so central to Christian teaching and practice (consider the Parable of the Sower, and the Eucharist), that one can quite reasonably argue that the semantic parameters that describe the structure of *Andreas* need never be more than intellectual, textual and linguistic. A reader with horizons that do not reach beyond the cloister, scriptorium and library could still understand *Andreas* fully. What one may suggest beyond that, however, is that the whole semantic field of the poem is needlessly foreshortened without recognition of its real dimension. In particular it is this frame of reference that does most to make one conscious of the intermediary position of an actual, worldly Christian society between the bestial heathenism of the Mermedonians and the divine blessedness of the heavenly kingdom. One final image reinforces this point in a crucial way.

Andreas' parting gift to Mermedonia is to establish a church there: rather nicely, a recognizable minster church, with a bishop, Platan (lines 1636–94). Prior to that he has miraculously, but spiritually appropriately, resurrected the young men of the island who had given up their old lives in the baptismal torrent (1613–31; cf. 1530–1, quoted above). But not all were spared. When, answering the Mermedonians' entreaties, Andreas has, Christ-like, stilled the storm and caused the flood to sink, it happens in a manner mirroring its onset:

> Þā se beorg tōhlād
> eorðscræf egeslic, ond þǣr in forlēt
> flōd fæðmian.   (1587–9)

---

[48] It should be noted that the passage quoted here contains a number of editorial emendations of manuscript readings, and in particular that the thematically consistent translation of *sorgbyrþen* (line 1532) as 'brewing of grief' rather than the more obvious 'sorrow-burden' is a bold, although linguistically valid, interpretation.

> Then the hill/barrow parted,
> a dreadful grave, and allowed
> the flood to pour in there.

With it, the flood carried *in forwyrde* ('to damnation') the fourteen worst of that people. The term *beorg* is ambiguous in Old English. It is used of both a small, rounded, natural hill, and of constructed burial mounds: still called 'barrows' in English archaeology. The word *eorðscræf*, which could refer to any pit or fissure, commonly has the meaning 'grave' in Old English poetry and certainly does so on the two other occasions it is used in *Andreas*. It is truly impossible to encounter this collocation of *beorg* and the accursed burial places of condemned criminals without evoking the parallel late Anglo-Saxon use of what they perceived as heathen barrows as execution sites.[49] In this way, *Andreas* emerges as firmly rooted in the Anglo-Saxon organization and use of the landscape despite its idealism and its desire to transcend the worldly. Critical respect for its realistic dimension is absolutely justified.

Such a case can be made even more forcefully in respect of an exemplary, hagiographical tale set not on an imaginary cannibal island but on the coastal margins of eastern England, in the Fens. A man called Guthlac was born into a noble family in Christian England around the middle of the second half of the 7th century. We know he died in 714, but not at what age. After a military career between the ages of 15 and 24, he spent two years as a monk at Repton (Derbys.) before becoming a hermit on the island (strictly a promontory) of Crowland in the Fens, in the far south of Lincolnshire. His saintly deeds in life and death were recorded in an Anglo-Latin *Vita* (Life) during the first half of the 8th century by a monk, Felix. Two Old English poems also celebrate his deeds, *Guthlac A* and *Guthlac B*, preserved side-by-side in a vernacular poetic anthology, the Exeter Book.[50] This codex is judged to be of a similar date to the Vercelli Book. *Guthlac B* is derived from one long chapter of Felix's *Vita Sancti Guthlaci* (chapter L), describing his final days, but there are only occasional and minor close correspondences between *Guthlac A* and the *Vita*, which therefore appear independent of one another. It is thus possible that, like Felix's *Vita*, *Guthlac A* was written within the first few decades after Guthlac's death.[51]

Guthlac A focuses principally on Guthlac's struggle to establish his hermitage (most commonly referred to using the terms *hām*, *setl* and *wīc*: 'home', 'seat', 'habitation') on a *beorg* in the fenland wastes. Although the poem is not explicit on the character of this *beorg*, Felix's *Vita* (chapter XXVIII)

---

[49] Andrew Reynolds, *Later Anglo-Saxon England: Life and Landscape* (Stroud: Tempus, 1999), 96–110. A more detailed investigation and discussion can be found in Dr Reynolds's unpublished Ph.D. thesis, 'Anglo-Saxon Law in the Landscape' (University College London, 1998). I am grateful to the author for making a copy of this thesis available to me.

[50] Sources of all quotations and references here: Bertram Colgrave (ed. and trans.), *Felix's Life of Saint Guthlac* (Cambridge University Press, 1956); Jane Roberts (ed.), *The Guthlac Poems of the Exeter Book* (Oxford: Clarendon Press, 1979). On Crowland and these sources, see Audrey L. Meaney, 'Felix's Life of St Guthlac: hagiography and/or truth?', *Proc. Cambridge Antiq. Soc.*, 90 (2001), 29–48. On the Exeter Book, see Muir, *op. cit.* in note 42, esp. vol. I, 1–44, and Patrick W. Conner, *Anglo-Saxon Exeter: A Tenth-Century Cultural History* (Woodbridge: Boydell, 1993).

[51] See Roberts, *op. cit.* in note 50, 19–29 and 70–1.

identifies it as a constructed mound, with a kind of 'cistern' in its side: Crowland did in fact have a Bronze-age barrow cemetery.[52] The struggle is represented as being against a community of fiends, or devilish spirits, who had formerly inhabited the mounds undisturbed, although more practical considerations intrude into the contest too. While of course this hermitage is located within a Christian cosmology between Heaven and Hell, *Guthlac A* is noticeably less concerned to assert and reinforce the hierarchical contrasts in this scheme than we found *Andreas* to be. Indeed the phrase *hālig hām* ('sacred home') is here used of Guthlac's habitation on Crowland, not of Heaven (line 149; cf. *Andreas*, 1683, cited above). Guthlac certainly looks forward to occupying a *fægra botl* ('fairer home') in Heaven (382–3), and in the end goes to his *ēce geard* ('eternal space': 786) there, while Hell is once described as *þæt atule hūs* ('the dreadful house': 562). Altogether, though, one is led to believe that the *fægre gesceaft* ('fairer creation') that the devils lost by their ancient rebellion is not confined to Heaven above (629–36), but is repeatedly shown to have been extended to Crowland by Guthlac's settlement there.

Just as explicitly and no less emphatically recognized within the poem are the economics both of place and of political geography. It is in fact precisely in these terms that the fiends initially try to turn Guthlac away:

> Bi hwon scealt þū lifgan   þēah þū lond āge?
> Nē þec mon hider   mōse fēded;
> bēod þē hunger ond þurst   hearde gewinnan
> gif þū gewītest   swā wilde dēor
> āna from ēþele.   (273–7)

> With what shall you live even if you hold the land?
> No one will bring food to you here.
> Hunger and thirst will be your harsh enemies
> if you go alone like some wild beast,
> away from your homeland.

The answer that the poet gives Guthlac at this point may have been theologically correct, but is in practical terms downright evasive:

> Is mīn hyht mid God
> ne ic mē eorðwelan   ōwiht sinne.   (318–19)

> My joy is with God,
> and I do not care for earthly goods at all.

We would seem to have reverted to a familiar, bland and idealistic piety: a view that could appear eventually to be confirmed in the worldly climax of the poem, when Guthlac finally settles peacefully on his mound, which then transforms into a green, Franciscan utopia, where he feeds the hungry birds:

---

[52] Hall and Coles, *op. cit.* in note 33, 73. Roberts, op. cit. in note 50, firmly rejects this identification and sees the *beorg* in the poem simply as a hill.

Sigehrēðig cwōm
bytla to þām beorge;   hine bletsadon
monge mægwlitas   meaglum reordum,
trēofugla tuddor   tācnum cȳðdon
ēadges eftcyme;   oft hē him æte hēold
þonne hȳ him hungrige   ymb hond flugon,
grādum gīfre   geōce gefēgon.
Swā þæt milde mōd   wið moncynnes
drēamum gedǣlde,   dryhtne þēowde,
genōm him tō wildēorum wynne   syþþan hē þās woruld forhogde.
Smolt wæs se sigewong   ond sele nīwe,
fæger fugla reord,   folde geblōwen;
gēacas gēar budon;   Gūþlāc mōste
ēadig and onmōd,   eardes brūcan.
Stōd se grēna wong   in Godes wǣre,
hæfde se heorde   se þe of heofonum cwōm
fēondas āfyrde.   Hwylc wæs fægerra
willa geworden   in wera līfe
þāra þe yldran   ūsse gemunde
oþþe wē sylfe   syþþan cūþen?   (733–51)

Exultant he came,
the builder to the barrow; many species
and kinds of tree-birds blessed him
with ringing voices, gave signs to make known
the return of the saint; often he held out food for them
when they flew, hungry around his hand,
greedily ravenous, and were glad of his help.
Thus this gentle character left the joys
of human society, and served the Lord;
he betook himself to the happiness of wild creatures when he
                                                    rejected this world.
Calm was the site of victory and his hall for the first time,
fair the birds' song, the earth in fruit;
the cuckoos announced the new season. Guthlac was able,
blessed and resolute, to use that land.
The green plain remained in God's keeping;
the pastor who had come from Heaven
had put the fiends to flight. What fairer desire
has come true in the life of those men
whom our elders knew of
or we ourselves have since been able to know?

Especially if it is accepted that the term *beorg* denotes nothing more specific than a hill rather than the barrow familiar from Felix's *Vita*, it is possible to discern here echoes of authoritative, patristic literature on the lives of the first saintly hermits in the Syrian and North African deserts – particularly the 4th-century life of St Anthony by Athanasius.[53] The first 92 lines of *Guthlac A*

---

53 J.-P. Migne (gen. ed.), *Patrologia Graeca*, vol. XXVI (Paris, 1887), 837–976.

constitute a sustained 'gnomic' passage: a generalized moral introduction, constructed of proverbial maxims. This includes a survey of strategies of holy living, echoing both the New Testament and the 6th-century *Vitae Patrum* ('Lives of the Fathers') of Gregory of Tours.[54] Yet this is thoroughly interwoven with a recognition and acceptance of contemporary economic rules. The holy life merges completely and elegantly with both a commercial exchange system and with a gift-based exchange system that served to create social alliances and security:

> wuldres bycgað
> sellað ælmessan   (76–7)

> they buy glory, they give alms

Salvation thus has a set of economic relations of its own, as we are reminded once more at the end of the poem:

> earniað on eorðan   ēcan līfes
> hāmes in hēahþu   (795–6)

> upon earth they earn eternal life,
> a home above

This is no crude appropriation of economic facts of life to try to familiarize the holy: while the human subjects buy and earn their salvation, God operates differently as the great gift-giver, bringing His people back to Him. The word *giefu* ('gift') itself is repeatedly used to refer to God's grace (e.g. lines 100, 124, 357 and 530), and in its final appearance is imaginatively conceived of as something that is built in the human mind:

> Nis þæt hūru læsast   þæt sēo lufu cȳþeð
> þonne hēo in monnes   mōde getimbreð
> gǣstcunde gife.   (769–71)

> That is not, indeed, the least thing which that love makes manifest
> when it constructs in the human mind
> spiritual grace.

We should also note just how effectively the noun *getimbru* ('structures') and verb *getimbran* ('construct') form a key and recurrent theme in the poem (lines 18, 250, 485 and 770).

The use of realistic imagery in *Guthlac A* does not, then, merely assert and reinforce a rigid sense of hierarchical difference between the divine and its antithesis as may be suggested for *Andreas*. Rather it conveys a surprisingly subtle model of interpenetration between human endeavours and investment and gracious divine initiatives. All of this takes on a much enhanced significance when we look at Guthlac's foundation of the hermitage at Crowland in context. Felix tells us that Guthlac was succeeded there by another hermit, Cissa, but,

---

[54] Roberts, *op. cit.* in note 50, 26–7.

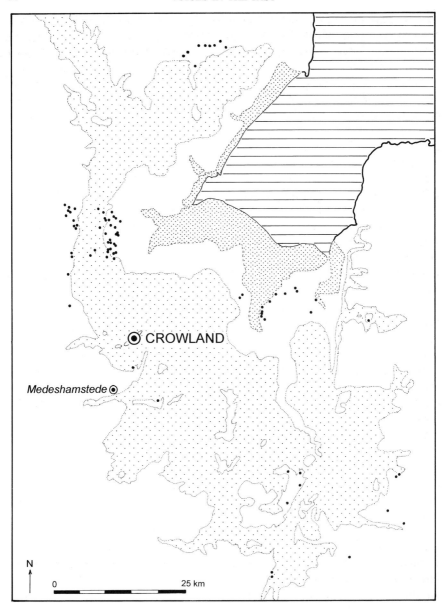

FIG. 4. Anglo-Saxon settlement sites in the Fens c. AD 700 (larger dots). Dark stippling: silt fen. Light stippling: peat fen. After Hall and Coles, *op. cit.* in note 33.

despite forged claims to the contrary fraudulently representing a more direct connexion with a saintly founder than seems to have been the fact, the late Anglo-Saxon Benedictine abbey of Crowland was, so far as we can tell, a later 10th-century foundation.[55]

Whether or not Guthlac had intended to found a monastery at Crowland, his occupation of the promontory in the Fens around the beginning of the 8th century was not the egregious act his hagiographical life-records would like to suggest. The history of settlement, and of the landscape, in the Fens has been carefully studied in recent years, largely through extensive field survey work but also through excavations. This has revealed considerable changes in the topography of the Fens and fluctuations in the human settlement and use of the area.[56] After extensive and increasing exploitation in the Roman Period, for the special fishing, grazing and above all salt-making the Fens could support, the previously settled areas were largely abandoned in the earliest centuries of the Anglo-Saxon Period. In a Middle Saxon Period, however, defined by the appearance of particular types of pottery at settlement sites, largely Ipswich Ware south of the River Nene and 'Maxey-type' wares north of it, the introduction of which coincides closely with Guthlac's settlement, there are clear signs of both the re-organization of settlement in this area and a greater exploitation of the Fens (Fig. 4).[57] The replacement of scattered small settlement sites with fewer, larger villages seems to have occurred first around the Fen Edge, later on inhabited silt-lands within the Fens. This process of nucleation renders it practically impossible to compare the density of settlement in terms of levels of population across the Anglo-Saxon Period, but it does appear likely that there was some increase in the population supported here in the Middle Saxon Period. No further Late Saxon increase is detectable, but by sometime in the 9th century the entire Wash had been faced with a Sea Bank, to protect the Fenlands from flooding. By the late 10th century most of the area formed part of great monastic estates – Crowland, Peterborough, Thorney, Ramsey and Ely. How far back such direct monastic interests might go can only be a matter of guesswork (and Anglo-Saxon fraud). Remarkably, though, the area of Crowland itself remains an archaeological blank for the Middle Saxon Period.

About 35 miles (55 km) east-south-east of Crowland, on the opposite edge of the Fens in north-western Suffolk, a settlement site contemporary with Guthlac's hermitage has been excavated at Brandon. This was situated upon a sand ridge, where, within an area of 12,000 square metres, the foundations of 25 buildings were excavated by the date of the only published report on the site, from 1988.[58] A timber causeway linked this periodical island to the mainland.

---

[55] All sixteen charters relating to Crowland and its property catalogued by Sawyer (*op. cit.* in note 24) and purportedly dating from the early 8th to the mid-11th century seem likely to be forgeries.

[56] Hall and Coles, *op. cit.* in note 33; Special section: 'Survey, environment and excavation in the English Fenland', *Antiquity*, 62 (1988), 305–76; David Hall, 'The changing environment of the Cambridgeshire silt fens', *Landscape Hist.*, 3 (1981), 37–49. Between 1985 and 1996 eleven volumes of reports from *The Fenland Project* have been published in the monograph series East Anglian Archaeology (vols. 27, 35, 45, 52, 55, 56, 61, 66, 70, 78 and 79).

[57] See especially Hayes, *op. cit.* in note 33.

[58] R. D. Carr, A. Tester and P. Murphy, 'The Middle Saxon settlement at Staunch Meadow, Brandon', *Antiquity*, 62 (1988), 371–7.

The buildings were typical Anglo-Saxon post-built structures, some of them with hearths. A three-celled, oriented, post-built structure which had been a focus for burial is identified as a church: the burials imply an organic community of both sexes and all ages. There was a large amount of Ipswich Ware and some imported pottery and metal-vessel fragments amongst the stratified finds from an occupation layer. Grains and seeds reflect the type of agricultural and gathering regime already outlined, and bone waste included not only domesticated animals but also fishbone and oyster shells indicating exploitation of the waterlands and coast. Textile production and dyeing were carried out at this site. Particular evidence of a sophisticated lifestyle at the site takes the form of styli, for writing, a considerable amount of glass fragments, and a decorated and inscribed gold plaque depicting St John the Evangelist, possibly from a book cover. Although one earlier Anglo-Saxon brooch-fragment has been found at the site, there is currently no basis for dating the founding of this settlement significantly before the introduction of Ipswich Ware around the beginning of the 8th century. There has inevitably been much debate over the possible monastic character of the settlement (the age- and sex-range of the burials notwithstanding), but, for the reasons given above (pp. 51–2), this seems doomed to be inconclusive. In many respects a comparable site, overlooking the flood-plain of the River Trent close to the Humber in North Lincolnshire rather than the Fens, is that of Flixborough.[59] Here a longer sequence of settlement, from the 7th to the 10th centuries, is represented, but the range of finds is distinctly similar, including styli and an inscribed 8th-century plaque. Especially striking amongst the finds reported from this site so far is the large amount of preserved bone, including a considerable proportion of fresh- and saltwater fish, and oyster shells, alongside netsinkers for fishing. Both Brandon and Flixborough give us a detailed insight into how thriving and recently established Middle Saxon fen-edge settlements would really exploit the land (*eardes brūcan*: *Guthlac A*, 745).

Why Crowland, though? Archaeologically, this spot would appear to have been conveniently available for a Guthlac around the year 700, uninhabited, except perhaps by phantoms. According to the early sources, Guthlac was attracted to the place by its wildness and isolation. Unoccupied though it may have been, at 8 miles (13 km) north-north-east of Peterborough (Cambs.) and the major monastery of *Medeshamstede*, founded by the second half of the 7th century, it was not quite as remote as Felix would have us believe. Besides this important monastery, the Peterborough area was well settled and thriving throughout the Anglo-Saxon period: this area has a number of furnished cemeteries of the 5th and 6th centuries, with some of the earliest Germanic finds from England, plus important excavated Early and Middle Saxon settlements at Orton Hall Farm and Maxey, on the Nene and Welland.[60] It is difficult to believe that Guthlac's occupation of Crowland could have been independent of the local

---

[59] Christopher P. Loveluck, 'A high-status Anglo-Saxon settlement at Flixborough, Lincolnshire', *Antiquity*, 72 (1998), 146–61.

[60] Donald F. Mackreth, *Orton Hall Farm: A Roman and Early Anglo-Saxon Farmstead*, East Anglian Archaeol., 76 (Nene Valley Archaeol. Trust, 1996); Peter V. Addyman *et al.*, 'A Dark-age settlement at Maxey, Northants', *Medieval Archaeol.*, 8 (1964), 20–73.

centre at Peterborough, and a reasonable guess that Guthlac and his family had prior links with this area. It is then impossible to overlook the fact that less than 5 miles (7 km) west of Peterborough on the Nene lay the Roman town of Durobrivae (Water Newton), best known publicly for spectacular late 4th-century hoards of gold coins and Christian silverware found there, but a large and important site upon Ermine Street, the Roman Great North Road, in its own right. There is evidence that this town enjoyed the status of a regional capital in the later 3rd century. Most interestingly, it has cautiously been inferred that it may have housed the administrative centre of an imperial estate in the Fens themselves.[61] The archaeological emptiness of the Crowland area in the Early and Middle Anglo-Saxon Periods reinforces the view that it was then a cultural border zone between the territories, or spheres of interest, of East Anglia and Lindsey – possibly reflected by the distribution of Ipswich and Maxey-type wares – and that the occupation of Crowland can be interpreted as an attempt to assert a claim upon this area.

By declaring in his Prologue that he has written the *Vita* at the request of King Ælfwald of East Anglia (713–749), Felix reveals his own connexion with that kingdom. He was thus in a position to know how the Fens were being developed at this date. Apart from the tentative suggestion that the independence of *Guthlac A* and the *Vita* could mean that they were separately composed around the same time as one another, we have no definite evidence as to the date and background of *Guthlac A*. Metrical and grammatical details support the case that *Guthlac A* may be one of our earliest surviving poems, but this evidence is not conclusive, nor does it suggest a clear absolute date of composition. The poem certainly could have been composed as early as the 8th century; the contrary, pre-emptive declaration that 'the burden of establishing an earlier [i.e. pre-Alfredian] dating for the poems [in the Exeter Book] lies with critics who wish to develop that thesis' is groundless.[62] But in whatever way – and however unconsciously – an understanding of the changing organization and exploitation of the relevant landscape zone came to the poet, *Guthlac A* most decidedly embodies those insights in a real and significant way. A remarkably well-rounded fusion of the economic considerations involved in the recolonization of difficult but resource-rich areas such as the Fens with the social implications those had in political and ecclesiastical terms, as well as the superordinate religious beliefs of Christian readers and writers in Anglo-Saxon England, informs *Guthlac A* from beginning to end, and transforms naïve hagiography into a rich artistic microcosm of a phase of Anglo-Saxon culture. That would not in itself make this into a great or even a good poem, but it certainly extends the range of its artistry, while at the same time much enhancing its functional weight. How this has been overlooked! Even one of the poem's few appreciative critics could refer to the poet's indifference to detail, and write that '*Guthlac A* is no place to go for a primary description of anything material: a barrow, the Fens (etc.).'[63]

---

61 Barry C. Burnham and John Wacher, *The 'Small Towns' of Roman Britain* (London: Batsford, 1990), 81–91.
62 Muir, *op. cit.* in note 42, vol. I, 44.
63 Laurence A. Shook, 'The burial mound in *Guthlac A*', *Modern Philol.*, 58 (1960), 1–10. See also

But we, like the poet, and early audiences too, can supply our own mental pictures from separate experiences. The poet did not *need* to describe the material world in order to use it carefully and meaningfully. Altogether, this indicates that this poem had substantial and ambitious goals, which it achieved with remarkable structural balance and efficiency. Its lack of modern critical appreciation may indeed be because the composition of the poem assumed an audience or readership that was better informed over a wider range of experiences than much of its modern readership has been.

Remaining within an interpretative paradigm of Old English poetry that contrasts realism and idealism, we may, consequently, note that idealism needs a concrete knowledge of reality to define itself against. We have seen, however, that realism can be introduced and used in thoroughly pious Old English poems in unexpected ways, while in the case of *Guthlac A* the level of implicit information that may underlie the text is remarkably high. We might even go on to suggest that the starkly dichotomous image of an Old English poetic corpus dominated by idealism, dramatized in highly unrealistic contexts and with little concern for features of practical contemporary life, and with just a few, covert forays into reality by way of contrast, is a distorting and reductive one. Crucial to our case for significant reference to material reality in *Andreas* and *Guthlac A* has been an identification of implicit – not just covert – realism. There is at least a good *prima facie* case to be made that an explicit-implicit dichotomy provides a much richer reading of this literature than an idealist-realist one. It is easy to understand that, in literature with a dominant, explicit Christian message, there is little need to invoke particular contextual understandings to make the point. For wider and implicit ranges of meaning and relevancy, as in *Guthlac A*, the text must rely upon some shared and assumed perceptions for those meanings to be grasped. Implicit meaning is 'hidden' meaning in a way, then, although not deliberately covert, nor necessarily doubtful. Rather, the idea of a clear, materially defined implicit meaning can be understood as an entirely consistent extension of standard linguistic semantics to include connexions and contrasts in the real and physical world amongst the syntagmatic and paradigmatic relationships that determine what a word or utterance can or cannot mean. It is hardly surprising that, at the distance we now stand from its original cultural circumstances, these references have too often eluded critical scholarship.

This study has been undertaken, however, to enrich our perception of the life and culture of the Anglo-Saxons, not to castigate modern scholarship. The positive point it makes is that a total rejection of the world (*contemptus mundi*) was no more sustainable in the Anglo-Saxon church and its ideology than it was in Anglo-Saxon economic and social life, or is in our own scholarly linguistics and criticism. The poets and visionaries of Anglo-Saxon England lived harmoniously with their natural world in many constructive ways, making constructive use of both their practical technology and their poetry.

Jennifer Neville, *Representations of the Natural World in Old English Poetry* (Cambridge University Press, 1999), esp. pp. 128 and 204.

3

Two Medieval Books

Manuscripts Digby 86 and Harley 2253

IN virtually every aspect of English history, the later 11th and earlier 12th centuries lie between periods of markedly different character. In the case of the English language and its literature, this is the boundary between the Old and Middle English periods. The language changed considerably, both in spoken and written form. Grammatically, the Old English system of gender and case-endings simplified greatly, and new syntactical structures appeared, while the pronunciation also changed. Together with a considerable influx of Scandinavian loanwords, ultimately attributable to Viking-period settlement and influence, and some French introduced by the Normans, these defined a new series of major dialect divisions within English. Where a standardized version of late Old English (known as Late West Saxon) had been successfully enforced, a regional character re-asserted itself in Middle English literature that was not to give way to a national norm again until the 16th century.

The overwhelming majority of known Old English poems survive for us in single manuscript copies. These, however, are clearly the products of collection into anthologies and copying, and the thinness of the surviving sample implies how high a proportion of Old English poetry has been lost. For Old English prose, we have rather more multiple manuscript copies, particularly in the case of the leading late Old English ecclesiastical authors Ælfric and Wulfstan. It is no surprise, then, that the Old English poem of which we have most early copies is 'Cædmon's Hymn', preserved in the context of a Latin prose text eventually translated into an Old English version.

Amongst the contrasts between the Old and Middle English periods is a much greater profusion of literature from the later period. This manifests itself in almost every conceivable form. There is a higher absolute quantity of surviving text, and it is far more common to have multiple copies of specific works that can be compared with one another, both in attempts, editorially, to establish an original form, and to investigate variations between them in terms of their possible functions. Generically, vernacular poetry occurs in a wider range of types, with the superseding of heroic epic by chivalric romance, and the burgeoning of lyric as especially prominent features. It is not possible to be sure how much of this contrast between pre- and post-Conquest literary survival is

FIG. 5. The South-West Midlands and southern Welsh Marches, showing sites referred to in this chapter. Boroughs and market centres in italics.

due simply to the factor of time; or whether, perhaps, the obsolescence of Old English was compounded in the crucial transitional period by its loss of status, and even deliberate cultural hostility in the period of early Norman rule.

One factor, however, which explains the growth of Middle English literature in more positive terms, was that literary texts escaped from almost entirely ecclesiastical contexts in the earlier period into the secular world in the later. In this chapter we shall consider two major manuscript books that were written no more than 60 years and 40 miles (65 km) apart from one another, in the South-West Midlands and Welsh border area of the historic counties of Worcestershire, Herefordshire and southern Shropshire (Fig. 5). These offer us substantial insights into the role of literature in neighbouring, and even related, though still separate contexts in this period.

BODLEIAN LIBRARY MS DIGBY 86

MS [the conventional abbreviation for *manuscript*: a hand-written text] Digby 86 is so-named because it came into the collection of Sir Kenelm Digby in 1632. He gave his collection of manuscripts to the Bodleian Library of the University of Oxford in December 1634, where this codex has been held ever since. It is known that it was formerly in the possession of an Oxford don, Thomas Allen, who had apparently bequeathed a collection of manuscripts to Digby on his death in 1632. The Dissolution of the monasteries under Henry VIII, and Protestant assaults on the materiality of the medieval (Roman Catholic) church, had dispersed manuscripts and stimulated the emergence of private antiquarian collections. However we have no evidence that this manuscript had been in an ecclesiastical library, nor any clear clues as to how it had come to Allen and to Oxford.[1]

The early history of the codex, however, lies with families known by association with localities as the Grimhills and Underhills, of south-western Worcestershire. A calendar in the manuscript from folios 68v to 74r[2] has, added to the usual list of church feasts, death notices (*obits*) for Alexander de Grimehull', on 18 July, in the writing of the main scribe of the codex, and for both Amiscie, wife of Simon Underhill (11 July), and Simon Underhill himself (23 July) added in later handwriting, datable to the first half or middle of the 14th century. William, a son of Simon Underhill, was responsible for several pen-trials – practice fragments of script – in the manuscript after it had been completed. Most of these involve a declarative formula, found in a particularly full form on folio 99r and v:

pateat univ[er]sis per p[re]sentes quod ego Will[elmu]s

may it be clear to all through these present [letters] that I, William

and:

sciant p[re]sentes & futuri quod ego Will[elmu]s filius simonis de und[er]hulle

may people now and in the future know that I, William son of Simon of Underhill

That this is his personal handwriting is confirmed by the statement *Will[elmus] de und[er]hulle scripsit* (William of Underhill wrote [this]) on folio 141v. The largest marginal addition of this character, on folios 39v–40r, records the will of one Robert son of Robert of Pendock (Worcs.), that his body be buried at Redmarley, now Redmarley d'Abitot (Glos.) and leaving a *pullus*, 'colt', to

1   A full facsimile and study of the manuscript, on which this section is based, has been published by Judith Tschann and Malcolm B. Parkes, *Facsimile of Oxford, Bodleian Library, MS Digby 86*, Early English Text Soc., Supplementary Ser., 16 (Oxford, 1996). The history of the manuscript is discussed on pp. lvi–lx of the Introduction. Tschann and Parkes draw substantially upon B. D. H. Miller, 'The early history of Bodleian MS. Digby 86', *Annuale medievale*, 4 (1963), 26–56.

2   Page references in manuscripts are usually given to the folio (leaf) number, recto (r) or verso (v), recto being the front of the leaf, and right-hand side of the spine of an open book, verso the back of the leaf and left-hand side.

William. This Robert, son of Robert, appears in a couple of pen-trials of his own (e.g. fol. 98v), as does John, lord of Pendock, on folio 111v.

The Amiscie whose obit was entered into the calendar can be identified as the Amice daughter of Richard of Grimhill, who died in 1307 or early in 1308.[3] This connexion brings us back to the period and thus the most likely source of the manuscript itself. A scribal exordium at the end of the last full quire,[4] folio 205v, states *scripsi librum in anno et iii me[n]sibus*, 'I wrote the book in a year and three months.' This immediately follows a list of the names of kings of England that ends with Edward [I], son of Henry III, with the letter *x*, apparently denoting the tenth, or possibly ten completed years, of his reign, and thus datable to the period November 1281 – November 1283. The whole codex was, however, subsequently re-organized and added to, so this date is not necessarily the *terminus ad quem* for the whole work.[5] If, however, the main scribe was Richard of Grimhill, as suspected, he would have written the bulk of it as a man with three daughters in their teens or early twenties. Extraordinary, in light of some of its more risqué contents!

The later marginal scribbles just referred to are not the only supplements to the manuscript work of the main scribe: far more substantial are one inserted leaf (fol. 16), and two whole quires (fols. 81–96) in the heart of a long single text, a French translation of a collection of moral exempla, the *Disciplina Clericalis* of Petrus Alphonsus. These two quires are not only in the handwriting of a different scribe, but even the type of parchment differs from the rest of the codex. Detailed study of the work of the main scribe, and of the markings of the codex, both the ruling on the pages and the labelling of the quires, tells a convincing story of how it was put together.

The current binding of the book is attributable to the period of 1632–4, when it was in Digby's possession; it maintains, however, the order of a full set of 26 quire signatures in a 22-letter alphabet (without our letters *j*, *k*, *u* and *w*), extending to *aa–dd*, marked on the leaves in 16th-century handwriting. Earlier quire signatures, meanwhile, reveal two series of gatherings, implying that the anthology was originally regarded as two separate collections subsequently combined into a single, longer one. The first eight quires still surviving have the quire signatures ii–v and vii–x, revealing that two quires (i and vi) have been lost. There is no evidence of what was lost at the beginning: quire ii (fol. 1r) begins with the opening of a complete text, a *Distinctio Peccatorum*. The abrupt interruption of one text at the end of quire v (fol. 33v) and jump to a point within a different text, unheaded, on the following recto at the beginning of the quire marked vii shows that material has been lost here. The remaining eighteen quires were marked in conspicuous capitals by the main scribe as A–F and L–Y: this sequence includes a W, but no separate U or V. At least three quires are now

---

3   *Calendar of Inquisitions Post Mortem and other Analogous Documents preserved in the Public Record Office. Vol. V: Edward II* (London: His Majesty's Stationery Office [HMSO], 1908), 2–3 (no. 8). She is identified as the wife of Simon Underhill in this document, and her age is given as 44 at that date.
4   A quire is a gathering of folios, created by folding and cutting the edges of a larger sheet of parchment. Two single leaves were latter added to the end of MS Digby 86.
5   Tschann and Parkes, *op. cit.* in note 1, xxxvi–l.

missing between F and L, namely G, H and I; if the scribe included K in his alphabet, a fourth. Again, the abrupt ending and beginning of texts between these quires (fols. 112v–113r) confirms the loss of material some time between the writing of the manuscript in the late 13th century and the re-lettering of the quires in the 16th. Two further leaves, folios 206–7, in the hand of the main scribe have been added at the end.

It appears that the quires were kept unsewn and unbound for some time. There is soiling on the outer leaves of the quires, and evidence of folding, implying that they were kept loose in a wallet of some kind. The signatures were therefore required to keep them in order, not just to put them in order for binding. It has been noted that the two sequences are associable with different kinds of text. Texts that are more serious in conventional ways, namely religious and practical learning, mostly in French though some in Latin, predominate in the opening series, ii–x; a more miscellaneous range of texts, including several that are less manifestly serious – or more entertaining – appears in the later sections. The discussion to follow in this chapter notes the pitfalls of making too superficial a classification of texts in just that way, but is sufficiently illustrative of the shift of genre to note that after the lacuna now following quire F, we enter quire L in a ribald French fabliau that is followed by a particularly salacious poem, 'La vie de un valet amerous' ('The life of a lusty lad').[6]

Within the second section of the whole compilation (quires A–Y) there is one anomalous quire of four leaves, R, which is nearly entirely occupied by one of the rare examples of a Middle English fabliau, *Dame Siriz*. This was written on smaller parchment leaves than the rest of the codex, and does not over-run quire boundaries. At the end of this quire there was slightly more than one blank page left for a metrical exercise listing 'Les nouns de un leure en englais' ('The names for a hare in English'), after which a French list of unlucky days of the year was eventually squeezed in. Another copy of that list appears on folio 68r of the first section (quire ix): this has been suggested to be the scribe's second copy, placed close to the calendar to which it was clearly relevant.[7] Quires A–Y also include one exceptionally long quire of twelve folios, [M],[8] which it has been suggested was deliberately constructed in order to fit in a set of texts from one long exemplar: the texts concerned are mostly Marian poems, plus a set of *dicta* attributed to Bede. While the clustering of these texts may well give us a glimpse of the sort of pre-existing collection the scribe was copying into Digby 86, it is not clear why the quiring should have been adapted at this point, when he was usually content to copy across quire boundaries. Quire R, with *Dame Siriz*, is a more convincing case of a separate booklet – though still by the same scribe – being physically incorporated into the compilation.

The major act of appropriation of such a kind visible in Digby 86 is the infixing of quires C and D, written by a different scribe (called scribe B). These quires provided the bulk of the French verse translation of *Disciplina Clericalis*. The main scribe (scribe A) altered his usual text layout of 32 long ruled lines per

---

6 John Hines, *The Fabliau in English* (London: Longman, 1993), esp. 37–44.
7 Tschann and Parkes, *op. cit.* in note 1, xlvi.
8 The quire signature in this case has actually been lost due to damage.

Quire and folio sequence

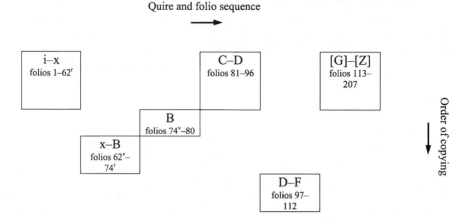

FIG. 6. Schematic diagram of the inferred sequence of copying of MS Digby 86. Note that a quire [G] can be assumed to have existed but has been lost; [Z] is used to denote the single sheets following the last full quire, marked Y.

page to scribe B's two columns of 33 lines at the start of this text, which he copied himself from folio 74v of quire B up to the end of that quire. As this text is in verse, it was an easy matter to calculate the amount of space required to reach the first complete quire provided by scribe B that could simply be incorporated in the compilation as quire C. There was space left for the rubric (heading) and a short Latin prose text on the computation of ecclesiastical feasts at the top of folio 74v. But this was still three pages from the start of quire B.

Scribe A's target appears to have been to fill in the space from here back to folio 62r, the end of a long French text on the care of hunting birds, in quire x, the last quire of the first sequence. It has been noted that the texts of psalms on folios 62v–67v consequently look compressed. Scribe A was then able to fit in a French hymn and the unlucky days of the year re-copied from quire R, before finally, on folio 68r and continuing back at the bottom of folio 67v, he squeezed in an introduction to Arabic numerals as best he could. This then left one page for each month of his calendar from folios 68v–74r.[9]

The implications of these observations are that quire x of the first section was incomplete – unfilled – when the main scribe, scribe A, decided to join the two sequences together, and worked out how to do so through the two incorporated bridging quires of scribe B and seven intermediary texts. *Disciplina Clericalis* was completed by scribe A on the first leaf of quire E, and is followed by a sequence of French verse texts with no obvious adjustment needing to be made to fit them in, up to the end of quire F (fol. 112) where the lacuna between quires F and L occurs (Fig. 6). It has been suggested that the character of scribe A's handwriting at the beginning of quire L looks rather different and perhaps represents an earlier, experimental, stage of his writing development. The one detail

---

[9]   See especially Tschann and Parkes, *op. cit.* in note 1, xlv–xlvii.

of the codex that still seems to have no commonsense and pragmatic explanation is why the scribe should then have decided to begin a new series of quire signatures (A onwards) after quire x, in the middle of a selection of psalms, rather than simply continuing the numeration. This apart, Tschann and Parkes offer a thoroughly coherent account of the composition of this manuscript compilation; only the missing quires of the second sequence could strengthen their case further.

BRITISH LIBRARY MS HARLEY 2253

The other codex to be considered in this chapter is British Library MS Harley 2253. It was purchased and added to the library of Sir Robert Harley, Earl of Oxford, in 1723, and sold on to the national collection in 1753. In surveys of the literature of medieval England, it is often paired with Digby 86, as the two manuscripts represent similar collections of diverse texts. 'Commonplace book' has been the rather dismissive-sounding term usually used to categorize them. Strictly this means collections of texts desired for special reference – memorabilia rather than memoranda, not the collection of ephemera and mundanities that the term *commonplace* might now seem to imply. Although the term is a later one, emerging first in Elizabethan English, it may point us towards their intended function. A broader but possibly more appropriate suggestion that has recently been made is to classify them as 'household books'.[10]

Like Digby 86, Harley 2253 is a composite codex, although of rather less complicated construction. The complete codex starts with four quires containing a total of 48 folios written by a scribe whose handwriting may be dated to the late 13th century or possibly the early 14th.[11] The texts here are seven devotional texts in French, two in verse followed by five in prose. The texts written by the scribe we are interested in are collected in the following 92 folios of eleven quires. It is not certain that the present ordering of quires represents the exact sequence of copying as there are no quire signatures. Five quires in this section start with new texts, so that this scribe's work can be subdivided into five potential booklets, three of single quires, one of three quires and one of five. A relative chronology is, however, suggested by a change of ruling at the start of the twelfth quire of the whole manuscript that seems to represent a habit adopted by the scribe as a later practice. The nature of the work gives the impression of following a relatively methodological order, at least in the simple sense of clustering like with like within a relatively restricted range of genres.[12] The fifth quire of the whole codex – the first by what we shall call for simplic-

10 Julia Boffey, 'Bodleian Library, MS Arch. Selden. B. 24 and definitions of the "household book"', in A. S. G. Edwards *et al.* (eds.), *The English Medieval Book: Studies in Memory of Jeremy Griffiths* (London: British Library, 2000), 125–34.

11 N. R. Ker, *Facsimile of British Museum MS, Harley 2253*, Early English Text Soc., Original Ser., 255 (Oxford, 1965). Malcolm Parkes (personal communication) suggests a slightly later date for the writing of the first four quires than Ker.

12 This opinion differs a little from the conventional view of a relatively haphazard and unstructured ordering, recently summarized and discussed by Theo Stemmler, 'Miscellany or anthology? The structure of medieval manuscripts: MS Harley 2253, for example', in Susanna Fein (ed.), *Studies in the Harley Manuscript: The Scribes, Contents, and Social Contexts of British Library MS Harley 2253* (Kalamazoo: Medieval Inst. Pub., 2000), 111–22.

ity's sake 'the Harley scribe' – is the most discrete booklet, with two solemn French poems, leaving space where some recipes were added by a later hand.

The key difference from Digby 86 that not only allows us to discern a history of the Harley scribe, but also to locate him firmly in time and place, is the fact that many more documents and manuscripts can be identified as being in his distinctive hand.[13] While standard palaeography (the study of past handwriting) suggested a dating of Harley 2253 some time after 1330, much closer dating has been made possible by the identification of the writing of the Harley scribe in a series of short legal documents (deeds) – as well as in two other major manuscripts – dated from December 1314 to April 1349. Comparing details of letterforms in dated documents with various parts of the Harley codex supports the view that the sections in the hand of the Harley scribe were written gradually, but with nothing earlier than 1329. Most of this copying was probably done in the period 1338–42, but the final entry, a short Latin prose account of the martyrdom of a Shropshire saint, Wistan, on the final page (fol. 140v), appears to be no earlier than 1343. *Probably 1347-49*

The deeds also locate the scribe quite precisely. They are overwhelmingly associated with the south Shropshire town of Ludlow. Many of them were explicitly drawn up at Ludlow, or its suburb Ludford; other locations that recur in these deeds are the manorial sites of Overton and Ashford Carbonell, just a few miles to the south of Ludlow and still within Shropshire. It is interesting that most of these 41 deeds were drawn up on behalf of a wide range of different people, although there is a group of four produced for Thomas de Overton or his son John. In the earliest codex attributable to the Harley scribe, British Library MS Harley 273, there is a liturgical calendar including a celebration of the date of dedication of the church of St Laurence, the parish church of Ludlow, establishing a direct link with that church.

It is the two later, extended codices of the Harley scribe, both compiled gradually and probably successively from the 1320s to the 1340s, that reveal the scribe's connexions with and involvement in a somewhat wider world. In the 1320s and 1330s the scribe was compiling British Library MS Royal 12 C.xii. A major item of manifestly local interest here is the French prose historical romance *Fouke Le Fitz Waryn,* imaginatively interweaving historical material from the mid-12th to mid-13th century with fantastical elements, but starting with an account of the building, and struggles for control of, the castle of Ludlow.[14] The later focus of attention in that text is the activities of a border baron in the Welsh Marches to the north of this area during the reign of King John. With a focus to the south, however, the scribe copied in a couple of seal-mottoes of Bishops of Hereford, dating from the period 1282–1327, on folio 6v.

[13]   For our knowledge of the Harley scribe we are deeply indebted to the extensive and productive work of Carter Revard, which is summarized in his 'Scribe and provenances', 21–109 in Fein (ed.), *op. cit.* in note 12.

[14]   E. J. Hathaway *et al.* (eds.), *Fouke Le Fitz Waryn*, Anglo-Norman Text Soc., XXVI–XXVIII (Oxford, 1975).

Concerns with the Diocese of Hereford are also evident in Harley 2253. The manuscript includes hagiographical texts on three local saints: Ethelberht, of Hereford; Etfrid, of Leominster (Herefords.); and Wistan, of Wistanstow. Further evidence of links comes from parchment leaves re-used in the binding, as flyleaves, of the codex, one of which has fragments of the service book (Ordinal) of Hereford Cathedral on one side, and accounts from an Irish estate associable with the dominant local baronial family, the Mortimers, on the other. The Mortimers were in fact lords of a moiety of Ludlow, and held Ludlow Castle. At the time of writing Harley 2253 the castle seems to have been in the possession of Joan, widow of the Roger Mortimer executed by Edward III in 1330.[15]

Harley 2253 was therefore the last major textual work of a literate man – a *clericus*, in 14th-century terminology. This need not imply that he was in ecclesiastical orders, although that has long been considered most likely, not least on the grounds of the diversity and minuteness of ecclesiastical interests reflected in the three major manuscripts. Christopher Hohler has pointed in particular to items on confession and details of masses in Harley 273 and Royal 12 C.xii as probably practical entries, copied by a priest for his own use, while also arguing that the devotional pieces in French represented here are otherwise only found in high-quality Books of Hours, implying an association with noble circles, presumably as a household chaplain.[16] Carter Revard has further shown how the interests implicit in the contents of Royal 12 C.xii and Harley 2253 could be consistent with the patronage of the Harley scribe by a Shropshire knight, Sir Lawrence de Ludlow, holder of Stokesay Castle in the same county.[17] This concerns not only *Fouke Le Fitz Waryn* but also political and satirical verses in Harley 2253. Stokesay Castle lies just 6.5 miles (10.5 km) north-east of Ludlow, and just a couple of miles (4 km) south of the Wistanstow associated with the martyred Wistan. The de Ludlow family were prosperous wool merchants who also had significant property in the town after which they were named.

The key issue is, not that we can claim to know, or even that we need to know, specifically who the Harley scribe was, who his patrons, and where he worked. The degree to which he was compiling these miscellanies for his own use rather than by commission is an important issue, but these two alternatives are not incompatible, and the length of time over which he appears to have been adding to them shows that he retained control over them for extended periods. In the case of both Digby 86 and Harley 2253, we can locate the production and initial use of these manuscripts remarkably closely in both time and place, and with that we can characterize their immediate material circumstances substantially. This significantly enhances our insight into the role of the English literature they contain.

---

[15] Michael Faraday, *Ludlow 1085–1660: A Social, Economic and Political History* (Chichester: Phillimore, 1991), esp. 4–9.

[16] In unpublished letters. My thanks to Malcolm Parkes for sharing copies of this valuable correspondence from Hohler with me. See also Revard, *op. cit.* in note 13, 65–73.

[17] *Ibid.*, 77–81.

Provincial Life, Rural and Urban

MSS Digby 86 and Harley 2253 introduce us to a broad transect of life in the South-West Midlands of England from the later 13th to the mid-14th century. Historically, this period falls between the reign of Edward I, a time distinguished especially in relation to the area of immediate interest by Edward's successful military campaigns in Wales, and the Black Death, a devastating epidemic of bubonic plague that reached England in 1348 and which was responsible for the abrupt death of about one-third of the population. After a writing career of nearly 35 years to April 1349, the Harley scribe would have been relatively elderly; all the same, his disappearance after that date renders it likely that he too was swept away in the plague. The spectrum of contexts to which these manuscripts pertain ranges from the rural and manorial to the urban and bourgeois; through the Harley scribe too, irrespective of his precise clerical status, we see the direct and pervasive presence of the Church in all aspects of medieval life.

THE GRIMHILLS, UNDERHILLS AND DE PENDOCKS

We cannot now identify a relevant Grimhill where we should expect to find it, in the vicinity of Pendock and Redmarley – unlike Underhill Farm, which lies just a mile east of the crossroads of the modern village of Pendock (Figs. 5 and 7). There are several places in Worcestershire whose names could appear as *Grimehull'* or some variant of that in the relevant historical records, and it is consequently impossible to be sure how many different families and even individuals called de Grimhill we may have information on. In the case of the property of the Richard father of Amice, we know that the portion of his estate that was the inheritance of his wife Agnes was taken into the king's hands on his death, and subsequently divided between his three daughters.[18] He may have been the man deriving his surname from the place now known as Greenhill (Worcs.) who held one hide of land – an area of anything between about 50 and 200 acres: essentially a unit of tax assessment – which was liable to provide a portion of a knight's fee to the Bishop of Worcester.[19] The register of documents of the Bishop of the period 1308–13 lists a Grimhill amongst thirteen manors whose yields had allegedly been lost to the prior and convent of the see at some previous date.[20] As a result the convent was allowed to appropriate the income of the church of Dodderhill in the north of the county, to which it already had the right to appoint the priest. Irrespective of the problem of identifying precisely who and where these fragmentary records refer to, they give us a useful impression of both the fluidity of possession and the variety of institutional interests in

[18] *Calendar of the Fine Rolls, preserved in the Public Record Office. Vol. II: Edward II, A.D. 1307–1319* (London: HMSO, 1912), 16 and 21–2.

[19] M. Hollings (ed.), *The Red Book of Worcester*, 4 parts (London: Worcestershire Hist. Soc., 1934–50), 432 and 443–5.

[20] R. A. Wilson (ed.), *The Register of Walter Reynolds, Bishop of Worcester, 1308–1313* (London: Worcestershire Hist. Soc. and Dugdale Soc., 1927), 75–6.

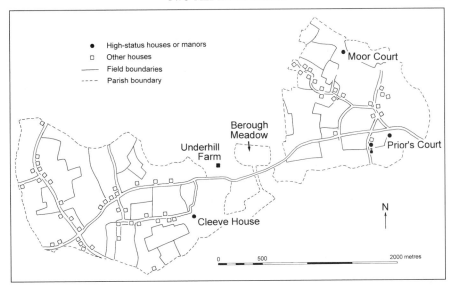

FIG. 7. Medieval Pendock. After Dyer, *op. cit.* in note 21.

the agrarian landscape of this period: in particular the clearly defined pecuniary returns the land was expected to deliver to a hierarchy of proprietors.

We are, meanwhile, fortunate in that a detailed archaeological survey of Pendock around this date has been made, from a perspective concerned primarily with the typology of English medieval rural settlement, in which Pendock can be taken as an example of dispersed settlement as opposed to the nucleated village.[21] Alongside this a much broader history and characterization of the settlement emerges. There is evidence that the population here fell dramatically in the early Middle Ages from that of the Roman Period, to rise again sharply after the Norman Conquest. This inference is based largely upon the evidence of occupation provided by surface scatters of pottery from the Roman Period and of the 12th–15th centuries, correlated with documentary sources indicating that much of the area had become woodland, with a population of only some three dozen, at the time of Domesday Book (1086). In both the Roman Period and the later Middle Ages the types of pottery found are primarily local, simple, domestic wares. Unbroken settlement at Pendock is implied partly by its place-name, a rare example of a surviving Welsh name in this particular area and probably meaning the hill or promontory associated with cultivation. An 11th-century record at Worcester refers to Pendock in the year 967 as being in the possession of a manor in the Severn valley, which presumably exploited it for its woodland resources, while some 11th-century Saxo-Norman pottery has been picked up from the eastern part of Pendock parish.

21 Christopher C. Dyer, 'Dispersed settlements in medieval England: a case study of Pendock, Worcestershire', *Medieval Archaeol.*, 34 (1990), 97–121. Repr. in *idem, Everyday Life in Medieval England* (London: Hambledon and London, 2000), 47–76.

Unusually, the parish of Pendock is in two parts, east and west, with a tongue of land and an isolated meadow almost linking them. It is logical to infer that Pendock parish was portioned off from a larger land-unit – not necessarily already a parish itself – of Berrow. The nature of the division nicely reflects the crucial importance of providing a practical range of resources to the land-unit, which in the case of the parish was not simply designed to meet spiritual needs but had also to be economically viable so as to support its church and priest through tithes. The western part of Pendock would have been mostly woodland at Domesday; the eastern part offered more meadow resources alongside the Longdon Brook, a tributary of the Severn. The isolated Berough Meadow, immediately beside the present Underhill Farm, was a further concession to strike a balance. With the evidence of late Anglo-Saxon occupation in the eastern area, it is plausible that the parish map represents the linkage of the existing settlement there with an area of woodland to the west that Domesday records as belonging to the manor of Overbury, a site on the far side of the Severn-Avon confluence.

The re-settlement and growth of population at Pendock in the 12th and 13th centuries was dramatic: truly a transformation of the area. The parish came to contain at least two manor houses, possibly a third: those of the de Pendocks at a site now known as Prior's Court and the Abitots about half a mile north at Moor Court; possibly too the de Clyve family in the west, where there is still a Cleeve House. The whole area, meanwhile, also retains the physical traces of a fully occupied, and even at one time or other fully cultivated, landscape, with a series of hollow-ways, representing tracks between houses and fields, and house-platforms, boundary-ditches and pottery concentrations revealing a number of peasant messuages (essentially a house plus yard, or *toft*) that may have numbered as many as 60 and have housed a population as high as 250. The precise plot of the settlement earthworks shows that the settlement pattern was that of interrupted rows of settlement: peasant dwellings that formed clusters of a sort, but as strings of homesteads along a lane, with open, worked land between the individual tofts.

The pressure on cultivated land at this period, and a rotation system between different types of crop and fallow stages, required strict control and management, which was achieved through a variety of settlement and field patterns in different parts of England. In comparison with the nucleated village and large open-field system that was predominant in contemporary southern and eastern England, Pendock's dispersed but still densely packed pattern would have allowed individual peasant farmers more freedom and flexibility in their cultivation strategies, yet with that have imposed an overriding need for careful self-management and cooperation. The population of Pendock appears to have included a high proportion of free tenants, paying rent to the relevant manorial lord for their land, and the great increase in the population would for the most part have been achieved by attracting such tenants in as settlers to clear the land. The Underhills were probably originally amongst their number. It is salutary to compare the considerable amounts of money recorded as changing hands in rent within and from Pendock with the material finds from this period. As Dyer notes, the high rents of the largest holdings in the parish imply that those farmers were selling produce at a substantial market: the nearest major site would be Tewkesbury. However the pottery picked up here is overwhelmingly of the standard, local Malvernian type:[22] there is little material evidence of a significant inflow and consumption of any more special goods or commodities. The implication must rather be that the intensification of agricultural production was largely being converted into a cash surplus, that itself was used to cement social obligations and ties rather than to make any further difference to the material circumstances of life.

The surge in population between the 12th and mid-14th centuries was to be reversed again from the mid-14th to 16th century. The reasons for this are anything but clear or simple, and strictly lie beyond the range of our current interest in this area: in very broad terms, though, the process can be understood as a continuation of the long-term search by a few individuals for maximal cash profits from the land held, which now turned towards the amalgamation of farming tenures and more extensive pastoral farming, and a drift of population towards the slowly growing towns and industrial employment. By no means a cause of this, but certainly a factor that accelerated it, was the sudden population drop resulting from the Black Death. The context in which MS Digby 86 was probably produced, and that in which it was certainly handed down, re-opened and written in, in the succeeding generations, was therefore one of considerable structural and tenurial fluidity. The codex itself could thus naturally have changed hands in the dynamic circumstances in which families and households were striving for status and security.

LUDLOW

To turn our attention now to Ludlow, the borough with which the Harley 2253 scribe is associated, is to broaden our perspective on settlement, economy and life in the medieval Welsh Marches – but not to contrast country with town. It was inferred that Pendock must have depended significantly upon a major urban market, even if its trade there was channelled primarily though the richest holdings of the parish. The relative sophistication and complexity of the economic and social system of this period is literally manifest in the fabric of the town of Ludlow – as, indeed, is the dramatic level of change and development in this area of the post-Conquest period.

For such a strategically well-placed site as that in which the medieval town of Ludlow could thrive, it is remarkable that nothing is known of pre-Domesday settlement here. It was long thought that the origins of the castle and borough of Ludlow must post-date the Domesday survey, for there is no definite reference to the site there. However the argument that a reference to *Lyde* in the survey represents some sort of ancestral vill of Ludlow is an attractive one.[23] This

22 Discussed in detail in Alan Vince, 'The medieval and post-medieval ceramic industry of the Malvern region: the study of a ware and its distribution', in D. P. S. Peacock (ed.), *Pottery and Early Commerce: Characterisation and Trade in Roman and Later Ceramics* (London: Academic Press, 1977), 257–305. On the sources of this ware, John D. Hurst, 'A medieval ceramic production site and other medieval sites in the parish of Hanley Castle: results of fieldwork in 1987–1992', *Transactions of the Worcestershire Archaeol. Soc.*, 3rd ser., 14 (1994), 115–28.
23 Derek A. Renn, ' "Chastel de Dynan": the first phase of Ludlow', in John R. Kenyon and Richard

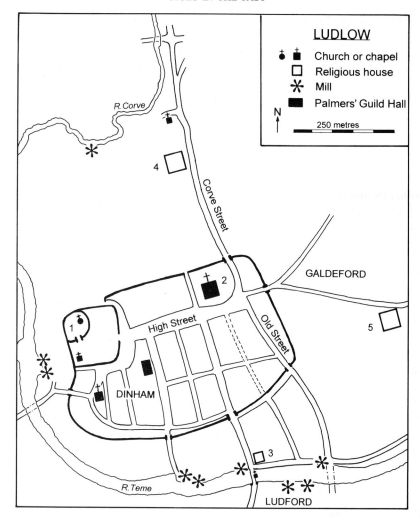

FIG. 8. Medieval Ludlow. 1 Castle. 2 St Laurence's church. 3 The Hospital of St John the Baptist. 4 Lawrence de Ludlow's house and the Carmelite priory. 5 Austin Friars.

identification would allow for the construction of a castle at Ludlow to have been commenced by Walter de Lacy, a follower of William FitzOsbern, a leading lieutenant of William the Conqueror in 1066, sometime in the mid-1070s, although its construction was still probably largely the business of his son and successor, Roger, between 1085 and 1096. The first castle would have been timber, and it was probably Roger who started rebuilding it in stone.

Avent (eds.), *Castles in Wales and the Marches* (Cardiff: University of Wales Press, 1987), 55–74, at p. 56; Ron Shoesmith and Andy Johnson (eds.), *Ludlow Castle: Its History and Buildings* (Logaston: Logaston Press, 2000), esp. 9–11. The recent finding of a 7th-century Anglo-Saxon garnet-inlaid cloisonné gold pommel by the River Teme in Dinham, Ludlow, now in Ludlow Museum, confirms that this was a ready focal point of regional activity.

As we would expect, the castle went through considerable extensions and reconstructions, especially in the 12th century, by the end of which it had both an inner and outer bailey essentially as we see today (Fig. 8). The inner bailey, the original kernel of the castle, is relatively densely packed, with a combined keep and gatehouse on its southern side, a hall, chamber and service block on the north side, and an architecturally unusual and important detached round Romanesque chapel within its area.

The outer bailey may have been completed as much as a century after the castle was founded, if that was as early as c. 1075, but interestingly there is little if any direct evidence that the expansion of the area of the castle ran over areas occupied by the extra-mural settlement of the embryonic town. Ron Shoesmith postulates that the primary settlement of this kind was in the quarter known as Dinham, south of the castle, and that a separate trading settlement grew up along the north–south road from Chester and Shrewsbury to Hereford and Chepstow in between the rivers Teme and Corve here: an area preserved in the modern Old and Corve Streets. Excavations at the site of the later Carmelite Priory in Corve Street have traced a building there back, it is suggested, to the earlier 12th century;[24] this evidence, regrettably, does not come down conclusively on one side or the other of Shoesmith's hypothesis. Whether the reasons for the re-orientation were a need for more space, or a desire to absorb the trading area, if not both, by the later 12th century a borough of familiar elongated form, with a main street running away from the castle gate, in this case towards the east, had been established. Many similar boroughs, large and small, successful and failing, were established in the post-Conquest Marches.[25] Medieval boroughs were legally defined entities, whose populations enjoyed rights and responsibilities that distinguished them from the rural populations with their customary rights and obligations along with the widespread condition of villeinage – a bond status that we could also call serfdom.

The exact date and circumstances of the establishment of a borough at Ludlow are not known. As a large and successful town of its time, though, medieval Ludlow developed its own form of local self-government, including councils of select individuals known as the Twelve and the Twenty-Five.[26] A characteristic feature of the medieval English borough was the laying out of burgage plots for tenements, usually elongated strips measured out in multiples of the perch (16.5 ft; 5.03 m), those on the eastern side of Corve Street, for instance, measuring 2 perches in width and 18 in depth. The parish church of Ludlow stands in the corner between Corve Street and the eastern end of the High Street leading from the castle gate. Again, it is not known precisely when this church was founded, although it is recorded as undergoing substantial modification in 1199–1200, and a little 12th-century carved masonry remains within the building. Its position must form part of a common, coherent plan, with the

24 Peter Klein and Annette Roe, *The Carmelite Friary, Corve Street, Ludlow: Its History and Excavation*, Historic Ludlow Research Paper, 6 (Ludlow Hist. Research Group and Birmingham Univ. Field Archaeol. Unit, n.d.).

25 Trevor Rowley, *The Welsh Marches: Archaeology, History and Landscape*, rev. ed. (Stroud: Tempus, 2001), 89–115.

26 Faraday, *op. cit.* in note 15, 20–8.

High Street leading to the eastern gate of the outer bailey, while reflecting also the importance of the Corve Street/Old Street quarter by this time. As well as the chapel – eventually chapels – within the castle, a chapel-of-ease dedicated to St Thomas of Canterbury was sited in Dinham. Its dedication cannot pre-date 1177, and 12th-century fabric of the building survives, but it is possible for there to have been an earlier church here.[27] A subsequent development of the town plan was the addition of further lanes, with burgage plots, at right-angles to the High Street and running south down the hill to the River Teme.

This layout catered for a multiplicity of activities. The High Street was laid out wide, so that the town and its lords could profit from regular markets. Rather than the lords collecting tolls directly from traders, the town agreed to pay an annual 'farm' – effectively a rent – so that surplus income remained with the urban community. A market place of this kind was the natural place for specialist producers to come to, or even to settle beside, to sell their goods. Interestingly, however, the list of craft gilds represented at the 1368 Corpus Christi procession of the town reveals the dominance of crafts associated with the textile and leather industries: fullers, weavers, dyers, tailors and drapers; skinners, barkers, saddlers, glovers and shoemakers. The millwards would have been largely associated with the fulling (washing) of woollen cloth. Butchers and bakers represent the sort of service industries that would automatically follow the concentration of population in a town, while the one remaining profession in this list is that of non-specific merchants. The key to Ludlow's prosperity was its role in medieval England's flourishing wool trade, a well-documented phenomenon and the background to the international connexions that could have brought to the town imports such as French wine and the pottery that followed it known in small quantities from Worcester.[28] The fleeces were not simply channelled through Ludlow, however. The town is sited at the confluence of the rivers Teme and Corve, whose waters then flow swiftly through a constricted gorge.[29] This is a stretch ideal for watermills, several of which are known along its banks, some for grinding grain, others as fulling mills for cleaning newly woven cloth. The multiplication of activity in the developing townscape is reflected by the way that millponds and weirs constructed then supported more controlled fishing.[30] The horizontal treadle loom that eventually supported a centralized urban weaving industry had been introduced to England as early as the 12th century, although we do not have evidence of specialist weavers in Ludlow earlier than the mid-14th century.[31]

Other significant elements in the topography of medieval Ludlow were its

[27] Faraday, op. cit. in note 15, 53–8.

[28] K. J. Barton, 'The medieval pottery of the City of Worcester', Transactions of the Worcestershire Archaeol. Soc., 3rd ser., 1 (1965–7), 29–44; G. C. Dunning, 'The pitcher imported from Saintonge found at Rich Street, Worcester', Transactions of the Worcestershire Archaeol. Soc., 3rd ser., 1 (1965–7), 45–6; Elaine Morris, 'Medieval and post-medieval pottery in Worcester: a type series', 221–54 in M. O. H. Carver (ed.), 'Medieval Worcester: an archaeological framework', Transactions of the Worcestershire Archaeol. Soc., 3rd ser., 7 (1980).

[29] The Lud- element of Ludlow and Ludford is derived from Old English hlȳde, 'a noisy stream'.

[30] Faraday, op. cit. in note 15, 108–13.

[31] Penelope Walton, 'Textiles', in John Blair and Nigel Ramsay (eds.), English Medieval Industries (London: Hambledon, 1991), 319–54, esp. 327–9; Faraday, op. cit. in note 15, 119–26.

suburbs: Galdeford to the east, and Ludford across a bridge to the south. To the east lay one set of town fields, and Galdeford housed barns, as well as at least one tanner and other leather workers. Beside Ludford was the town common for grazing on Whitcliffe Hill. Ludford was a separate parish. At the Ludlow end of the bridge was established the Hospital of St John the Baptist, an early 13th-century foundation whose endowments came to include a mill in Ludford. Parts of the structure of this hospital remain, incorporated into still-occupied buildings. While the hospital was a charitable foundation, its location reflects the typically ostentatious character of medieval care for the poor and sick: partly to reflect favourably on the benefactors involved; partly too as a conspicuous reminder of human frailty and mortality. An increasingly important element in the activity of the hospital was intercessionary prayer for its benefactors, especially after their deaths. There was a leper hospital in Ludford, and in the early 15th century there was even a small chapel occupied by a penitential hermit on the bridge itself.

Later medieval displays of charity and piety of this kind can be cynically deconstructed, but it is crucial to appreciate the extent and impact of communal concern for spiritual and material welfare within this urban community, and how extensively that was embodied within the very fabric of the town. In Ludlow such forces were put into effect most markedly by the institution of the Palmers' Gild. The proliferation and flourishing of gilds was a distinctive feature of the later Middle Ages whose importance has long been appreciated in social history, and which is now coming to be recognized in late-medieval architectural history and archaeology.[32] Two complementary types of gild can be distinguished: the craft mysteries, associated with specific professions, and the religious lay confraternities. Membership of both types of society was a controlled privilege. There were craft gilds in Ludlow, represented by the list associated with the Corpus Christi procession of 1368, but the most influential and powerful gild in the town was of the latter type. Palmers were, strictly, pilgrims who had made the journey to Jerusalem: the Palmers' Gild itself claimed legendary associations with heroically devout visitors to the Holy Land.[33] The history of the Palmers' Gild can be traced back to the 1270s at least; in the lifetime of the Harley scribe it was conspicuously consolidating its position. In 1329 it gained formal recognition and a royal licence to acquire property: this was of great importance in releasing property from payments that were customarily made when one tenant died and was succeeded by another – sure enough, a major donation of property followed in 1330. Even before this, the gild had been accruing extensive interests in Ludlow property through endowments of rent charges. Its guildhall can be traced back to 1283, and much of a dendrochronologically dated, late 14th-century reconstruction of the building survives

[32] Gervase Rosser, 'Going to the fraternity feast: commensuality and social relations in late medieval England', *Journal of British Studies*, 33 (1994), 430–46; Katherine Giles, *An Archaeology of Social Identity: Guildhalls in York,* c. *1300–1630*, British Archaeol. Reports Brit. Ser., 315 (Oxford, 2000).

[33] Faraday, op. cit. in note 15, 77–95. See also Christian Liddy, 'The Palmers' gild window, St Lawrence's Church, Ludlow: a study of the construction of gild identity in medieval stained glass', *Transactions of the Shropshire Archaeol. Hist. Soc.*, 72 (1997), 26–37.

behind a Georgian façade in Mill Street. The gild became a significant employer in the town, not least of chaplains for the purpose of maintaining chantries – masses sung for the souls of the departed who left money for that purpose. The influence of the gild is manifest in the parish church, largely rebuilt in the mid-15th century, where special chapels were set aside for chantries, in one of which a large Palmers' window celebrates the gild's legendary origins. A college of priests founded by the gild was housed immediately to the west of the church, and we should remember that MS Harley 273 records the date on which the dedication of this church was celebrated.

Ludlow had two further conventual houses, both of them occupied by friars: the Austin Friars, to the east of the town in Galdeford, and a Carmelite priory north of the town centre in Corve Street. The site of the Carmelite house is of particular interest both as a microcosm of developments in Ludlow in the Middle Ages and also for its direct link with the Lawrence de Ludlow Carter Revard suggests to have been the patron of the Harley scribe. The excavations at this site already referred to show the sequence and character of events here well. A series of three successive houses have been found on the site from the 12th century until the foundation of the priory in the mid-14th. These buildings are also successively grander; the last, which became Lawrence's own town house, included a main hall with a highly decorated glazed tile floor and a large tiled central hearth. Immediately after the Black Death, and the disappearance of the Harley scribe, in 1350 Lawrence was permitted to give this plot to the Carmelite order: a different, but still characteristically medieval form of investment, establishing what was intended to be a private, memorial, chapel and mausoleum, simultaneously doing what he could assure what worldly immortality might be possible for him and the eternal repose of his soul. In all respects it proved a struggle to achieve his ambitions: just four years later there was an unseemly pecuniary dispute over where his funeral should take place.[34] Down to the Dissolution in 1538, the priory saw various swings of fortune, and a number of later benefactors were able to get in on the act of supporting construction, repairs and modifications. Having been surrendered to King Henry VIII in August 1538, the priory was demolished within four years.

STOKESAY, AND OTHER PLACES OF OCCUPATION

Lawrence de Ludlow also had a country seat at Stokesay, north-west of the town, a truly astonishingly well-preserved medieval building. Although known as Stokesay Castle, it is more accurately described as a fortified manor house – and even then, the elements of fortification should be understood to have been included for display rather than for serious military purposes. It is recorded that a house here was purchased by Nicholas de Ludlow in 1281, and that rebuilding followed by his son Lawrence the elder, the grandfather of our Lawrence de Ludlow, who in 1290 obtained a licence to crenellate the house – nominally, to fortify it – from the king. It is a matter of debate how much if any of the house bought by the socially ambitious merchant Nicholas may survive, and to what

---

[34] Klein and Roe, *op. cit.* in note 24, 6.

FIG. 9. Interior view of Stokesay Castle, showing the windows on the western side and the staircase leading to the solar in the north tower.

extent the surviving building reveals stages of development concluded by Lawrence the elder or is a complete rebuilding for which he was responsible. The complex consists of a moated courtyard, on the western side of which stands the house. This has a hall open to the roof, with a service area at the southern end, and a northern tower in three storeys. Attached to the service area only by a passageway is a southern tower. It has long been thought that the north tower is the earliest element of the building, and dendrochronological dates of 1261–3 from its undercroft hint at a phase preceding the current structure both here and in the hall which is dated by the same method to the period 1284–1290. What is not a matter of dispute is that Lawrence the elder rebuilt the hall with spectacular, half-glazed windows along both sides, while in the northern tower a jettied upper storey or *solar* chamber was constructed on the second floor (Fig. 9). This north tower now also includes, on the first floor, a large number of the same glazed tiles as were found in Lawrence's house in Corve Street, Ludlow. These were relaid at Stokesay in the course of 19th-century restoration of the building: it is not known where they came from, but one can cautiously presume it was from this site. The continuing importance of Stokesay after the Middle Ages is reflected in an early 17th-century timber framed gateway that was added on the eastern side of the courtyard, and the panelling of the same century of a room at the southern end of the hall. Stokesay Castle was still a major prize at the time of the Civil War, although again arguably more as a matter of prestige than of strategic significance. Subsequently, however, the site and building slipped into obsolescence, until deliberate preservation began in the mid-19th century.[35]

Much though the architecture of medieval buildings can tell us, they nevertheless remain essentially the shells of constructed and divided space, whose full significance resides ultimately in the activities that went on inside and around them. The documentary sources of the later 13th and 14th centuries are invaluable in associating sites and developments with specific people and episodes, as we have seen; meanwhile archaeology can produce equally important information about material life in the context of these places of occupation and work. There have been few large-scale modern excavations on either urban or rural sites of the later Middle Ages in this area as at the Carmelite priory in Ludlow. However a number of exploratory excavations on long abandoned sites now in the countryside provide a consistent and illuminating picture on many important points.

As at Pendock, the dominant impression provided by a diachronic perspective across the post-Conquest Middle Ages from the 11th century to the 15th is one of persistent, and really quite dramatic, change – including the contrastive movements of colonization and developmental construction followed by retrenchment and abandonment. There can never be a single comprehensive explanation of the 'deserted medieval village' phenomenon, although in the Welsh Marches there is no doubt that a contributory factor was the profitability of land devoted to the pasturage of sheep at the expense of settlements cultivating fields.[36] In several cases, meanwhile, the attempts to establish successful settlements, either farming units or boroughs, appear simply to have been over-ambitious from the start. The *Nonarum Inquistiones*, or *Inquisitions of the Ninths*, a national taxation document of 1342 that in effect granted a second tithe to the king, can be compared with an equivalent assessment for a papal tax in 1291, and records a marked drop in taxable yield, in Shropshire in particular.[37] An excavated rural settlement in the hills of north-western Herefordshire at Hampton Wafer seems to have been a small village and manor, occupied from about the end of the 11th century to c. 1300.[38] Finds here indicate material life with a degree of special quality: a coin of William II (1087–1100) and a gilt bronze finger ring somehow lost on site, and glazed ridge tiles from the roof of one building. It is known that this manor passed in to the possession of a FitzAllen family in 1330, who concentrated their interest and investment at the

[35] Julian Munby, *Stokesay Castle* (London: English Heritage, 1993); Anthony Emery, *Greater Medieval Houses of England and Wales*, 2 vols. (Cambridge University Press, 2000), vol. II, 574–6; Derek Renn, 'Two views from the roof: design and defence at Conwy and Stokesay', in John R. Kenyon and Kieran O'Conor (eds.), *The Medieval Castle in Ireland and Wales: Essays in Honour of Jeremy Knight* (Dublin: Four Courts, 2003), 163–75.

[36] Rowley, *op. cit.* in note 25, 155–62.

[37] J. L. Bolton, *The Medieval English Economy 1150–1500* (London: Dent, 1980), 180–206; Alan R. H. Baker, 'Evidence in the "Nonarum Inquisitiones" of contracting arable lands in England during the fourteenth century', *Economic Hist. Review*, 2nd ser., 19 (1966), 518–32; cf. John Ampthill (ed.), *Lay Subsidy Roll, A.D. 1332–3, and Nonarum Inquisitiones, 1340, for the County of Worcester* (Worcestershire Hist. Soc., 1899).

[38] S. C. Stanford, 'The deserted medieval village of Hampton Wafer, Herefordshire', *Transactions of the Woolhope Naturalists' Field Club*, 39 (1967), 71–92.

site of Hampton Court (Herefords.), a few miles west on the banks on the River Lugg. The stately home now at this Hampton Court goes back to the mid-15th century, although much remodelled since.

There is evidence of a general development in the structural architecture of buildings at most levels of society and sophistication in this period, as buildings with earth-fast posts – like the first one on the Carmelite priory site in Ludlow – were superseded by structures with at least stone footings to the walls, if not stone walls up to roof height. While we have to try to infer the superstructure of such buildings from small numbers of surviving early examples, it is reasonably supposed that this development represents timber-framed buildings, principally of the cruck type, resting on stone foundations rather than earth-fast posts that would rot relatively quickly. This is turn implies a development of specialist carpentry skills, with obvious social and economic implications.[39] Julian Munby identifies the use of crucks in the hall of Stokesay Castle as an element of advanced building skill ostentatiously used in that structure. As seen in a grand manner both in this manor house and in Corve Street, Ludlow, even humble peasant houses were often of a bicameral pattern, with a larger 'hall' area and smaller chamber at one end. The longhouse, with animal stalls in line with the residential rooms, seems to have been a relatively rare variant. Better appointed buildings could have had tiled roofs with glazed ridge tiles, and tiled floors.[40]

The main material traces left by medieval agriculture are the extensive ridge-and-furrow field systems, with hollow-ways, as in the case of Pendock, and occasional ditches revealing field boundaries. A few carbonized grains of oats were found in an oven at the Herefordshire manor site of Tretire,[41] while the finds at Hampton Wafer included a rare hoe. Although it survives in a highly fragmentary form, the near-ubiquitous evidence for small-scale, practical ironworking at excavated settlement sites is important. Both Tretire and Wallingstones yielded slag indicating that iron blooms were worked on the site, a form in which newly smelted metal could have been brought there, although what have been identified as small bowl furnaces for smelting were also found at Wallingstones. A consistent range of utilitarian iron products is represented amongst the finds: horseshoes and nails, knives and keys. Most broken or worn-out metal implements must have been recycled, and finds of tools are particularly rare. Textile working is represented by spindle-whorls, while a weaving comb indicates weaving on site at Wallingstones in the later 13th/early 14th centuries.

Finds of pottery are common, especially of local jugs and cooking pots for

[39] Christopher C. Dyer, 'English peasant buildings in the later Middle Ages', *Medieval Archaeol.*, 30 (1986), 18–45; repr. *idem, op. cit.* in note 20, 133–66. Mark Gardiner, 'Vernacular buildings and the development of the later medieval domestic plan in England', *Medieval Archaeol.*, 44 (2000), 159–79. N. W. Alcock (ed.), *Cruck Construction: An Introduction and Catalogue*, Council for British Archaeol. Research Report 42 (York, 1981).

[40] In addition to Hampton Wafer (Stanford, op. cit. in note 36), see also the finds at Breinton and Wallingstones (Herefords.): F. G. Hays, 'Excavations on a medieval site at Breinton, Herefordshire', *Transactions of the Woolhope Naturalists' Field Club*, 37 (1963), 272–94; N. P. Bridgwater, 'The medieval homestead of Wallingstones', *Transactions of the Woolhope Naturalists' Field Club*, 40 (1970), 75–116.

[41] N. P. Bridgwater, 'The manor of Tretire', *Transactions of the Woolhope Naturalists' Field Club*, 39 (1969), 447–55.

domestic use; more impressive glazed wares from further afield tend only to be recovered from sites with higher pretensions, such as Wallingstones, or the failed borough of Richard's Castle close by Overton.[42] The latter site also produced evidence of glass vessels. Of course, we cannot set up a hierarchy of site-types and assume that only at certain levels in that gradation would certain goods be encountered; we can nonetheless accept that the survival of fragments is likely to be correlated in a broad way with the relative frequency of such items at the site when it was occupied. Coins were, understandably, carefully kept, and the excavation of lost coins at settlements is rare, although not unknown.[43] Amongst the most unusual finds at Wallingstones were iron arrowheads, the boss of a shield and a rowel spur, all of which had apparently been discarded as rubbish. In this case the arrowheads can be identified as a military type rather than a specialized hunting one: altogether, then, this small assemblage provides more than a tantalizing glimpse, rather a salutary reminder, of the equestrian military obligations that late-medieval culture placed upon men in the higher ranks of society.

We can thus say a good deal about the sort of contexts with which MSS Digby 86 and Harley 2253 were originally closely associated, without it being necessary to pin them down to specific times, places and characters. The codices were transportable and subject to exchange and modification, and it is not the peculiar but rather the general characteristics of their original circumstances that matter. The summary overview of medieval Ludlow, and the manors and countryside of Shropshire, Herefordshire and Worcestershire here, largely ignores other major poles of the relevant world, such as the thriving international port of Bristol, and the diocesan sees and cathedrals of Hereford and Worcester. Another important, carefully excavated and analysed archaeological site, meanwhile, is that of Bordesley Abbey, in north-eastern Worcestershire, where a series of watermills adapted specially for metalworking (the mills driving hammers and bellows) dating from the late 12th to the later 14th century has been found. This site served as a centralized, specialized production and repair place, not least for work on weapons and armour.[44] Yet it is also manifest, not least from the type of pottery found at Bordesley and its wider distribution, that this area of Worcestershire and Bordesley formed a separate economic sub-region from the Ludlow and Pendock areas.

At a local level, in consequence, even within a much broader administrative and economic framework, we see a picture of considerable self-reliance. The sites we look at were practical, functioning sites, varying considerably in their individual histories although subject to common trends of development. They changed in ways that reflect individual decisions and the particular levels of success and failure that those contributed to. Survival and success required

---

[42] P. E. Curnow and M. W. Thompson, 'Excavations at Richard's Castle, Herefordshire, 1962–1964', *Journal of the British Archaeol. Assoc.*, 32 (1969), 105–27.

[43] Christopher C. Dyer, 'Peasants and coins: the uses of money in the Middle Ages', *British Numismatic Journal*, 67 (1997), 30–47.

[44] G. G. Astill, *A Medieval Industrial Complex and its Landscape: The Metalworking Watermills and Workshops at Bordesley Abbey*, Council for British Archaeol. Research Report 92 (York, 1993).

work, and climatic and economic vicissitudes could create times of real hardship. But we should not picture to ourselves households and communities battling grimly on in the face of constant crisis. It is equally hard to conceptualize this period – in the southern Welsh Marches at least – as the somnolent early centuries of the medieval *longue durée*. The archaeological record of this area in the later 13th and 14th centuries shows an active community, constructing, adapting and re-constructing its material circumstances. The writing and use of MSS Digby 86 and Harley 2253 made a special and dynamic contribution to its life.

Representation and Performance

The diversity and hierarchy implicit in medieval cultural life in the south-western Midlands of England also found direct expression in language and literature. Both Digby 86 and Harley 2253 are trilingual compilations, with Latin as the formal, international language of the Church and of learning; French – here anglicized to a degree, and in some cases bearing traces of a distinct Norman dialect – the language of the higher social classes since the Norman Conquest; and English, the indigenous vernacular, by the time these manuscripts were written well in the process of re-establishing itself as a respectable literary language and on the brink of superseding French in a succession of formal social domains. There would also have been another language in local use, certainly a familiar one in the Ludlow area, Welsh: a language which haunts the study of these manuscripts, appearing in place- and personal names, as well as in a couple of rare cases of Welsh words used in Middle English lyrics in Harley 2253.[45] Despite the prevalence of Latin and French texts in both manuscripts, in this area the highly marginalized position of Welsh roots both collections in essentially English milieux.

The linguistic hierarchy is also reflected by the types of text written in the different languages. Prose rather than verse was the conventional mode of the most self-consciously serious texts at this time, and it is striking that, apart from minor later additions in both codices, neither of them contains any English prose; the Latin texts of Harley 2253, meanwhile, are all prose. It is salutary to note both the quantity of French in both collections and the range of genres in this language. Since the long lost section of three or four quires in Digby 86 both begins and ends with secular French texts, it is possible that this entire section was in French, which would have substantially increased the preponderance of that language. French also accounts for the highest proportion of text in the work of the Harley scribe in Harley 2253. Unlike English – and indeed Latin in the latter manuscript – the French texts include both prose and verse. The prose texts are generally religious, or learned, offering advice and examples for pious

---

[45] These are *miles*, 'animals', and *croup*, 'fiddle'. In both cases the use of the words can be explained as poetic licence to achieve desired alliteration or rhyme. The words must be familiar and understood, but need not have been adopted as regular vocabulary in the local Middle English dialect, and would thus imply familiarity with Welsh itself.

and noble behaviour. The verse covers a much wider range, from moral and exemplary tales and devotional lyrics to love songs and the fabliaux and other bawdy verse. While initially it might appear to be evidence of its strength and superiority for French to have been acceptable across the whole range of literary expression, upon reflection the language's lack of direct association with any special domain could actually have been its weakness in comparison with English and Latin. French was the language of a dominant elite, but there was no area of discourse for which French was the only available option. There was no topic or literary genre that by precedent one would associate exclusively with the use of French in England.

Neglected and fascinating though the topic of French literary culture in medieval England is, our focus of attention here is the English literature of these two manuscripts. How usefully can we generalize about what purposes that literature served? The character conveyed by the collection of English texts as a whole is, just like the two compilations in their entirety, that of an overwhelmingly religious and moral anthology. Even less encouragingly, gloomy warnings about the transitory nature of good fortune in this world, the judgment of the soul and the horrors of Hell, seem to dominate the Christian verses, especially in Digby 86.[46] A more positive and heartening view of the demands of Christianity is provided by a few exemplary biographies, and affective meditations on Christ's passion and the salvation that provided, but there is still nothing here to suggest that the life of a good Christian can be at all easy, let alone readily assimilated to the day-to-day world. The English verses in Digby 86 also include several different collections of precepts and proverbs, reinforcing the insistent but highly generalized moral tone. The booklet of quire R, with *Dame Siriz* and the names of the hare, thus stands out all the more as an oddity.

Harley 2253 includes some of the same pious poems as Digby 86: a dialogue between the soul and the body; a penitential monologue of Maximinian; and the proverbs of Hendyng the Hende. Harley 2253 is particularly well known in the history of English literature for a collection of some thirty Middle English lyrics it contains, the lyric here being defined as a short, stanzaic poem, apparently intended for singing although capable of being appreciated as a read or recited poem too. A distinction can be drawn between the lyric and the ballad with the former usually being an encapsulation of and reflection upon some particular moment or state; the latter a more extensive, narrative piece. This is not, however, a useful distinction to make in the case of Harley 2253. What we may call the Middle English lyrics of Harley 2253 include not only Christian devotional pieces and nearly a dozen love lyrics, but also a number of political and satirical poems referring to specific and identifiable events or features of the contemporary world from the late 13th century to around 1340. However, just as

---

[46] There is no comprehensive edition of the contents of these two manuscripts, even of the texts in any one language. For major selections of the English texts see J. A. W. Bennett, G. V. Smithers and Norman Davies (eds.), *Early Middle English Verse and Prose* (Oxford: Clarendon, 1968); Carleton Browne (ed.), *English Lyrics of the XIIIth Century* (Oxford: Clarendon, 1932); *idem*, rev. G. V. Smithers, *Religious Lyrics of the XIVth Century* (Oxford: Clarendon, 1952); G. L. Brook (ed.), *The Harley Lyrics* (Manchester University Press, 1968). Readable Modern English translations of many of the texts can be found in Brian Stone, *Medieval English Verse* (Harmondsworth: Penguin, 1964).

Dame Siriz stands out amongst the English texts of Digby 86 (though not, generically, amongst the French), Harley 2253 also has one isolated, largely secular oddity in the romance of *King Horn*: the story of a young prince driven into exile, who eventually wins back his rightful position.[47] Horn does this, however, as an exemplary Christian king, most of whose enemies are brutal Saracens.

Although the political and satirical pieces in Harley 2253 include material critical of the king and government of England, and even superficially sympathetic to the difficulties and injustices of life faced by the peasant in the case of poems known as 'The Song of the Husbandman' and 'The Man in the Moon', it has not proved hard to offer explanations of the inclusion of these lyrics in the anthology as congruent with the interests of even a privileged landowner and merchant such as Lawrence de Ludlow, as well as of the conservative, clerical scribe.[48] It is similarly difficult to make the case for any real multiplicity of sympathies being implied by the interspersed religious and amorous lyrics. The love lyrics almost all speak of frustrated, unrequited love, and can therefore easily be understood in terms of a familiar, anti-feminist tradition, being used as warnings against the seductive appeal of women and the sorrows such desire brings. Their tone is uniformly misogynistic and pessimistic, but the controlling attitude is nicely summed up by a pair of lyrics written towards the end of the codex on folio 128, given the modern titles of 'The Way of Christ's Love' and 'The Way of Woman's Love', and drawing an obvious evaluative contrast between the two. Both poems have a refrain:

> Euer ant oo, niht ant day, he haueþ us in is þohte
> he nul nout leose þat he so deore bohte.

> Ever and ever, night and day, he keeps us in his thought.
> He does not want to let anything go that he so dearly bought.

in the former case, and:

> Euer ant oo for my leof icham in grete þohte
> y þenche on hire þat y ne seo nout ofte.

> Ever and ever for my love I am in heavy thought.
> I think on her whom I do not see often at all.

Not only is the permanence of Christ's love contrasted here with the hurtful indifference of women, the common use of the noun *þohte*, 'thought', makes the point that the distracted lover is himself treating Christ just as the cruel and unresponsive object of his own desires treats him. What this also shows us, however, is how the meaning of individual texts is developed by the context in which they are placed. They do not just say what they themselves have to say,

---

[47] See Rosamund Allen (ed.), *King Horn: With an Analysis of the Textual Transmission* (New York and London: Garland, 1984).

[48] Revard, *op. cit.* in note 13, 73–7; John Scattergood, 'Authority and resistance: the political verse', in Fein (ed.), *op. cit.* in note 12, 163–201; Richard Newhauser, 'Historicity and content in the *Song of the Husbandman*', *ibid.*, 203–17.

but enter into a dialogic discourse, which further enjoins the reader or listener to think about and interpret them.

Thus far, then, the relationship between the literature and its external, physical context would appear to be a classic specimen of the contrastive complementarity of real and ideal. We may, however, claim that the dynamic and constructive character of the associated material culture alerts us to features of significant critical potential within the literature. Let us take the case of *Dame Siriz*. This 450-line poem tells the earthy tale of a clerk, Wilekin, who lusts after a merchant's wife, Margery. She rebuffs his advances. Wilekin therefore goes to the crone, Dame Siriz, who eventually agrees, for payment, to help him have his will: she feeds her bitch mustard so that her eyes run, and persuades the wife that this is her daughter, grieving for the revenge a sexually frustrated clerk has wreaked upon her by turning her into a dog. Margery then, remarkably enthusiastically, yields to Wilekin's desires. While there are many characteristic features of the fabliau, it is the combination of a trick leading to an indulgent misdeed here that can be taken as most definitive of this genre. The fabliau was recognized as a particular type of narrative in the Middle Ages themselves, as reflected in the heading to the poem in the manuscript: 'Cil commence le fablel e la cointise de dame siriz' ('Here begins the fabliau and the trickery of Dame Siriz').

This is not the only fabliau in Digby 86, however. As noted above, the lacuna created by the lost quires ends at an early point in a well-known Old French fabliau, *Les quatre souhais saint Martin* ('The four wishes of St Martin'), which is followed, without a break or a heading, by anti-feminist extracts from *Le blasme des femmes* ('The reproach of women') and *Le Chastie-musart* ('The bawd punished').[49] Also entitled *fablel* in the manuscript is *Le fablel del gelous* ('The fabliau of the jealous man'), an abusive tirade against jealousy; similar to the fabliau in its lack of respect for conventional propriety and its scatological language, but not a text we would ourselves classify as a fabliau. These works thus represent conscious anthologization from contemporary literary tradition, and in the rubrication of *Dame Siriz* itself almost certainly the conscious categorization of the text by the Digby scribe in person. We can infer more about the background of *Dame Siriz* from evidence within the text. The story is set, not in the South-West Midlands but in the east, as the merchant husband is absent at the fair of Boston (Lincs.). Several features of the language of the text also represent a well-attested East Midland dialect. There are, however, also spellings suggesting that an intermediary exemplar may have been copied in the south-east of England before this version was produced in or near Worcestershire.[50] Although we know of Old French and Anglo-Norman fabliaux in

---

[49] W. Noomen and N. van den Boogard (eds.), *Nouveau recueil complet des fabliaux*, 9 vols. to date (Assen and Maastricht: Van Gorcum, 1982–), vol. IV, 189–216 and 403–11. See also Hines, *op. cit.* in note 6, 6–7 and 25–30.

[50] Bennett, Smithers and Davies (eds.), *op. cit.* in note 46, 303–6. In the early 14th century, Worcester monks are known to have been buying cloth and spices on a large scale from Boston; Christopher C. Dyer, 'Trade, towns and the Church: ecclesiastical consumers and the urban economy of the West Midlands, 1290–1540', in T. R. Slater and Gervase Rosser (eds.), *The Church in the Medieval Town* (Aldershot: Ashgate, 1998), 55–75, at pp. 61–2.

England by this date, there is no evidence of any other fabliau in English as early as *Dame Siriz*. Unless we assume that its presence in the codex is merely the blind result of the compiler-scribe collecting whatever he could, we can regard this text as a carefully sought out acquisition, imported to make its distinct contribution to the literary collection that man was beginning to put together. *Dame Siriz* is not, in any ordinary sense, representative of the codex as a whole. Along with its French counterparts, however, it defines the parameters of the collection in an important direction, and thus contributes substantially to its overall character.

A further feature of *Dame Siriz* that becomes especially salient when we place this copy in its physical context is the fact that it is a performable text, arguably even marked up for performance, with changes of speaker indicated by marginal capital letters. It is effectively structured as a brief play or interlude, with most of the lines falling into dialogues between one pair of the three main characters or another, and some fifty lines left in the voice of a narrator-presenter. Such a text could amusingly be acted out by a single performer. This distinctive character of *Dame Siriz* is corroborated by the fact that, although none of the French or Anglo-Norman fabliaux is especially suited to dramatized performance in the same way, a related tale appears in a possibly truncated form in a 14th-century Middle English interlude in the Northumbrian dialect, *Interludium de clerico et puella* ('The interlude of a clerk and a girl'), while the dialogic structure of one of Chaucer's fabliaux, the Shipman's Tale, is of essentially the same pattern and textual prevalence. We should not, in consequence, regard *Dame Siriz* as a risqué text that came to the houses of Grimhill or Underhill only to be discreetly read and enjoyed: its form presupposes that it should constitute a fictional performance there, literally enacted within the homestead.

An equally prominent performative character resides in the Middle English lyrics of which we have a few examples in Digby 86 and many in Harley 2253. As already noted, the lyric genre implies performance in the form of song, even if we have no musical notation or reference to tunes with the texts in the manuscripts. Furthermore, as they eschew the narrative character of the ballad, the lyrics typically require an imaginative association with one or more characters in the particular situation they represent on the part of the performer, reader or audience of the lyric. The overwhelming majority of the lyrics use a first-person narrator, normally with the pronoun *I*, constituting a persona for the reader to adopt or empathise with. Sometimes the pronoun is *we/us*; sometimes too the listener/reader is addressed directly, and individually, as *thou*. Although, to all appearances, more as a guide to a contemplative reader than to a potential performer, the Harley 2253 'Harrowing of Hell' (fols. 55v–56v) has changes of speaker marked in the margin like the text of *Dame Siriz*. There are, moreover, dialogic poems of which we have copies in both manuscripts whose dramatic format is especially well adapted to an imaginative involvement of the reader or listener: a dialogue between the soul and the body, and a lyric headed 'Chauncon de noustre dame' ('Song of Our Lady') in Digby 86, which proceeds from a dialogue between Christ on the cross and Mary to two concluding stanzas from a narrator, who addresses Mary and prays for 'us'.

The 'Song of Our Lady' is also an outstanding example of the 'affective' technique, a poetic device designed to engage the imagination and affect the emotions of the reader through the sensuous use of familiar, usually physical, imagery. Thus Mary directs our eyes and feelings at the same time:

> Y se þin fet, y se þin honde
> nayled to þe harde tre . . .   (lines 5–6)

> I see thy feet, I see thy hands,
> nailed to the hard wood . . .

> Y fele þe dedestounde . . .   (line 10)

> I feel the point of death . . .

> Y se þe blody stremes erne
> from þin herte to my fet . . .   (lines 23–4)

> I see the bloody streams run
> from thy heart to my feet . . .

> Sone, I se þi bodi byswngen
> fet and honden þourhout stongen . . .   (lines 28–9)

> Son, I see thy body scourged,
> feet and hands stabbed through . . .

– before her later words show less emotion but lead us rather into prayerful resolution. This lyric calls upon essentially the same active and creative engagement of both experience and imagination on the reader's part as some of the rich uses of imagery that appear from time to time in the love lyrics. One known as 'Annot and John', for instance, opens with:

> Ichot a burde in a bour ase beryl so bryht,
> ase saphyr in seluer semly on syht,
> ase iaspe þe gentil þat lemeþ wiþ lyht,
> ase gernet in golde ant ruby wel ryht . . .

> I know a lass in a bower as bright as beryl,
> fine for to look upon like sapphire in silver,
> like jasper the noble which gleams with light,
> as garnet in gold, and ruby full rich . . .

The lyric continues from such similes likening the beloved woman to gems, on through similes with flowers and herbs, birds, and spices; and finally, within this sequence of recondite but not alien experience, to a series of romance heroines and heroes:

> . . . rekene as Regnas resoun to rede,
> trewe ase Tegeu in tour, ase Wyrwein in wede,
> baldore þen Byrne þat oft þe bor bede . . .

> . . . as ready as Regnas to give good advice,
> as faithful as Tegeu in the tower, like Girwain in dress,
> bolder than Bern who oft faced the boar . . .

These references show off a knowledge of some now deeply obscure corners of English and Welsh literature.

The lyrics of Harley 2253 include a version of the *De clerico et puella* vignette, a lyric that is usually referred to by that name although it has no title in the manuscript. This poem too is entirely in dialogue, with either speaker easily identified by what they say:

1. 'My deþ y loue, my lyf ich hate, for a leuedy shene.
   Heo is briht so daies liht, þat is on me wel sene.
   Al y falewe so doþ þe lef in somer when hit is grene.
   Ȝef mi þoht helpeþ me noht, to wham shal y me mene?

2. Sorewe ant syke ant drery mod byndeþ me so faste
   þat y wene to walke wod ȝef hit me lengore laste.
   My serewe, my care, al wiþ a word he myhte awey caste.
   Whet helpeþ þe, my suete lemmon, my lyf þus forte gaste?'

3. 'Do wey, þou clerc, þou art a fol, wiþ þe bydde y noht chide.
   Shalt þou neuer lyue þat day mi loue þat þou shalt byde.
   Ȝef þou in my boure art take, shame þe may bytyde.
   Þe is betere on fote gon þen wicked hors to ryde.'

4. 'Weylawei! Whi seist þou so? Þou rewe on me, þy man!
   Þou art euer in my þoht in londe wher ich am.
   Ȝef y deȝe for þi loue, hit is þe mykel sham;
   þou lete me lyue ant be þi luef ant þou my suete lemman.'

5. 'Be stille, þou fol, y calle þe riht; const þou neuer blynne?
   Þou art wayted day ant nyht wiþ fader ant al my kynne.
   Be þou in mi bour ytake, lete þey for no synne
   me to holde and þe to slon, þe deþ so þou maht wynne!'

6. 'Suete ledy, þou wend þi mod, sorewe þou wolt me kyþe.
   Ich am al so sory mon so ich was whylen blyþe.
   In a wyndou þer we stod we custe us fyfty syþe;
   feir biheste makeþ mony mon al is serewes myþe.'

7. 'Weylawey! Whi seist þou so? Mi serewe þou makest newe.
   Y louede a clerk al par amours, of loue he wes ful trewe.
   He nes nout blyþe neuer a day bote he me sone seȝe;
   ich louede him betere þen my lyf, whet bote is hit to leȝe?'

8. 'Whil y wes a clerc in scole, wel muchel y couþe of lore;
   ych haue þoled for þy loue woundes fele sore,
   fer from hom ant eke from men under þe wodegore.
   Suete ledy, þou rewe of me; nou may y no more!'

9. 'Þou semest wel to ben a clerc, for þou spekest so stille.
   Shalt þou neuer for mi loue woundes þole grille.
   Fader, moder ant al my kun ne shal me holde so stille
   þat y nam þyn ant þou art myn, to don al þi wille.'

1. 'My death I love, my life I hate, for a lady gleaming.
   She is as bright as the day's light: on me that is clearly seen.

I turn all pale as does the leaf in the summer when it is green.
If my mind helps me not at all, to whom shall I be pleading?

2. Sorrow and sighing and desolate mood tie me up so fast
    that I expect to go quite mad if this should longer last.
    My sorrow, my care, all with one word she could cast away.
    What good does it do you, my sweet beloved, thus my life to
                                                           destroy?'

3. 'Get off, you clerk, you are a fool, I don't want to squabble with you;
    you shall not live unto the day when you shall have my love.
    If you are taken in my room, shame will you befall.
    It is better for you to go on foot than ride a wicked horse.'

4. 'Woe and alas! Why say you so? Take pity on me, your man!
    You are ever in my thought, wherever in the land I am.
    If I die for your love, it is to you great shame:
    let me live and be your love and you be my dear own.'

5. 'Silence, you fool – I address you right: can you never give in?
    You are watched for, day and night, by my father and all my kin.
    If you are taken in my room, there is no evil they will eschew
    to imprison me and you to slay: thus may you gain your death!'

6. 'Sweet lady, change your mind: you want to show me mercy.
    I am altogether as sad a man as formerly I was happy.
    At a window where we stood we kissed each other fifty times.
    A fine promise makes many a man hide away all his sorrows.'

7. 'Woe and alas! Why say you so? You make my sorrow anew!
    I loved a clerk with real love, and he was a lover true.
    He was no way happy any day until the moment he saw me.
    I loved him better than my life; what good does it do to lie?'

8. 'While I was a student at school, I learned a lot of lore.
    I have suffered for your love many grievous sores
    far from home and also from men under cover of the shaw.
    Sweet lady, take pity on me: I can now do nothing more!'

9. 'It suits you well to be a clerk, for you speak so firmly.
    You shall never, for my love, suffer dreadful wounds.
    Father, mother and all my kin shall not keep me so closely
    that I am not yours and you are mine, to do all you will.'

This dramatic dialogue starts in a familiar enough manner, with the clerk
making his pleas in a clichéd, courtly style: his unfulfilled desires have become
a sickness that has brought him close to death. The girl's first reply, in stanza 3,
immediately identifies this wooer as a clerk, and again initially appears to be the
conventional, hearty scorn of a sensible girl who is not taken in by high-flown
lamentations. 'Do wey' is the same colloquial rejection that the girl in the
Interludium opens her speech with, and this girl goes straight on to call the clerk
a fool; a term repeated in her next speech, in stanza 5. Even in her first stanza,
however, there is an ambiguity in her fears for discovery. Although she says the
clerk will never enjoy her love, she can imagine only too acutely the situation of

them being caught together in her 'bower' – it would bring shame to him; and
oddly she seems to refer to herself disparagingly as a 'wicked horse', a
dangerous companion. In her second speech the situation becomes much
clearer: the clerk is already being watched suspiciously, and the consequences of
their being caught together will be physically grievous for both of them. In this
way the clerk can all too really expect the death he has rhetorically anticipated in
the opening words of the poem.

In stanza 6, the clerk reveals that the pair has already kissed – 'in a window',
that symbol of restricted access between inside and outside. The clerk's words
effectively manipulate the girl:

> Weylawey! Whi seist þou so?

she responds, one of several instances where we find her echoing the clerk's
words; and at this point his verbal recollection of the past brings also a confession of her continuing love. The clerk's response to this, in the eighth stanza, is
curious. He recasts himself in two other stereotyped roles, one past, one potentially future if he is exposed and punished although again a situation he claims
he has already fallen into. The first is as the student, learning what was taught
('lore'), which he then contrasts with the unteachable experience of love and its
wounds. Then he is an outlaw, in a patch of forest. The girl's response, which
concludes the dialogue, is that his eloquence fits him best to be a clerk – and the
successful lover-clerk of literary fiction whom she will love, physically, despite
her family's hostility. This stanza particularly focuses on the clerk's words as the
effective force in bringing her to this resolution – a resolution not just to admit
her feelings, but to act upon them.

We cannot in any justifiable way talk about any one specific purpose and
intention of this piece. From what we know about the circumstances of the
production of MS Harley 2253 we are able to realize just how differently the
vignette could appear to various individuals associated, or associable, with the
codex. We can picture to ourselves a Lawrence de Ludlow, and members of his
household, hearing the words and looking at the splendid windows of the hall at
Stokesay, glazed and unopenable above but shuttered and penetrable below,
hearing in the poem a clear 'lock-up-your-daughters' message in one case, and a
sympathetically romantic endorsement of dreams, or maybe even of secrets, in
another. And what of the clerical scribe, the outsider to the family? Did this
poem vicariously embody fantasies or even memories of his own, or would he
have seen it as a satire on young men's weaknesses – and on the inability of
young women to stop being temptresses? The lyric known as 'De clerico et
puella' forms a concrete enactment of speech-acts, which in turn refer to potential realities, past and future. That it remains a secret whether any such episodes
actually were realized adds to the impact of the poem. The story itself may be
familiar to the point of banality, but that makes it all the more congruent with
the total cultural circumstances of the writer and original readers of MS Harley
2253.

For something comparable in Digby 86 we may point to the lyric which has
the enticing heading in the manuscript, 'Ci comence la manere quele amour est

pur assaier' ('Here begins the way in which love is to be experienced').[51] In fact, how love is experienced here is as a word, and as the basis of a poetical and rhetorical exercise: the first 23 of the 28 lines of the poem offer a profusion of tersely listed aspects and effects of love, elegantly ordered with assonance, alliteration and rhyme, and contrasting attractive and adverse views, as in the opening couplet:

> Loue is sofft, loue is swet, loue is goed sware;
> Loue is muche tene, loue is muchel kare . . .

> Love is soft, love is sweet, love is fine words;
> love is great regret, love is great care . . .

The poem ends in a *dissuasio amoris*, a disuassion from love:

> Were loue also londdrei as he is furst kene
> hit were þe wordlokste þing in werlde were ich wene.
> Hit is isaid in an song, soþ is isene,
> love comseþ wiþ kare and hendeþ wiþ tene,
> mid leuedi, mid wiue, mid maide, mid quene.

> Were love as rock-steady as first it is passionate,
> it would be the worthiest thing to find in the world, I suppose.
> It is said in a song, as truly is seen,
> love begins with distress and ends in regret,
> for lady, for woman [or wife], for maiden, for queen.

What is startling here is that rather than being anti-feminist, the suffering is explicitly attributed to the female, across social boundaries and age-groups. The poem focuses itself into a simple but eloquent statement of how love is concurrently an integrative and a disruptive experience, throughout the social range.

The proposition is, then, that rather than merely contrasting the dreams of medieval people with the reality of their surroundings, or indeed depending on the recognition of specific material allusions for us to unlock the 'real' meaning of the texts, the literature of MSS Digby 86 and Harley 2253 – especially the English texts, with their performative character – forms a continuum with its exterior circumstances. The texts fit perfectly into a context of flux and a dynamically constructive approach to life. These were circumstances of uncertainty and pressure, but not of all-pervasive anxiety. The collection and anthologizing of literary texts in Digby 86 and Harley 2253 was part of the general, endless, accumulation and re-ordering of material culture in these households. Agreed, as the result of being written down, the texts became permanently fixed, in an intrinsically inactive form. For us actively to re-contextualize them, historically and materially, is also for us to re-activate the processes of writing and reading that explain why they were there in the first place. It is a modern critical choice to decide whether or not to see these manuscripts merely as

---

[51] Ed. Carleton Browne, *op. cit.* in note 46, 107–8, who gives it the slightly less tantalizing title of 'What Love is Like'.

repositories of inert writing – as collections of texts, not of performances. This is a matter of approach, not a non-negotiable fact.

Even material faithfully copied and unaltered from an exemplar can take on a special meaning in context. At one stage in *King Horn*, for instance, the hero disguises himself as a traveller – a pilgrim, specifically a palmer, in fact. To make this adopted character convincing, Horn makes himself ugly and dirty:

> Horn toc bourdon ant scrippe,
> ant gan to wrynge his lippe.
> He made foule chere,
> ant bicollede his swere.

> Horn took the bundle and wallet,
> and began to twist his lip.
> He put on a foul face,
> and made his neck all black.

Shortly afterwards, when the beautiful princess and his love Rymenild serves him in the hall, she offers him a huge amount of brown ale:

> A bolle of a galoun;
> hue wende he were a glotoun.

> A bowl for a gallon;
> she assumed he was a glutton.

In an area where the Palmers' Gild was so strongly established and influential, the local comic potential of this can hardly be missed.

These qualities of relevancy and materiality are not restricted to the English texts, nor just to the lyrics and *Dame Siriz*. All of the texts in their own way can engage a reader, right from the most utilitarian recipes to the most earnest devotional pieces. Remembering the definition of a commonplace book as a collection of memorabilia, these were indeed repositories of a variety of texts with diverse functions that were there if you needed them. Hitherto, examination of the historical circumstances of these manuscripts has always, understandably, looked for the most comfortable fit between the character and spirit of the literature and the probable interests of an original patron and reader of the texts. But maybe, in these compilations, we both can and should allow for a striving beyond the complacent satisfaction of reading texts that are as agreeable as possible and give the least offence to the socially most powerful patron. It is particularly intriguing that the sharper critical edge of the two codices is found in Harley 2253, not least in the political and satirical verses.

It is a valid observation, nonetheless, that when, in a lyric like 'Annot and John', the material and familiar imagery used is esoteric and culturally marginal such as the catalogues of precious stones, flowers and spices rather than the more practical material realities of day-to-day life, we do seem to be faced with confirmation that art – in this case literary art – is dangerously closely associated with the ephemera of life. However there is no need to be particularly dismissive of the materialist relationship in such terms, especially if one recognizes that a key feature of the continuum between material life and literature was the that the latter represents precisely the same striving to overcome the limits of technology in the later 13th and 14th centuries that is reflected in the archaeological record, and constituted the sense of value and ambition that made those rare and expensive objects special. It is genuinely hard to accept that there was a deep and dominant cleft between reality and idealism in the literature of these manuscripts. The ideal, be it the form of comforts of daily life or of religious beliefs, was a horizon towards which life really was directed.

Of course, we do not know who, if anyone, actually read the texts in these codices, nor whether or not they actually were performed, let alone how; we can, however, identify what sort of persons were involved with them, what their range of experience would have included, and the character of the contexts in which the literature could have been experienced. The literature thus vivifies the material culture, at the same time as the material cultural context expands the range of possible critical reading. We can not only add insights into the minds of people to our inert surviving archaeological remains, we can follow how they could imaginatively have perceived and used rooms and windows, spices and jewellery, as well as recognizing even in the gentry some perception of the physical hardships of the peasantry. In considering MSS Digby 86 and Harley 2253, we are primarily concerned – as far as we know – with the copying and reception of literature, not with its authorship. However, the literary tradition was not just transmitted in this way, but genuinely recreated. After the Black Death had taken off a large number of his contemporaries, the Harley scribe probably with them, Lawrence de Ludlow founded the Carmelite priory in Corve Street. He most certainly had in mind the eternal destiny of his soul, as so many of the texts in Harley 2253 would have enjoined him to:

> Nou icham to deþe ydyht
>   ydon is al my dede.
> God us leue of ys lyht
> þat we of sontes habben syht
>   ant heuene to mede! Amen.

> Now I am ready for death,
>   all my deeds are done.
> God grant us a portion of His light
> that of the saints we have our sight
>   and Heaven as a reward! Amen.

4

Medieval Medievalism and the Onset of the Modern

The Making of the Middle Ages

THE Great Hall of Winchester Castle was built in the earlier 13th century, and stands a short distance from the west gate of the medieval town. This is on a high point, looking down over Winchester, which stretches away towards the River Itchen, and its imposing cathedral. The hall continued in use as a court of justice until the 1870s, and served in that capacity again from 1938 until as recently as 1974. At the west end of the hall, above the medieval dais and more recently the judge's bench, the board of a huge round table is suspended – supposedly the Round Table of King Arthur and his knights (Fig. 10).[1]

After the court vacated the hall for the second time, in the mid-1970s a process of restoration of its interior, and the conservation and analysis of the round table, was begun. Attempts to date the table were made, using the radio-carbon method and dendrochronology. While the radiocarbon datings initially indicated that the table was probably constructed some time in the first half or around the middle of the 14th century, the dating based on tree-ring measurements in the timber, an intrinsically more precise method, has produced a series of dates consistently about a hundred years earlier than this, suggesting construction in the period c. 1250–80. This discrepancy is genuinely puzzling, but in such circumstances the greater trust has to be placed in the dendrochronological dates. Martin Biddle reasonably suggests, considering a wider range of historical evidence, that a tournament held in Winchester by Edward I in April 1290 would have been an appropriate occasion for making the table. The implication would then be that the oak used had been prepared and stored for several years. This is not implausible, and would not imply that the round table itself had been so long in the planning.

The table may never have left the hall. There is a reference to it hanging there in 1464, and the suspension of the table upon the wall – where it would serve solely for display, an exceptionally superior counterpart to the hung and displayed shields with their heraldic devices that were a familiar feature of

---

[1] Martin Biddle *et al.*, *King Arthur's Round Table: An Archaeological Investigation* (Woodbridge: Boydell, 2000).

FIG. 10. The Round Table, Winchester Castle. Photo: IBM.

late-medieval England – may have taken place as early as 1348–9, when the hall was substantially renovated. At this early date the table may have had a decorative leather or textile covering, carrying symbols and texts to declare its attributed identity and meaning. The wood of the table itself shows no evidence of having been painted before 1516, when we have records of extensive repairs being done. Then, or soon afterwards, it was painted with the current design, which centres on a double Tudor rose, red enclosing white, above which sits an enthroned king named as King Arthur. Alternate green- and white-painted segments of the table, and names around the edge, identify places for 24 more knights of the Round Table, while around the rose it is written: 'Thys is the rownde table of kyng Arthur w. xxiiii of hys namyde kny3ttes.' There is ample evidence in the iconography that this image was intended to portray the then king, Henry VIII, as Arthur's legitimate and effective successor. Henry indeed became heir to the throne in April 1502 when his elder brother Arthur unexpectedly died at the age of fifteen.

The word *icon* is an overworked one in contemporary jargon, but if ever an artefact merited designation as iconic it is the Winchester round table. It actually is the top of a usable round table, but also represents another round table – the fictional one of Arthur, first recorded in Wace's Anglo-Norman verse *Brut* of the mid-12th century. The purpose of its reproduction, preservation and adaptation, meanwhile, was to represent and endorse a set of values: an ethical code that is familiar from Arthurian literature. In this case these virtues are particularly those of sovereignty, good order, and patriotism. Superficially, the Round Table reflects fraternal egalitarianism, but there is nonetheless a point that becomes the head of the table: wherever the king was placed. The social dynamics of a table such as this hinder interaction between individuals and anyone other than those immediately beside them, so that the design in practice reinforces the reality of a hierarchy with graded ranks that it purports to reject.

The round table is also iconic of the phenomenon of medievalism. By medievalism is meant a historical enthusiasm for a past Middle Ages, reflected especially in revivalist artistic movements, such as the particularly strong one of the middle to later 19th century issuing, inter alia, in a Gothic Revival in architecture and pre-Raphaelite painting. Just a few decades before the Tudor painting of the round table, Sir Thomas Malory had written his Tales of Arthur, inspired by a nostalgic respect for the world of Arthur as a lost Golden Age:

> But nowadayes men can nat love sevennyght but they muste have all their desires. That love may nat endure by reson, for where they bethe sone accorded and hasty, hete sone keelyth. And ryght so faryth the love nowadayes, sone hote sone colde. Thys ys no stabylyté. But the olde love was nat so. For men and women coude love togydirs seven yerys, and no lycoures lustis was betwyxte them, and than was love, trouthe and faythefulnes. And so in lyke wyse was used such love in kynge Arthurs dayes.[2]

bethe: are; *keelyth*: cools; *lycoures*: lecherous.

Yet one of the most valuable things that the study of the Winchester round table reveals is how such medievalism goes back into the Middle Ages itself. The archaeology of the later Middle Ages shows considerable investment of this kind, to make both material and manifest a memorial version of the period's social and spiritual values.

As the round table as a practical object demonstrates, the values of chivalry were thoroughly elite and exclusive. The order of knighthood saw itself as the brotherhood of a special few who, in an idealized feudal scheme, were serving

---

[2] Quotations from Malory are taken from Eugene Vinaver (ed.), *The Works of Sir Thomas Malory*, 3 vols. (Oxford: Clarendon, 1947). Here pp. 1119–20.

the world at large morally, protecting that social system along with its Christian religion and the economic privileges they themselves enjoyed as a result. In military terms, the heavily armoured mounted knight remained a central feature of strategy and force, despite the disastrous defeat of the French knights at the Battle of Crécy in August 1346, usually noted as the first major demonstration of the vulnerability of armoured cavalry to a sufficient force of longbowmen, a lesson to be repeated even more decisively at Agincourt in the same Hundred Years' War nearly 70 years later.[3] As we saw in the previous chapter, some of the financial charges that the great landlords were due from their estates were calculated in terms of knights' fees – originally an obligation to provide a man to do military service, commuted to a money payment for a professional – while at the manor of Wallingstones a few items of military equipment were retrieved, albeit objects that had apparently unceremoniously ended up in rubbish deposits. Much medieval military equipment survives, in armouries, and in the form of a surprisingly large number of swords retrieved from rivers – usually presumed to be accidental losses, but probably in some cases ceremonially deposited there in practices similar to Bedevere's final discarding of Excalibur.[4] Another still common material reflex of the importance of late-medieval chivalry is the portrayal of knights in armour on stone monuments and memorial brasses. Noticeably, these use as their definitive material types accoutrements that are especially closely linked to the person: often body armour and spurs on the tombs, with a buckled sword, and the shield with a personal coat of arms.[5]

A significant element in the training of knights that was challenging enough for it even to be substituted – part as ritual, part as dangerous sport – for battle itself, was the joust. Tournaments like that in Winchester in 1290 could be arranged with a great deal of pomp, and historical records testify to ever more elaborate pageantry being orchestrated for the staging of these displays: continuing up to a self-conscious attempt to reach an unsurpassable peak when Henry VIII met Francis I of France at the Field of Cloth of Gold in northern France (but in English territory) in June 1520 – perhaps around the same time as the Winchester round table was painted.[6] Corroborating the hypothesis that the round table is an instance of the sort of material construction that accompanied such events, there are records showing that Edward III also intended to have a round table at Windsor – possibly considering taking the one from Winchester – an intention first announced at a tournament organized there in January 1344. That specific plan did not come to fruition, but Edward's aims in this respect

3   Richard Barber, *The Knight and Chivalry* (London: Longman, 1970), 182–3.
4   Malory, ed. Vinaver, *op. cit.* in note 2, 1238–41.
5   Brian and Moira Gittos, 'Motivation and choice: the selection of medieval secular effigies', in Peter Coss and Maurice Keen (eds.), *Heraldry, Pageantry and Social Display in Medieval England* (Woodbridge: Boydell, 2002), 143–67; Nigel Saul, 'Bold as brass: secular display in English medieval brasses', *ibid.*, 169–94.
6   Helmut Nickel, 'The tournament: an historical sketch', in Howell Chickering and Thomas H. Seiler (eds.), *The Study of Chivalry: Resources and Approaches* (Kalamazoo: Medieval Inst. Pubs., 1988), 213–62; Maurice Keen, 'Chivalry and the aristocracy', in Michael Jones (ed.), *The New Cambridge Medieval History. Vol. VI:* c. *1300* – c. *1415* (Cambridge University Press, 2000), 209–21; Joycelyne G. Russell, *The Field of Cloth of Gold: Men and Manners in 1520* (London: Routledge & Kegan Paul, 1969).

were realized in the establishment of the select Order of the Garter by 1349. The ostentatiously frivolous and romantic anecdote of the garter – how Edward rescued and treasured this personal item of the lovely Countess of Salisbury, which unfortunately slipped down while she was dancing – in fact links the Order with Edward's successes at Crécy and subsequent taking of Calais after nearly a year's siege, as the latter port is where the incident supposedly took place. As a sacred home and focus for the Order, the old St Edward's Chapel in Windsor Castle was reconstructed and rededicated as St George's Chapel – including stalls for 12 knights on either side of the altar: a close parallel to the 24 places for knights on the Winchester round table, although in this case including the king and his heir on either side, and a separate pew for the queen.[7]

Orders of this kind also expressed their existence and fellowship, and their distinctness from the remainder of the community, by the adoption of symbolic garb: usually both uniform clothing, often referred to as livery, and other symbolic dress-accessories, such as a replica of the unlucky Countess of Salisbury's garter. In a process in which expense and consumption were clearly themselves at a premium rather than thrift, wardrobe accounts of Edward III indicate the continual variation and re-issue of liveries associated with the Garter. Initially, a rather surprising adoption of blue as the key colour of the livery can be traced, but by 1364 the significance of the unusual colour seems to have been much reduced. The types of garment were typical of the fashion of the time, namely tunics as the principal item, and coats to be worn over them, with the hood as a separate piece; later on the gown: a rather heavier and fuller form of over-tunic. As well as being carefully controlled, uniform suits, these garments were explicitly linked to the Order by being decked with representations of the garter symbol: in the most elaborate cases in full three-dimensional model form, complete with silver buckle and pendants. The commissioning of textile products in the livery could extend as far as bed covers.[8]

Edward III's successor, Richard II, followed the same policy by distributing badges to his friends and adherents quite literally as a mark of his favour, eventually adopting the symbol of the white hart as his own particular motif following a tournament in Smithfield, London, in 1390. The white hart, a symbol of purity, spirituality and mystery, is particularly beautifully represented on the famous Wilton Diptych in the National Gallery in London, where one can seen the badge worn by Richard himself and by the angels of the court of Heaven.[9] Richard did not institute an Order of the White Hart as such, but the badge was explicitly associated with the king's livery, as in the case of one of his

[7] St George's Chapel was extensively rebuilt again under Henry VII and Henry VIII. Sir William St John Hope, *Windsor Castle: An Architectural History*, 3 vols. (London: Country Life, 1913), vol. I, 117–77, and vol. II, 374–477; Colin Richmond and Eileen Scarff (eds.), *St George's Chapel, Windsor, in the Late Middle Ages* (Leeds: Maney, 2001).

[8] Stella Mary Newton, *Fashion in the Age of the Black Prince* (Woodbridge, Boydell: 1980), esp. 43–6. Blue dyes based on woad were considered characteristic of the clothing of the clergy and the poor.

[9] The precise date and function of the Wilton Diptych has been much discussed. See Pamela Tudor-Craig, 'Panel painting', in Jonathan Alexander and Paul Binski (eds.), *Age of Chivalry: Art in Plantagenet England 1200–1400* (London: Royal Academy of Arts and Weidenfeld and Nicolson, 1987), 131–6, esp. pp. 134–5.

most loyal supporters (or henchmen), John Holland, Earl of Huntingdon and Duke of Exeter, whose valuables were listed as including *un livere de cerf* when he was put to death soon after Richard was deposed by Henry IV.[10]

The personal history of Richard II proved to be an extreme and ultimately tragic example of the attempt to realize and live out high courtly ideals. His actions, however, took the tendencies of his age to an extreme rather than cutting disastrously against the grain. The later 14th century was a time of heightened consciousness about costume and the significance of any individual's dress – a situation which understandably was reflected in an increased tempo of changes in fashion together with intermittent excesses, such as the vogue for shoes with ludicrously long pointed toes (*poulaines*) that appeared in the late 14th century.[11] A related phenomenon is a series of 'sumptuary laws' passed by parliament, and supplemented by various local ordinances. On the one hand these made explicit a basic set of beliefs as to how the structure of society should be construed and how that ought to be reflected in apparel; at the same time they reveal what strains such simple and prescriptive ideas were under. Whatever their intention, the sumptuary laws were ineffective as intrusive instruments of social and cultural control. The first Sumptuary Law of 1336 was of limited scope, and appears to have had little impact, while the second, of 1363, was almost immediately repealed. Further legislation sought by parliament in 1378 did not gain the assent of the young King Richard II.[12]

The usual view of the sumptuary laws is that they sought to enforce fixed identities within an ordered and hierarchical society. The notion that this was an appropriate issue for legislation was by no means unique to England, which indeed would appear to have had almost a *laissez-faire* attitude compared to some European governments at this time. The laws had rudimentary economic motives too, seeking to limit expenditure in certain areas and thus to direct the market, protecting indigenous production and discouraging imports. The second Sumptuary Law of Edward III, of 1363, is particularly interesting in that, for the more affluent and powerful in society, it permitted income to qualify them to bear certain qualities of clothing and dress-accessory as well as their social rank achieved by birth or promotion. Even gentlefolk (*gentils gentz*) who were not of a knightly rank, for instance, with an income below £100 per year were supposed not to wear silk or embroidered garments; merchants, London citizens and burgesses with £500 a year could, however, wear silver. The dominant style of these laws is, however, proscriptive rather than prescriptive: attempting to lay down a series of prohibitionary limits, not to impose uniforms for given classes. A noteworthy exception is the requirement in several town ordinances for prostitutes to wear distinguishing clothing.

Within such an atmosphere of conspicuous investment in garb, it was, of

May? clarke?

[10] Mary V. Clark, *Fourteenth-Century Studies* (Oxford: Clarendon, 1937), 276–8.
[11] Francis Grew and Margaret de Neergaard, *Shoes and Pattens*, rev. ed., Medieval Finds from London, 2 (Woodbridge: Boydell, 2001), 28–39.
[12] Alan Hunt, *Governance of the Consuming Passions: A History of Sumptuary Law* (Basingstoke: Macmillan, 1996), esp. 22–8 and 295–324. The texts of the laws of 1336 and 1363 can be found in *The Statutes of the Realm*, 11 vols. (London: Dawson, repr. 1963), vol. I, 280–1 and 378–83.

course, also possible to indulge in conspicuous denial and 'modesty'. There is nothing in the portrayal of the Knight in the General Prologue to the Canterbury Tales to suggest that his was a contrived air of negligence rather than genuine indifference to superficial splendour:

> But for to tellen yow of his array,
> His hors were goode, but he was nat gay.
> Of fustian he wered a gypon,
> Al bismotered with his habergeon,
> For he was late ycome from his viage,
> And wente for to doon his pilgrymage.   (I, 73–9)[13]

> *fustian*: a relatively coarse cloth; *gypon*: a padded, protective tunic; *bismotered with his habergeon*: stained by his chest armour; *viage*: travelling

Nonetheless such a pregnant interpretation and evaluation of the Knight's dress at the end of his portrait immediately provides a model – as if one were needed – for artificial emulation. The white hart image of Richard II, as on the Wilton Diptych, offers a poignantly creative twist to such studied humility. The stag's head has its own natural crown of antlers, and the stag consequently wears the crown as the chained collar of a restrained beast, prisoner or slave. Moreover such a collar could not have been put on after the antlers had grown to any size, implying that the fetter of kingship is one imposed from immature youth – as indeed was the case with Richard – if not from birth or by predestination. By the time the General Prologue of the Canterbury Tales was written, it had long been realized that dress and accoutrements were no silent and innocent embodiments of character. Costume and personal adornment were recognized to be matters of conscious choice, and media through which many different statements could be made.

Such creative and artistic currents had no less impact upon the fabric and adornment of the Church than in the secular world. While the Canterbury Tales tends to give the impression of the pilgrims as varied and variable characters moving between fixed points on a solidly built constructed stage, any real group making the pilgrimage from London to Canterbury would in fact have found major ecclesiastical building-sites at both the beginning and the end of their journey in the later 14th century. On the opposite side of the road to the Tabard Inn in Southwark High Street south of London Bridge, for example, lay the priory complex of St Mary Overie.

The church of this priory became Southwark Cathedral in 1905. It, and its surrounding area, have undergone so much rebuilding in the later Middle Ages and since the 19th century that the architectural history of the building, and its form and condition at any given time, can only be determined to a limited degree. From the 13th century to the earlier 15th century, however, reconstruc-

---

[13] All quotations from Chaucer are taken from Larry D. Benson (gen. ed.), *The Riverside Chaucer*, 3rd ed. (Oxford University Press, 1988). On costume in the Canterbury Tales, see Laura F. Hodges, *Chaucer and Costume: The Secular Pilgrims in the General Prologue* (Cambridge: Brewer, 2000), esp. 22–54 on the Knight.

tion here appears to have been a virtually constant process, if, implicitly, at a somnolent pace between a few well-recorded bursts of energy. The priory had been badly damaged by a fire in 1212, and was again affected by a fire of less certain magnitude in the 1390s. Amongst other things we know that (re-)building work on the south transept began in 1310, but was repeated, along with work on the nave, in 1420. In 1397 the bishop, William of Wykeham, who had a palace immediately to the west of the priory, took over direct responsibility for the building works.[14]

As we have already seen in medieval Ludlow, the need or opportunity for such rebuilding was a perfect pretext for secular benefactors to take a stake in the church. A detail of interest for English literary history is that the poet John Gower was resident within the precincts of St Mary Overie in Southwark from at least 1398, and it has been thought that his close involvement here could go back to the 1370s and coincide fully with his serious writing career. Gower's will, which has been preserved, endowed a chantry for his soul and bestowed vestments, liturgical books and a chalice upon the church. It stipulated, too, that he should be buried in a particular place, in the chapel of St John the Baptist within the church. His tomb has subsequently been moved more than once within the building, and in its present colourful state represents the results of restoration in 1958 following early descriptions as closely as possible. It is, however, probably now back in its original position, although the chapel itself has long since disappeared.[15]

We are rather better informed about the state of Canterbury Cathedral, containing the shrine of St Thomas à Becket, at the other end of the journey. Here, the entire nave of the cathedral had been demolished in 1377, at the start of a process of reconstruction that was to last until 1455. This rebuilding undoubtedly had more essentially to do with the precarious state of the 300-year-old nave constructed under Archbishop Lanfranc (1070–1089) than with ambitions to reshape the world; but such mundane necessities would hardly have been advertised, and the opportunity to rebuild in the most imposing style possible was certainly not missed.[16]

As far as visitors and pilgrims were concerned, however, during the period of rebuilding all the more attention would inevitably have been attracted to the massive choirs and transepts of the cathedral, and the extended eastern end, which included the Trinity Chapel with the shrine of St Thomas at its centre. Right alongside the altar of this shrine, on the southern side, Canterbury pilgrims of the later 14th century would have found the newly constructed tomb of Richard II's father, Edward the Black Prince, heir to the throne when he died

14 Martha Carlin, *Medieval Southwark* (London: Hambledon, 1996), 67–75.
15 John H. Fisher, *John Gower: Moral Philosopher and Friend of Chaucer* (London: Methuen, 1965), 58–60; John Hines *et al.*, '*Iohannes Gower, Armiger, Poeta*: records and memorials of his life and death', forthcoming in Siân Echard (ed.), *A Companion to Gower* (Cambridge: D. S. Brewer, 2004). For the text of the will, see G. C. Macaulay (ed.), *The Complete Works of John Gower*, 4 vols. (Oxford: Clarendon, 1899–1902), vol. IV (*The Latin Works*), xvii–xix.
16 Tim Tatton-Brown, 'The rebuilding of the nave and the western transepts 1377–1503', in Kevin Blockley *et al.*, *Canterbury Cathedral Nave: Archaeology, History and Architecture* (Dean and Chapter of Canterbury Cathedral and Canterbury Archaeol. Trust, 1997), 128–46.

the year before his own father, Edward III, in September 1376. It is not merely the good fortune of excellent preservation, but also the historical importance of the Black Prince at the juncture at which he died, that makes this tomb such an outstanding example of a late-medieval chivalric memorial. The tomb itself is in many respects severely typical, both in the sarcophagus, a rectangular marble chest with coats of arms around the sides representing the prince both as warrior and peace-bringer, and the recumbent figure of a praying knight, in his armour, that lies upon it. The whole monument, however, is of very high quality in terms of both workmanship and materials. The figure of the knight is stylised, conveying a sense of solemnity, piety, and the power both of arms and of prayer, yet still done with a sufficiently humane touch for some to wonder if it might be considered a portrait. The pageant of the Black Prince's funeral procession was scripted in his death-bed will, and included the bearing of a set of objects to be placed by the tomb as 'achievements': artefacts supposed to represent the accomplishments of the deceased knight in his life. Most of these items are still preserved in the cathedral, and include body armour – a helmet and separate crest, an heraldically ornamented tunic or *gypon*, and gauntlets – and weaponry in the form of a sword and scabbard, a dagger, and two shields.[17]

In the southern transept of the cathedral, such pilgrims would also have found the completed results of another recent piece of rebuilding: in this case a pair of chantry chapels built by and for the Black Prince and his wife Joan to expiate the sin of having married within the forbidden degrees of kinship. Chantry chapels such as these appeared to be creating a plethora of privately patronized churches within the Church. An exceptionally well-preserved example is the very late pre-Reformation chantry chapel constructed around the tomb of Henry VIII's elder brother Prince Arthur in Worcester Cathedral.[18] While the multiplication of chantries came in for a great deal of criticism in contemporary satirical literature, however, the main focus of these objections was the mercenary attitude of the chantry priests who neglected the living to pray for the once rich dead, not the physical imposition upon the space of the churches they involved.

This does not, however, mean that there was no explicit debate in the period of Chaucer and Gower about the material construction of an ideologically highly charged context for life in ways such as these. The sheer range of material evidence reviewed here, and the level of investment it involved, testify to the fact that the later Middle Ages had a heightened awareness of the ideological implications of material culture: both how artefacts and architecture could express identity and power, and how they could embody particular values and direct respect to specific foci. A logical consequence of this situation was a higher level of investment in what we should now distinguish as art: the elaboration of objects and structures for the purpose of making a statement or making an impression. A gap between the practical requirements of the item concerned

---

[17] Christopher Wilson, 'The medieval monuments', in Patrick Collinson *et al.* (eds.), *A History of Canterbury Cathedral* (Oxford University Press, 1995), 450–510, esp. 494–8; also pls. 118–20 in the same volume. See also Alexander and Binski (eds.), *op. cit.* in note 9, 479–81.
[18] Mrs Edmund McClure, 'Some remarks on Prince Arthur's Chantry in Worcester Cathedral', *Reports and Papers of the Association of Architectual Societies*, 31 (1912), 539–66.

and the attention given to aesthetic demands being made of it was beginning to open.

The feebleness of the first attempts to constrain the use of material objects in a struggle for social power represented by the 14th-century English sumptuary laws should not mislead us as to the seriousness of this issue, either as it was appreciated at the time, or in its historical consequences. This was a period in which the separation of art and artefact was a bewildering and disruptive development, affecting how influential individuals saw their world. Art ceased to be a mere skill, critically appreciated as the production of especially well-wrought or highly decorated objects that were themselves practical and functional requirements of the culture. Instead, art had moved a long way towards becoming a separate and compartmentalized category – something that was therefore all the more open to critical attention in itself, especially when used as a medium for making political statements, and for seeking or exercising power. An unhappiness with the enhanced materiality of ideology in this period appears in a telling form in Wycliffite, or Lollard, thinking. This was a reformist movement within the Church, whose values anticipated many of the characteristics of the Protestantism that came in with the 16th-century Reformation.

The concerns are illustrated in a text known as the Testimony of William Thorpe, the prose account of a trial of a cleric before Thomas Arundel, Archbishop of Canterbury (1396–7 and 1399–1414), for his Lollard opinions contrary to the practices and teaching of the Church.[19] The author of this text, Thorpe, was, of course, able to script this account as he chose, and it is therefore evidence of his views within the context of his time rather than a reliable verbatim record of specific historical exchanges, which he dates to 1407 (lines 166–71). The second of the five accusations, or *questiones*, put by the Archbishop concerns images:

'But what seist þou to þis secunde point þat is recordid aȝens þee of worþi men of Schrouesbirie, seiinge þat þou prechedist þere openly þat ymagis owen not to be worschipid in ony wise?' (1056–8)

aȝens: against; *Schrouesbirie*: Shrewsbury; *seiinge*: saying; *owen*: ought

There is a crucial ambiguity in the word 'worship' in this question: at this date it could mean 'to adore, to treat as divine', as in its usual modern sense, but also 'to honour, to treat with great respect' in an effectively non-religious sense. The Archbishop's question could be interpreted as a reasonable attempt to draw Thorpe to concede that there is more than one 'wise' in which religious images can be regarded.

Thorpe, however, flatly rejects any such pragmatism: he has a black-and-white view of the world on the relevant issue, with no half-tones in between. In terms that were discussed above, in Chapter 1,[20] he sees an absolute opposition between culture and nature here – a nature, however, that is not

---

[19] In Anne Hudson (ed.), *Two Wycliffite Texts*, Early English Text Soc., Original Ser., 301 (Oxford University Press, 1993).
[20] Pp. 10–15.

intrinsic to the physical universe itself, there from whatever beginning it had because of mindless scientific laws, but rather a nature that is, we might say, God's culture: it is the nature of the world as He created it and wills it to be, and that fact guarantees its sanctity, truth and goodness:

'. . . For lo, þe Lord witnessiþ bi Moisees þat alle þingis whiche he made were riȝt goode, and so þanne þei weren and ȝit ben and schulen ben goode and worschipful in her kynde. And þerfore to þe eende þat God made hem þei ben alle preisable and worschipful; and speciali man, þat was made aftir þe image and lickenesse of God, is ful worschipful in his kynde – ȝhe, þis holi ymage þat is man God worschipid. And herfore euery man schulde worschipe oþer in kynde, and also for heuenli virtues þat man vsiþ charitabli. Also I seie þat tree, stoon, gold, siluer or ony oþer mater þat ymagis ben maad of, alle þe creatures ben worschipful in her kynde and to þe eende þat God made hem fore. But þe keruynge, þe ȝetynge, neiþer þe peyntynge of ymagerie wiþ mannus honde, al be it þat þis doinge be accept of men of hiȝeste astaat and dignite, and ordeyned of hem to be a kalender to lewde men þat neiþer kunnen, ne wolen be leerned to knowe God bi his word, ne bi his creatures, neiþer bi his wonderful and diuerse worchyngis, ȝit þis ymagerie owiþ not to be worschipid in þis foorme ne in liknesse of mannes crafte, al be it þat euery mater þat peyntours peynten wiþ, siþ it is Goddis creature, owiþ to be worschipid in þe kynde, and to þe eende þat God made it, and ordeyned it to serue man.' (1061–80)

her: their; *ȝhe*: yea; *keruynge*: carving; *ȝetynge*: casting; *lewde*: common, uneducated; *worchyngis*: acts, products; *siþ*: since

Every man should therefore revere each other *in kynde* – for their divinely created nature, and any heavenly inspired virtues in their behaviour – and like-wise the material world is to be revered *in kynde*, but not as it is externally, culturally, modified. Logically, it is not easy to understand why Thorpe will not regard artistic skill – especially when it is used for the spiritual welfare of the Christian flock – as a heavenly gift placed in Man by God: this was certainly a view acceptable to the medieval Church, as its many legends of transcendentally skilled saintly craftsmen indicate. Historically, however, Thorpe's attitude is readily understandable in the context of a corrupt and acquisitive Church that exploited the trust of the faithful, while in cultural terms we can now see that the materiality of the Church at the beginning of the 15th century was a matter of habit that went beyond mere selfishness, greed and luxury.

A crucial juncture in the dialogue is Arundel's next response, in which he is made to concede a vital point:

'I graunte wel þat no liif owiþ to do worschip to ony siche ymage for itself'
(1081–2)

For him again, the range of the word *worschip* is crucial here, as his answer has to be construed as essentially a re-affirmation of the second Commandment: 'Thou shalt not make to thyself any graven image . . . Thou shalt not bow down to them.' *Worschip* is thus used in its most religious sense. Yet from the Wycliffite point of view the issue of the multiple meanings of the word can be sidestepped, and the Archbishop has conceded a separation between the work of art and its purpose: the image is not to be revered for itself, but for its Christian function. Arundel notes the educative and memorial roles of ecclesiastical imagery, and attempts to justify and explain those by using an analogy. As the seal of a great lord commands respect because of his secular authority, the imagery bears the authority of God (exercised through His Church). But Thorpe, with his acute consciousness of the peculiar, God-given nature of things, simply cannot recognize an analogy. For him, such things, even if superficially similar, are essentially different in nature. As the debate then proceeds, with Arundel arguing for the pragmatic usefulness of imagery, Thorpe consistently retorts that the best examples and inspirations to put before 'the people' would be holy lives and the (textual) teachings of Christianity. For him, then, these constitute pure and natural Christianity, and a direct, moral reality. Any material image can at best be a distraction (see especially lines 1133–8 and 1146–9).

We should not take this dispute between the radical fundamentalist Thorpe and the conservative prelate as evidence of a profound and comprehensive, philosophical cleavage within late-medieval cultural life and society.[21] It does, however, offer an unusually sharply focussed insight into a developing critical consideration of materialism and art, in the very period that saw Middle English literature suddenly leap to a pinnacle of quality in output, represented primarily by three great contemporary authors, Chaucer, Gower and Langland. All of these were, or became, closely associated with London, and were writing in a period from the 1360s to around 1400. Within their work, as we shall now see using examples from Chaucer and Gower, this context created and reveals deeper currents. Their writings embody the drama of the changing material circumstances in which they were writing, and are sharpened by their perhaps even unconscious involvement in the ideological implications of this new materialism.

Troilus and Criseyde and the Use of Space

The characterization of the later Middle Ages in England just offered would appear to confirm the proposition within Anders Andrén's scheme,[22] that, in a literate culture, a text-centred structure – in which life imitates art more than art reflects life – eventually supersedes object-centred and integrated relations. It would, however, be disappointing if, in such circumstances, the productive interplay of material culture and literature, and with that a productive integration of archaeology and literary criticism, were restricted to esoteric and elaborate fantasies such as the rituals of chivalry. The following examples show how far from the case that may be.

---

[21] The shades of opinion concerning such matters are well portrayed in Jeremy Dimmick *et al.* (eds.), *Images, Idolatry, and Iconoclasm in Late Medieval England: Textuality and the Visual Image* (Oxford University Press, 2001), especially in the papers by James Simpson, Nicholas Watson and Sarah Stanbury.

[22] Above, pp. 32–3.

At first sight, Chaucer's *Troilus and Criseyde* looks deeply unpromising as an example of a literary text that reflects significant issues in the material circumstances of its composition. Scholars are confident that Chaucer wrote this long narrative poem in the early to mid-1380s. It is a highly idealistic, even philosophical, romance, set in the ancient past, during the siege of Troy. It is refined and elaborate in style, with more than 8,000 lines in complex 'rhyme-royal' stanzas, divided into five books. It is not a translation, but is closely adapted from a work by the slightly earlier Italian author Boccaccio, *Il Filostrato* ('The victim of love'). None of this, however, need mean that the work is merely a piece of historical-fictional escapism, a sort of costume-drama; we can rather expect it to have had some metaphorical meaning for the time and circumstances in which Chaucer rewrote it. Unusually for Chaucer, the work was completed, and the text presents relatively few major editorial problems.[23]

Troilus and Criseyde is set in the city of Troy under siege as a consequence of the disastrous elopement of Paris, one of the Trojan princes, with Helen, wife of the Spartan king Menelaus. Troilus, a brother of Paris, has hitherto scorned love and its unmanning effects, but sees and falls in love with the young widow Criseyde. Her position in Troy has been compromised by her father, Calkas, who has foreseen the destruction of the city and treacherously fled to the Greek side. The tale proceeds from Book I to Book III as the story of Troilus's love-sickness and courtship, aided by a go-between, Pandarus, a friend of his and uncle of Criseyde. Eventually the couple are brought together at night, and consummate their relationship, at Pandarus' house. In Books IV and V, however, Criseyde is 'released' from Troy to join her father in the Greek camp, in exchange for a Trojan prince, Antenor, whom the Greeks had captured. Despite promising to escape and return to Troilus, she fails to do so; rather she is herself amorously besieged and eventually won by a Greek champion, Diomede, as Troilus learns. The tale ends after Troilus is killed in battle by Achilles, and rises to the eighth (penultimate) sphere of Heaven, from where he looks down pityingly upon the *blynde lust* of human, carnal desires that lead men to devote themselves in a religious manner to a worldly love, *eros*, in ignorance of a higher love, *caritas*, that lies beyond that.

For most critical readers of the poem, any reference to realism in *Troilus and Criseyde* would most readily be understood in terms of the psychological presentation of Criseyde and her responses to her dilemmas.[24] Meanwhile the use of architectural space as the setting for the drama has attracted some attention, albeit in a relatively selective way.[25] The main focus of such studies has,

---

23 For historical surveys of the literary and editorial criticism of *Troilus and Criseyde*, see Benson, *op. cit.* in note 13, 1020–5 and 1161–77. For a translation: Geoffrey Chaucer, *Troilus and Criseyde*, trans. Nevill Coghill (Harmondsworth: Penguin, 1971). On the date and Italian source also Derek Pearsall, *The Life of Geoffrey Chaucer* (Oxford: Blackwell, 1992), esp. 168–77; Robin Kirkpatrick, *English and Italian Literature from Dante to Shakespeare: A Study of Source, Analogue and Divergence* (Harlow: Longman, 1995), 60–79.

24 See, e.g., C. David Benson, *Chaucer's* Troilus and Criseyde (London: Unwin Hyman, 1990), 103–12; Barry Windeatt, *Troilus and Criseyde*, Oxford Guides to Chaucer (Oxford: Clarendon, 1992), 279–88.

25 H. M. Smyser, 'The domestic background of *Troilus and Criseyde*', *Speculum*, 31 (1956), 297–315; Saul N. Brody, 'Making a play for Criseyde: the staging of Pandarus's house in Chaucer's *Troilus and Criseyde*', *Speculum*, 73 (1998), 115–40. Valuable papers by Derek Brewer, 'House and garden in *Troilus*

understandably, fallen on Pandarus' house, where an elaborate series of contrivances and coincidences is exploited to allow the couple to spend the night
together unbeknown to anyone else but Pandarus. Criseyde and her male and
female servants come to Pandarus' house to dine; a rainstorm persuades them to
stay, with Pandarus yielding his private bed-chamber to Criseyde while the
others bed down in the hall just outside it. However Troilus has hidden access to
this chamber from a 'stewe', apparently a ground-floor wash- or bath-house immediately below it. Saul Brody's recent interpretation of this central part of the
poem is to see the setting as a readily recognizable form of theatrical stage, on
which Criseyde found herself both as spectator, as Troilus 'makes a play' for her,
and as one playing out her own scripted role.

Such studies inevitably take an essentially literary approach to architectural
detail, starting with the story, and seeing how realistic facets of contemporary
material culture are selectively referred to and used for the needs of the drama.
Barbara Nolan laid more stress on how architectural and public space in Troy
could be a recalcitrant and troublesome ambient rather than a readily adaptable
one, but concluded all the same that in the end this urban context dissolves, as
Calkas had foreseen before the action of the poem starts. Her approach was also
to compare Chaucer's handling of the setting with that of Ovid in *Ars Amatoria*
('The art of loving') and Boccaccio's *Il Filostrato*, thus examining the poem
within a series of comparative literary perspectives on the phenomenon of social
space. A materialist reading of the text remains to be undertaken: not to under-
mine or to correct these literary approaches but rather to add to and complement
them. In particular, it can be argued that the material context is not an inert one,
only to be vivified through literary imagination. The text-centred approach
tends to attribute control over the organization of space, and thus the ability to
direct events there, to Chaucer, just as Chaucer attributes it authorially to his
character Pandarus. The situation is, however, intrinsically less subjective.

Even though the consummation scene in Pandarus' house truly lies at the
centre of the poem, this is only one of a series of buildings that are presented,
primarily with reference to their domestic aspect. Each of these has a different
character, and the contrasts between them form a meaningful pattern. After
Troilus has first seen Criseyde in the public space of a temple, and been smitten
with love for her, the first domestic building we enter as a scene in which the
drama is played out is his home, a princely palace. Here, in fact, the division of
space is presented in extremely simple terms, consisting of a public space –
which in a princely household should have been *very* public – and his private
chambre, or bedroom, to which he can escape to think and to indulge his feelings:

> And whan that he in chambre was allone,
> He doun upon his beddes feet hym sette,
> And first he gan to sike, and eft to grone,
> And thought ay on hire so, withouten lette,

and other Chaucer poems', and Barbara Nolan, 'A phenomenology of social space in Chaucer's poetry',
were read at the London Chaucer Conference, Inst. English Studs., University of London, 8–9 April 2002.

That, as he sat and wook, his spirit mette
That he hire saugh a-temple, and al the wise
Right of hire look, and gan it newe avise.   (I, 358–64)

sike: sigh; *ay*: ever; *withouten lette*: without hindrance; *wook*: stayed
awake; *mette*: dreamed; *avise*: review.

Although private, this is not a place of complete seclusion. It is also a space for a
particularly close social tie with his friend, Pandarus, to express itself: he can
join Troilus here, and Troilus can confide in him:

Bywayling in his chambre thus alone,
A frend of his that called was Pandare
Com oones in unwar, and herde hym groone,
And say his frend in swich destresse and care:
"Allas," quod he, "who causeth al this fare?
O mercy, God! What unhap may this meene?
Han now thus soone Grekes maad yow leene?"   (I, 547–53)

oones: one time; *unwar*: unsuspecting; *say*: saw; *fare*: carry-on;
unhap: misfortune; *han . . .?*: have . . .?; *leene*: lean, drawn.

We can characterize the presentation of architectural space here as
'unmarked'. It reduces the conceptualization of the building and its rooms to the
equivalent of a child's naïve drawing of a house: a square with a triangular roof,
a door in the middle, and a window in each corner. The basic bicameral division
between hall and bedchamber was a template for houses ranging from humble
vernacular cottages to manor houses and urban palaces, and it is significant that
the Trojan princes' palaces are represented reduced to this highly traditional and
conservative form.[26] Indeed we have the same fundamental disposition of space
in Troilus' brother Deiphebus' house, where Criseyde and Troilus are first
brought to meet by Pandarus. Troilus lies sick with love in a small bedchamber,
which is presented to us as simply lying off the 'grete chaumbre', possibly to be
understood as a solar rather than a single public hall, from which Pandarus can
bring Criseyde: indeed Troilus can hear them whispering outside (II, 1646–7,
1709–15 and 1751–7). An additional space here, to which Deiphebus and Helen
can be sent to read over a letter, is the garden, to which they have to descend,
realistically, from the first-floor hall. This is an important extra element, but it
does nothing to modify the strikingly simple subdivision of the house itself into
a larger public and a smaller private room.

Meanwhile the reader, following Pandarus, has paid a visit to Criseyde's
house, where, we were told very early on in the poem (I, 127–31) she has dwelt
discreetly and honourably after Calkas has fled. Yet we first meet Criseyde here
in a new type of room, a 'paved parlour', which we can take then to be on the
ground floor:

[26] Above, pp. 88–91; Jane Grenville, *Medieval Housing* (London: Leicester University Press, 1997),
66–120 and 134–56; Margaret Wood, *The English Medieval House* (London: Phoenix House, 1965), esp.
16–98; Eric Mercer, *English Vernacular Houses: A Study of Traditional Farmhouses and Cottages*
(London: HMSO, 1975), 8–22; Gardiner, *op. cit.* in Chapter 3, note 39.

> Whan he was come unto his neces place,
> "Wher is my lady?" to hire folk quod he;
> And they hym tolde, and he forth in gan pace,
> And fond two othere ladys sete and she,
> Withinne a paved parlour . . .   (II, 78–82)

gan: began, did; *sete*: seated

John Schofield's study of medieval London houses identifies the parlour as a 14th-century innovation there, belonging to larger and more imposing houses: certainly a feature that had been around for half a century by the time *Troilus and Criseyde* was written but still one that conferred a modern urbanity on Criseyde's palace (a term that is used of her house) conspicuously absent in the princes' houses.[27] Dramatically, in fact, it is events in Criseyde's house, far more than in Pandarus', that reveal how subtly space, architectural features and furniture can be manipulated by the characters living in them to negotiate their business with one another and their course through life. In fact, as we see when Pandarus first arrives, even the additional room does not automatically provide Criseyde with privacy for the conversation a parlour was nominally set aside for. By seating Pandarus on the bench beside her, however, Criseyde can signal an intention to converse with him, which should push others away:

> Quod Pandarus, "Madame, God yow see,
> With youre book and all the compaignie!"
> "Ey, uncle myn, welcome iwys," quod she;
> And up she roos, and by the hond in hye
> She took hym faste, and seyde, "This nyght thrie,
> To goode mot it turne, of yow I mette."
> And with that word she doun on benche hym sette.   (II, 85–91)

iwys: indeed; *in hye*: directly; *thrie*: three times; *mot*: may.

At the same time, this action attracts the reader's voyeuristic attention. Criseyde also has a bedchamber or *closet* to which she can retire for private thought, and eventually to write to Troilus (II, 1215–18). Yet there is a quite deliberate paradox in this too, for it is shut away here that she starts to unfetter her heart out of the prison of resistance to love. Essentially we see that there is no true individual freedom in any genuinely private space. In her bedchamber, Criseyde is subject to the subliminal persuasion of a nightingale singing outside her window (II, 918–22), just as, immediately beforehand, her amorous propensities have accidentally been stimulated by her niece Antigone singing a love song in the same garden (II, 812–903).

The bedroom window has served an even more important function a little earlier on, offering Criseyde a view of Troilus returning, heroically, from battle (II, 610–16 and 649–62). The windows come back into play as crucial sites of activity twice more in this book, when Pandarus tells Troilus he will lead

---

[27] John Schofield, *Medieval London Houses* (New Haven: Yale University Press, 1994), esp. 66–7; Wood, *op. cit.* in note 26, 81–94.

Criseyde to a window to see him again the following day (II, 1009–22), and then when he brings her to the hall window to look across at a finely arrayed house opposite but uses this as a private conversation space in which to speak of Troilus (II, 1184–96). What we are observing here, acted out in a fictional microcosm, are tensions that were crucial to developments in architectural form and the use of space within buildings in the later Middle Ages. The idea that display was intrinsic to the construction of major town houses, be it in the form of ostentatious jettying over street fronts to maximize the available space or the placement of daises in guildhalls, is a familiar one.[28] It is important to be no less alert to the equal importance of being able to observe and scrutinize others on the part of those with higher social positions to maintain: to design and build an environment in which they could see as well be seen. There was a desire for both display and privacy, but these are antithetical objectives – as the current British royal family has learnt in a painful way.

Pandarus' house also has an upper storey of the classic, simple, hall-chamber model. Here we also encounter the pragmatic detail that it is possible to divide the hall into a 'middel chaumbre' and an 'outer hous' with a partitioning curtain or screen, the 'travers'. *Troilus and Criseyde* actually affords the first recorded example of the noun in this sense in English. However the most crucial detail is that Pandarus' bedchamber, on the first floor, has what is in effect a secret access to it through a trap-door in the floor from the 'stewe' in which Troilus has been hidden so that he can come, secretly, to Criseyde. The term *stewe* is related to our word 'stove'. It implied a heated place, and seems to have been used primarily in the 14th century to refer to special bath-houses – which were also, in fact, notorious as brothels. It is perfectly realistic to see Pandarus' *stewe* as a functional wash-house in the ground-floor undercroft, although less immediately obvious why that should also have direct vertical access to and from the bedchamber. At an abstract level, meanwhile, the contrivances in Pandarus' house – and contrivances they most emphatically are – clearly represent the desire to control, channel and restrict access to private spaces, for almost covert activities. This is a feature of developing design that the introduction of access-diagram analysis to architectural theory and history has done much to explicate.[29]

A plan of the Bishop of Ely's Inn, or House, off Holborn in London, survives from 1776, but in certain important details agrees with a survey of the buildings dated to 1357 (Fig. 11).[30] There are even records of rebuilding work here in the period 1374–88, precisely when *Troilus and Criseyde* was being written. The survey of 1357 refers to the hall, three principal chambers, and further chambers *pro secretis episcopi*, which (avoiding innuendo) can be translated as 'for the private business of the bishop'. It is clear enough that we can see such chambers in the plan, with highly controlled access, both in respect of doorways between rooms and of access to whole ranges of rooms from (as well as to) the

---

[28] Grenville, *op. cit.* in note 26, 181–93; Giles, *op. cit.* in Chapter 3, note 32, 62–4.

[29] E.g. Graham Fairclough, 'Meaningful constructions: spatial and functional analysis of medieval buildings', *Antiquity*, 66 (1992), 348–66.

[30] Schofield, *op. cit.* in note 27, 35–6 and 191–2.

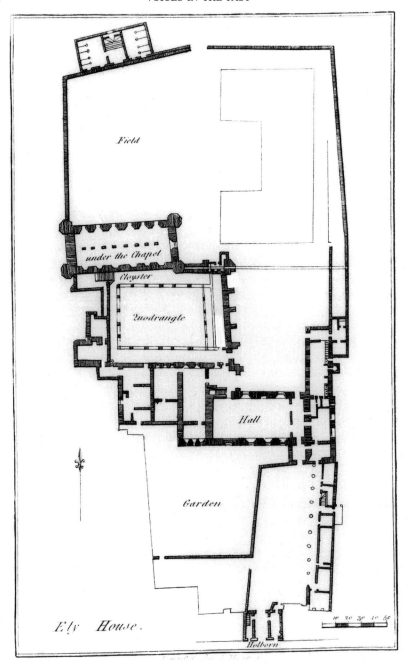

FIG. 11. Ely House: the former Bishop of Ely's Inn, Holborn. Plan of 1776.
Copyright: Guildhall Library, London.

quadrangle/courtyard and the garden. The plan shows us only one floor. But it is unlikely that the upper-storey arrangements simply negated the controls built into the ground floor.

It is also interesting to look at this plan and see what in 1776 was a garden at the front of the property, with a 'field' beyond the chapel at the rear. This is not to make anything of the spatial separation between the two items, which cannot be attributed to the medieval layout, but there is a point that both the church – or in *Troilus and Criseyde* the temple – and the garden appear as crucially important public spaces in the poem. The temple, appropriately, bears a high ideological significance. But we learn that precisely because it is also a natural meeting place: this is where Troilus first sees Criseyde, and makes a religion of his love for her; here too Pandarus finds Troilus in Book IV, reflecting philosophically on destiny when he has learnt that Criseyde must leave Troy for the Greek camp. The garden too is an open space, where people can meet in an unconstrained way, yet also enclosed, so that only the privileged can have access to that facility. Here again the public-private paradox is acted out as Pandarus tells Criseyde the story – a fiction within the fiction, in fact – that he has learnt of Troilus's love for her by overhearing Troilus talking in his sleep, as he lay dreaming in the garden.

We have already noted the significant functioning of furniture within these spaces, with reference in particular to the way in which the occupation of a bench or a window-seat creates, in a gestural way, a relatively private space in which two people can speak – cautiously – between themselves. It may seem rather naïve also to make a point of referring to the bed as a significant functional meeting place, but worth taking that risk to note that the bed is not just a place in which Troilus and Criseyde can consummate their love. Pandarus in fact repeatedly joins Troilus in bed, sitting on his bedside, even lying down with him. The curtained-off bed should have been about the most private space available – though it would have been closely rivalled or even beaten by the oppressively dark, narrow and unpleasant privies; yet again, it was a private space that allowed secret inter-personal dealings to go on. From a material-cultural perspective, a striking point is that in this poem we are persistently faced with constructed furniture literally built into the houses and gardens. The development of readily movable furniture in the early modern period, particularly from the later 17th century onwards, had great implications for the social use of architectural space.

There is, however, a further example of dwelling space that makes its appearance only in Book V, the final book of the poem. This is Greek camp of tents, providing yet another intrinsically negative contrast to the urbane sophistication of Pandarus' and Criseyde's houses in the town. This contrast can be argued to be highly significant, and indeed essential to the denouement of the story. The tent is an undivided and readily accessible space, where Diomede, the Greek champion who has scurrilously pledged himself to win Criseyde's favours, has all-too-easy access to her:

> But for to tellen forth of Diomede:
> It fel that after, on the tenthe day

> Syn that Criseyde out of the citee yede,
> This Diomede, as fressh as braunche in May,
> Com to the tente ther as Calkas lay,
> And feyned hym with Calkas han to doone;
> But what he mente, I shal yow tellen soone.
>
> Criseyde, at shorte wordes for to telle,
> Welcomed hym and down hym by hire sette –
> And he was ethe ynough to maken dwelle!
> And after this, withouten longe lette,
> The spices and the wyn men forth hem fette;
> And forth they speke of this and that yfeere,
> As frendes don, of which som shal ye here.   (V, 841–54)

syn: since; *yede*: went; *han to doone*: to have business; *ethe*: easy;
yfeere: together

The ease with which the luxurious commodities of spices and wine are fetched into them here bears its own connotations. These were goods available from London shops, and Chaucer himself was a vintner's son. Shops were another distinctive feature of London architecture, adapting the repertoire of conventional room-types such as the solar chamber around an accessible, street-front space where the vendor and customers could conveniently meet.[31] Whether or not one sees the analogy of tent and shop as a little too stretched, it remains a fact that the tent presents an undifferentiated space in which Criseyde has to remain, live, and do everything. At one point we are told that she just goes to bed 'inwith hir fadres faire brighte tente' (V, 1022). In this place, where the hierarchy of conventionally organized and controlled space has completely broken down, she is easy prey for Diomede.

One's sense that the contrast between the Greek camp and the streets, houses and gardens of the town in which the action has been set hitherto is a thematically vital one is gradually reinforced by a series of comparisons and scene-shifts from town to camp and back again in Book V. We are shown Troilus looking out on the camp from the walls of Troy:

> Upon the walles faste ek wolde he walke,
> And on the Grekis oost he wolde se;
> And to hymself right thus he wolde talke:
> "Lo, yonder is myn owene lady free,
> Or ellis yonder, ther tho tentes be."   (V, 666–7)

ek: also; *oost*: host

and Criseyde looking back on the towers, halls and walls of the town:

> Ful rewfully she loked upon Troie,
> Biheld the toures heigh and ek the halles;
> "Allas," quod she, "the plesance and the joie,

---

31 Schofield, *op. cit.* in note 27, 71–4; cf. Grenville, *op. cit.* in note 26, 165–74.

> The which that now al torned into galle is,
> Have ich had ofte withinne yonder walles!"   (V, 729–33)

When she decides to 'dwelle' in the camp, however, she casts a rather briefer glance, not upon the substance of the town, but only upon its predicament: 'the perel of the town' (V, 1023–9). Perhaps the most emphatic passage in this book, meanwhile, is that from lines 519 to 553 (it really extends beyond this to line 679 with the *Canticus Troili*, Troilus' song of lamentation), in which Troilus goes to look upon Criseyde's palace, only to see its shut windows and doors. He apostrophizes the palace – that is, he addresses it directly – as a now extinguished lantern, the crown of houses, a ring without its gem, an empty shrine: a series of realistic, material images that is exceptional for this poem. Of course it is psycho-dramatically realistic for someone in Troilus' position to respond to his grief by visiting places associated with his lost lady. But this is precisely where and how, for Troilus, the fate that Calkas fled – 'that Troie sholde destroied be' (I, 64–84) – has come true. The form it has taken is not the conquest of the town but its voiding: the disappearance of life and spirit from within its built environment. After Troilus finally looks in vain for Criseyde from the gates (V, 1112–13 and 1192), he himself emblematically starts to go mad, or 'wood', and searches frantically amongst the hedges, trees and groves (V, 1144; cf. 1170–6). Finally he finds a secure place to 'dwelle' himself, in the highest sphere of Heaven to which an enlightened pagan could be assigned (V, 1807–27).

By virtue of being a romantic fiction set in an imagined, Classical city, in exceptional circumstances, *Troilus and Criseyde* was not constrained by the demands of strict realism and could thus dramatize in an especially clear way priorities and concerns that lay in the minds of the people who were adapting or constructing the built environment of later medieval England – and particularly in London. Much light is thus shed upon how these people saw that space could be put to different uses, and the potential they recognized in details such as windows, doors and furniture. One of the most striking insights to emerge from a re-reading of this familiar poem from the materialist perspective is an appreciation of the constant struggle to maintain one's position in the social and cultural environment it represents. While it has been relatively easy for archaeologists, historians, and art-historians alike to talk about elites, power and display, we can also see how even those who seem to have enjoyed real social and material success were dogged by insecurities embodied within the physical infrastructure of their culture, and needed to be watchful as much as to be watched with respect.

What we gain from an interdisciplinary, archaeological and literary, reading of *Troilus and Criseyde* is not the discovery of new examples of direct realism in the poem. As suggested above,[32] such illustrative links between text and material context can hinder the progress of integrated studies more than they promote them. A more profound relationship between the two forms of expression allows us to claim that the drama of *Troilus and Criseyde* is based essen-

---

32 Pp. 28–9.

tially, perhaps even totally, upon two fundamental 'scales of modality' in medieval domestic architecture. By that term is meant an axis of variation between competing objectives, in respect of which building design has to adopt a position, and must do so in concrete form. One of these scales is the opposition between public and private, which was gradually resolved in English domestic architecture in favour of the private house over the hall. For us now, a *hall* is usually a small passageway where one may leave one's shoes or hang one's coat; where one can greet and say farewell to visitors, but a place of only transitory use. The other fundamental modality is the range of access between the restricted and the open, the forbidding and the inviting. Privacy and restricted access are self-evidently closely associated phenomena, and might perhaps be seen not as separate modalities but as a particular objective and the form in which it could be realized respectively. Yet as we have seen, it is illusory to suppose that relatively inaccessible places are securely private while open spaces are insurmountably public; and large open spaces may be ostentatiously reserved for a privileged few while complex access arrangements can be employed to impress a general public that is allowed to pass through them. It would be poignant if we could identify the drive for privacy and seclusion as the pursuit of a chimera – recalling, perhaps, the paradox of the early 15th-century hermit who occupied a cell on the bridge leading into Ludlow.[33] This does not mean that secrecy, restricted access to information, is an impossibility. But as the discussion of the 'De clerico et puella' dialogue in MS Harley 2253 implies, secrecy takes on a powerful dramatic force when secluded places, unguarded passageways, and verbal hints enable suspicion to form.

Where the structures that embody these modalities are seen to exist is within the city of Troy. In the Greek camp we have only tents, which offer a plain inside/outside dichotomy. The space inside these tents is necessarily much more variable in function, more easily redesignated at will or at need as a living space, a dining space, or a sleeping space. This is consequently much more like the emergent domestic architecture and furnishings of the early modern period.[34] This is not to suggest that Chaucer wrote *Troilus and Criseyde* primarily as some sort of covert or repressed architectural theorist, who, had he lived nowadays, would have expressed his insights in a more explicit but less artistic way. Rather it is to infer that he was at least subconsciously aware of the issues involved in his built environment, and of the force of the pressures that eventually and gradually brought about a radical change.

In the final analysis, though, one may wonder just how innocent, historically, we should allow Chaucer to be. It is difficult to conceive of his description of Criseyde's shuttered palace as solely a product of his literary imagination, unaffected by direct experiences of a London where, as in other English and Euro-

---

[33] Cf. Matthew Johnson, 'Rethinking houses, rethinking transitions: of vernacular architecture, ordinary people and everyday culture', 145–55 in David Gaimster and Paul Stamper (eds.), *The Age of Transition: The Archaeology of English Culture 1400–1600*, Soc. Medieval Archaeol. Monographs, 15 (Oxford: Oxbow, 1998), esp. p. 154. I do not share Johnson's anxiety that it may be seriously anachronistic to attribute a 'sense of the individual [person]' and thus a concept of privacy to the late Middle Ages.

[34] Matthew Johnson, *Housing Culture: Traditional Architecture in an English Landscape* (London: UCL Press, 1993).

pean towns and cities, the population fell abruptly after the plagues of the middle and later 14th century;[35] not least when there was a national origin myth linking Britain with a Brutus who escaped from Troy, and even more specifically when the idea of London as Troy refounded, *Troynovant*, was a current one.[36] Just as, in the inter-war period of the last century, the para-patrician novelist Evelyn Waugh was to heap scorn upon the Metrolanders – the commuters of the new suburbs of the Home Counties – during another period of huge demographic relocation and metropolitan reconstruction, Chaucer may intuitively have turned his nose up at the unchivalric suburbanites camped outside the walls of his city, whose ability or destiny ultimately to invade and empty the ancient city and its structures was all too foreseeable.

A Poet at Work: John Gower

It was noted above how Chaucer's contemporary John Gower created a place for himself in the suburbs of London – on the south bank of the Thames, an area through which all travellers between the Cities of London and Westminster and south-eastern England, including the great sees of Canterbury and Winchester, would pass. We have less information about Gower's life than Chaucer's, but still enough to indicate that their backgrounds and experiences were similar in certain broad and significant respects. Both were of the gentry class, and are referred to in contemporary documents as *armiger* and *esquier*, 'squire'; both were of families that had or acquired a coat of arms; both made careers in professional, clerical service in one of the twin cities of the capital. The only direct link between Gower and the royal court we know of is the claim made in the first version of the Prologue to his *Confessio Amantis* that this English collection of moral tales was composed at the direct behest of Richard II (Prol., 24–92), while at the violent end of Richard's reign Gower expressed his support for Henry Bolingbroke, subsequently Henry IV. In 1393 Gower had accepted a collar – a form of livery – from Henry, and this is shown on his tomb effigy. Although unconfirmed, a brief biographical reference to the author wearing what could be a legal court official's robes in his French work *Mirour de l'omme* (c. 1375–8) supports the plausible conjecture that Gower made a career in the law. Other than that, the non-literary life records of Gower that we have reveal a man with a Kentish background but property interests in Essex and

---

[35] David Nicholas, *The Later Medieval City 1300–1500* (Longman, London: 1997), 50–3.

[36] This fanciful idea was made familiar by Geoffrey of Monmouth in his *Historia Regum Britanniae*, an Arthurian legendary history of the mid-12th century, where he claimed that London had been founded by Brutus and was first called *Troia Nova*. In the original version of the Prologue to *Confessio Amantis* of around 1390 Gower speaks of meeting King Richard II while rowing on the Thames:

Under the toun of newe Troye,
Which tok of Brut his ferste joye . . .   (37–8)

See also Gower's *Vox Clamantis*, vol. I, 879–1358, where Gower likens the assault on London during the Peasants' Revolt to the sack of Troy.

East Anglia too, and one who was acquiring more land, especially from the 1360s to early 1380s.[37]

Towns were places to do business. We would normally understand that expression in commercial terms, and, as we have already seen, the surge of borough-formation in post-Conquest England was largely economic in motivation. A different function of the town, and certainly a major factor in the origins of several English cities, is government and jurisdiction. There is, in fact, a broad concept of social exchange which may embrace both economic and administrative transactions, so that towns can be characterized essentially as sites of specialized exchange that acquire larger resident populations than the agrarian settlements of the same society. Gower – always an intriguing, and critically a much neglected author – provides us with a precious insight into the special adaptation of the craft and occupation of literary author to these circumstances in the later Middle Ages. Where the convention had been for poets and performers to portray themselves as visitors and guests in a noble court or hall, he tells us in *Confessio Amantis* of a supposedly accidental encounter between King and poet, where Richard:

> . . . bad me do my besynesse
> That to his hihe worthinesse
> Som newe thing I scholde boke,
> That he himself it mihte loke
> After the forme of my writynge   (Prol., 49–53)[38]

boke: put in a book; *loke*: look at

using a verb, *bad*, that ambiguously could mean either 'commanded' or 'requested'.

While the plagues from the mid-14th century onwards had a noticeable impact on the urban population, it is not the case that there was a direct and concomitant shrinkage in urban economic activity. It proved possible for the smaller number of people to maintain and enjoy greater profits from much the same range and level of production and trade as before. In the midst of the economic changes in the countryside that had been taking place at least since the late 13th century anyway, London succeeded in holding and even enhancing its dominant position in English economic life in the late 14th and 15th centuries. Much of this success depended on trade, with wool, and foodstuffs such as grain and cheese, being exported to the Continent, and exotic commodities such as spices and Venetian glass coming back in: London grocers came to dominate a national supply network. Yet manufacturing and craftwork were also important facets of London's economy. Some of these productive occupations could be highly specialized, such as the women silkworkers based in the Cheapside area; others involved more familiar, heavier work, such as the tanners and leatherworkers at various sites just outside the walls of the City supplying craftsmen such as shoemakers, glovers and saddlers. Metalworking is recorded princi-

---

37 *Opp. cit.* in note 15.
38 All quotations from Gower are taken from Macaulay, ed. cit. in note 15.

pally in the Aldgate area, although archaeological evidence has also been recovered from the Guildhall site. The London of Chaucer and Gower was thus economically dynamic, sustaining itself largely on the secondary trading and reworking of basic agrarian products. Meanwhile the historical evidence of the London gilds and companies shows conscious attempts to define and organize professional identities and communities within this swirl.[39]

The usual perception of Gower against this background, however, is as an awkwardly detached character. Responding to the Peasants' Revolt of 1381, for instance, he wrote a long Latin poem in stylized hexameters, appropriating for its title the words of Isaiah applied to John the Baptist at the beginning of the Gospel of Mark: 'vox clamantis in deserto' ('the voice of one crying in the wilderness'). In this form, Gower's *Vox Clamantis* must have been directed primarily at the clergy, and it evinces nothing but hostility and fear towards the common people. Before this he had written *Mirour de l'omme*, which is also referred to by a Latin title in colophons to *Confessio Amantis* and on Gower's tomb in Southwark Cathedral, first as *Speculum Hominis* and subsequently *Speculum Meditantis* ('The mirror of Man'; 'The mirror of one thinking'). This work contains a rigidly formal survey of vices and their contrary virtues, followed by a social exposé constructed according to the familiar Three Estates (knights, ploughmen, and clergy) model, and concluding with a devotional Life of Mary. The explicit character of Gower's perception and evaluation of his contemporary circumstances seems to preclude any major role for subconscious and implicit factors of the kind just noted in *Troilus and Criseyde*.

The *Mirour*'s structuration around the Seven Deadly Sins is repeated in the third and final work of Gower's trilingual trilogy, *Confessio Amantis*. In too many modern critics' view, despite now writing in English and intending, according to the revised version of his Prologue:

> to make
> A bok for Engelondes sake   (Prol., 23–4)[40]

Gower scarcely succeeds in being less formal, less remote or less autocratic a moralist in this collection of Classical and exemplary tales than elsewhere. A reading of the text looking for some equivalent evocation of the concrete, contemporary world to that in *Troilus and Criseyde* would initially appear to bear this out. Most of the imagery in the *Confessio* is conventional and non-specific: of warriors and strongholds, kings and emperors, and a noticeably frequent allegorical use of ships and sea-voyages. Contemporary material is

---

[39]   E. M. Veale, 'Craftsmen and the economy of London in the fourteenth century', in A. E. J. Hollaender and W. Kellaway (eds.), *Studies in London History Presented to Philip Edmund Jones* (Leicester: Leicester University Press, 1969), 133–51: repr. in Richard Holt and Gervase Rosser (eds.), *The Medieval Town, 1200–1540* (London: Longman, 1990), 120–40; Christopher Dyer, *Making a Living in the Middle Ages: The People of Britain 850–1520* (New Haven: Yale University Press, 2002), 303–7. The archaeological evidence is only partially published; a good conspectus is on display at the Museum of London. See also Geoff Egan, 'Some archaeological evidence for metalworking in London, c.1050 AD – c.1700 AD', *Journal of the Hist. Metallurgy Soc.*, 30 (1996), 83–94.

[40]   In the first version, line 24 reads 'A bok for king Richardes sake'.

rare, although not non-existent.[41] It does seem, therefore, that we could characterize Gower, or even accuse him, of being a detached writer, and a theoretical moralist rather than a practical one.

That critical assessment can, however, be challenged at its very root by an analysis of a passage from Book IV of *Confessio Amantis*. This book is concerned with the sin of Sloth (*Accidia*). The structure of the *Confessio* is that a character identified with the author, Amans ('Lover'), is being confessed by Genius, a priest of Venus, the goddess of love. While superficially done in respect of Amans' behaviour as a lover, this is inevitably the basis for reflections of much wider moral application in individual and social conduct. In this passage, quoted here in full, Amans exculpates himself from any guilt of Idleness, one of the branches of Sloth (IV, 1112–1223):

> '. . . Mi sone, if thou of such a molde
> Art mad, now tell me plein thi schrifte'
>   'Nay, fader, god I yive a yifte,
> That toward love, as be mi wit,
> Al ydel was I nevere yit,
> Ne nevere schal, whil I mai go.'
>   'Now, Sone, tell me thanne so,
> What hast thou don of besischipe
> To love and to the ladischipe   1120
> Of hire which thi ladi is?'
>   'Mi fader, evere yit er this
> In every place, in every stede,
> What so mi ladi hath me bede,
> With al myn herte obedient
> I have therto be diligent.
> And if so is sche bidde noght,
> What thing that thanne into my thoght
> Comth ferst of that I mai suffise,
> I bowe and profre my servise,   1130
> Somtime in chambre, somtime in halle,
> Riht as I se the times falle.
> And whan sche goth to hiere masse,
> That time schal noght overpasse,
> That I naproche hir ladihede,
> In aunter if I mai hire lede
> Unto the chapelle and ayein.
> Thanne is noght al mi weie in vein,
> Somdiel I mai the betre fare,
> Whan I, that mai noght fiele hir bare,   1140
> Mai lede hire clothed in myn arm:
> Bot afterward it doth me harm
> Of pure ymaginacioun;
> For thanne this collacioun
> I make unto miselven ofte,

---

[41] One example is an attack on Lombard bankers, II, 2077–2144.

And seie, "Ha lord, hou sche is softe,
How sche is rounde, hou sche is smal!
Now wolde god I hadde hire al
Withoute danger at mi wille!"
And thanne I sike and sitte stille,   1150
Of that I se mi besi thoght
Is torned ydel into noght.
Bot for al that lete I ne mai,
Whanne I se time an other dai,
That I ne do my besinesse
Unto mi ladi worthinesse.
For I therto mi wit afaite
To se the times and awaite
What is to done and what to leve:
And so, whan time is, be hire leve,   1160
What thing sche bit me don, I do,
And wher sche bidt me gon, I go,
And whanne hir list to clepe, I come.
Thus hath sche fulliche overcome
Min ydelnesse til I sterve,
So that I mot hire nedes serve,
For as men sein, nede hath no lawe.
Thus mot I nedly to hire drawe,
I serve, I bowe, I loke, I loute,
Min yhe folweth hire aboute,   1170
What so sche wole so wol I,
Whan sche wol sitte, I knele by,
And whan sche stant, than wol I stonde:
Bot whan sche takth hir werk on honde
Of wevinge or enbrouderie,
Than can I noght bot muse and prie
Upon hire fingres longe and smale,
And now I thenke, and now I tale,
And now I singe, and now I sike,
And thus mi contienance I pike.   1180
And if it falle, as for a time
Hir liketh noght abide bime,
Bot besien hire on other thinges,
Than make I othre tariinges
To dreche forth the longe dai,
For me is loth departe away.
And thanne I am so simple of port,
That forto feigne som desport
I pleie with hire litel hound
Now on the bedd, now on the ground,   1190
Now with hir briddes in the cage;
For ther is non so litel page,
Ne yit so simple a chamberere,
That I ne make hem alle chere,
Al for thei scholde speke wel:
Thus mow ye sen mi besi whiel,

That goth noght ydeliche aboute.
And if hir list to riden oute
On pelrinage or other stede,
I come, thogh I be noght bede,   1200
And take hire in min arm alofte
And sette hire in hire sadel softe,
And so forth lede hire be the bridel,
For that I wolde noght ben ydel.
And if hire list to ride in Char,
And thanne I mai therof be war,
Anon I schape me to ryde
Riht evene be the Chares side;
And as I mai, I speke among,
And otherwhile I singe a song,   1210
Which Ovide in his bokes made,
And seide, "O which sorwes glade,
O which wofull prosperite
Belongeth to the proprete
Of love, who so wole him serve!
And yit therfro mai noman swerve,
That he ne mot his lawe obeie."
And thus I ryde forth mi weie,
And am riht besi overal
With herte and with mi body al,   1220
As I have said you hier tofore.
My goode fader, tell therfore,
Of Ydelnesse if I have gilt.'

bede (1124, 1200): bidden; *naproche* (1135): do not approach; *in
aunter if* (1136): in case; *and ayein* (1137): and back; *somdiel*
(1139): partly; *collacioun* (1144): text; *danger* (1149): feminine
disdain; *afaite* (1157): train; *bit, bidt* (1161–2): bids; *clepe* (1163):
call; *sterve* (1165): die; *loute* (1169): bow down; *yhe* (1170): eye; *tale*
(1178): chatter; *pike* (1180): pick, select; *bime* (1182): by me; *dreche
forth* (1185): drag out; *port* (1187): bearing; *mow* (1196): may; *char*
(1205, 1208): carriage; *mot* (1217): must.

After denying the charge of idleness (line 1116), Amans is challenged to
declare how he has been busy in love (1118–21). The key note in his response,
and a recurrent one, is how he has served his lady obediently, diligently, and
subserviently (1122–32). The lady, however, apparently has no use to put all of
this devotion to, and the outcome is not some service or task gladly borne but
rather no more than a labour of imagination for him (1142–9). Yet while his
collacioun – a term with religious connotations, as an utterance of quasi-
patristic authority – is manifestly an evocation of the work of the love poet, it
equally manifestly fails to answer his immediate needs. It is a form of idleness,
turning his 'busy thought . . . into nought' (1150–6). This does not dissuade him
from continuing to try to serve his lady, following her about in a pathetic manner
– 'I serve, I bow, I look, I fawn' (1169) – and kneeling wherever she sits.

It is immediately after this that the word *work* is introduced for the first time, and ironically is associated with the lady rather than the busy lover:

> But when she takes her work in hand
> Of weaving or embroidery,
> Then I can only muse and pry
> Upon her fingers long and slim . . .   (1174–7)

His response is utterly characteristic of the conventional love poet, alternating song and sighs while she is busying herself (1179 and 1183). Paradoxically, his labour is now the opposite of productive, making 'tarryings, to while away the long day' (1184–5), and the counterpart to her work is for him to play, with her little dog, which we can also recognize as a poor substitute for the sexual play or labour he would rather be at with his lady, not least as this specifically takes place 'now on the bed, now on the floor' (1189–90). He then returns to the labour of serving his lady whether she wants it or not, placing her in her saddle and leading her horse around by its bridle (1200–4), a position in which he once more openly identifies himself as poetic, singing a song which Ovid had composed about the inevitable woe and enslavement of the man in love (1210–17).

Amans thus presents love as his occupation, as allegorically he must: he can only be 'the one who loves'. He asserts that he is not idle in this occupation. The association between Amans and Gower the poet – Gower the *maker*, to use a Late Middle English term for poet – is perfectly clear. The irony of the fact that the lover's toil is assiduous in a self-imposed and otherwise unwanted service to his lady is comically exploited, at the same time as, in a rather more sharp-edged manner, this labour of love is contrasted with the lady's active and material work, weaving and sewing. It is the realism that cuts into this mono-logue with the image of the lady, tellingly placed at the very centre of the speech, 'when she takes her work in hand', that is particularly significant. This is not simply a matter of the realism of her doing something that is concrete and practical, and indeed something that was still widely perceived as a female occu-pation at all levels of society. Textile production was growing into a major, urbanized industry of the later Middle Ages, and as a result weaving had become a male trade too, to the extent, indeed, that the weaver is perhaps the most common stereotype of the working man outside of the agricultural world at this time.[42] Just as realistically, however, the reader may be fully aware that a lady like Gower's lady would actually have been embroidering as a pastime as much as as an essential producer. In other words, her practical role in the mate-rial and commercial world she has evoked merely by picking up her embroidery as a sign of her indifference to her lover's presence and persistence is that of the consumer. The pretence implicit in her representation as an industrious worker

---

42 Jacques Le Goff, 'Le temps du travail dans la «crise» du XIVe siècle: du temps médiévale au temps moderne', 66–79 in idem, *Pour un autre moyen âge: temps, travail et c ulture en occident, 18 essais* (Paris: Gallimard, 1977): trans. A. Goldhammer, *op. cit.* in Chapter 1, note 12, 43–52; Dyer, *op. cit.* in note 39, 203 and 321.

thus evokes an awareness of the complexities of economic relationship and interdependency in the late 14th century that is genuinely sophisticated.

Where, meanwhile, does this leave Gower? In his equally ostensibly self-conscious self-portrait, is he so aloof from the practical world that he simply does not care about – or maybe does not even notice – the imputation of idleness and unproductiveness he lays himself open to? Or is this merely a straightforward piece of self-deprecatory irony, in the style of Chaucer, pretending to be such a helpless drone? Each of these explanations seems unlikely, or, to use the standard of critical evaluation, undesirably reductive. Firstly, and pertinently, the issue of idleness and non-productivity was a topical and a charged one in the late 14th century. When the industrious Piers sets the world to work towards the end of the opening *passus* of *Piers Plowman*, the very first thing he does (idealistically, and not realistically) is to get *all* the women sewing, spinning or weaving.[43]

More insight into Gower's own view of Idleness can be found in the relevant sections of *Mirour de l'omme*. Here the equivalent vice, *Oedivesce*, is portrayed in lines 5773–879,[44] and the opposite virtue, *Solicitude* ('Industry'), is portrayed in lines 14401–592. *Oedivesce* ('Idleness') is portrayed as an aversion to exertion in two spheres of activity: physical labour, which is represented specifically by agricultural work; and in the ecclesiastical and spiritual realm. Idleness prefers playing games, gambling, and begging, to honest labour and ploughing – although interestingly, the question of working for wages is not even mentioned here. Further suggesting an association with the poet, Idleness is likened to the grasshopper that uselessly and improvidently sings and dances throughout the summer, while in the depiction of Industry a contrast is provided in the figure of the worthy, labouring ant. A sexual element is introduced too, for at the end, where the break in the manuscript occurs, we are being told how Dame Oedivesce (the noun *oedivesce* is feminine) is a corrupting influence. This actually comes just after Idleness has been identified as the underlying cause of sodomy, one thing at least that Amans' futile industry in the passage from *Confessio Amantis* can claim as a benefit according to its own moral criteria.

The contrasting virtue, *Solicitude*, is portrayed in a way that repeats but determinedly balances the dichotomy of its material and spiritual aspects. Industry labours to provide food for both the body and the soul, but this is to be achieved in practice by a division of labour:

> Ascuns s'en vont les champs tenir,
> De qui labour le pain nous vient.
> Ascuns sont clers . . .   (14468–70)

> Some go out to tend the fields:
> From their labour bread comes to us.
> Others are clerics . . .

---

[43] The passage is common to all three major recensions of *Piers Plowman* (the A-, B- and C-texts): A VII, 6–22; B VI, 6–20; C VIII, 5–18. See also James Simpson, *Piers Plowman: A Reading of the B-Text* (London: Longman, 1990), 68–70.

[44] After line 5879 there is a lacuna in the sole surviving manuscript of *Mirour de l'omme*, so this section is not complete.

The ideal purpose of Industry is not to increase and to amass material wealth but rather just to provide sufficient for human needs. It consists, indeed, of a perfect balance between the active and contemplative lives.[45] Of these two, the contemplative life is here explicitly identified as the higher one, but active, practical work is nonetheless both needful and worthy.

In this historical and literary context, however, the contemplative life now means something very different from monastic asceticism and withdrawn study. By the later Middle Ages, intellectual activity had become a form of work. Both scholarship and art could be professions. Meanwhile poetry was regularly recognized, in a perfect or idealized conception at least, as being a venerable and even holy means of ethical guidance. Even a poet writing in the vernacular language could be a form of theologian.[46] But it must then have been a sensitive issue, how far this veneration of poetry might be compromised by an emergent commodification of both literature and the book implicit not only in the way Gower takes his commission from Richard, but also in the nature of the manuscripts in which both Chaucer's and Gower's works were reproduced in the 15th century.[47]

Gower's invocations of his social and economic context, though relatively few, are thus subtly exemplary and wittily alert. They are rooted in a profound awareness of the issues and pressures in his contemporary world that we can only fully share in by being as attentive to the significance of the material imagery and relevant allusions in his work as historicizing critics have been to, for instance, the references to King Richard II and Henry Bolingbroke. It was fully consistent for Gower's tomb, the design of which he may well have contributed to himself, to have combined the traditional form of his day with an innovation in memorializing him in his identity as a poet, the head of his effigy upon the tomb-chest pillowed by his three major books. In his writing, Gower's awareness enabled him to evoke vital factors within his world without embracing it in a worldly way. It remains elitist or aristocratic, and idealist; but read in this light has a conscious intellectual conservatism reinstated as a major element of its purpose – it does not embody reactionary social and economic conservatism in the automatic manner it as has so widely been supposed to.

Gower was as much engaged in the debate over the place and role of literature in his rapidly changing world as was Chaucer.[48] Then as now, it was easiest to see how the world was becoming modern in economic and social terms, with the inexorable rise of the urban bourgeoisie to which they were both so closely linked. Yet both of these great authors appear also to have grasped the ideolog-

---

[45] A tradition of ideological endorsement of the contemplative life can be traced back to Ancient Greek philosophy. A dilemma over the relative virtues of an active life of good works in the world, and a contemplative life of withdrawal, meditation and worship became a key one for medieval Christianity, for which authoritative sources were the Fathers of the Church, Augustine and Pope Gregory the Great.

[46] A. J. Minnis and A. B. Scott (eds.), *Medieval Literary Theory and Criticism c.1100–c.1375: The Commentary Tradition*, rev. ed. (Oxford: Clarendon, 1988), esp. 373–519.

[47] Malcolm B. Parkes and A. I. Doyle, 'The production of copies of the *Canterbury Tales* and the *Confessio Amantis* in the early fifteenth century', in M. B. Parkes and Andrew G. Watson (eds.), *Medieval Scribes, Manuscripts and Libraries: Essays Presented to N. R. Ker* (London: Scolar, 1978), 163–201.

[48] See Jocelyn Wogan-Browne *et al.* (eds.), *The Idea of the Vernacular: An Anthology of Middle English Literary Theory 1280–1520* (University of Exeter Press, 1999).

ical and cognitive changes that were associated with and embedded in those material and practical shifts. Neither embraced this incipient modernity with enthusiasm; both, however, reveal a mature understanding of it and attempted to mediate the force and direction of the flow of change through their literary art. Gower made a determined bid to negotiate a special place for literature as the very embodiment of an ideology that was independent of worldly events and fortune while still both aware of and relevant to them. By giving himself a more substantial role in the framed narrative of *Confessio Amantis*, Gower was able to dramatize the problems implicit in the incipient professionalization of literary authorship more directly and personally than Chaucer did in the Canterbury Tales. This may help us to explain why the critical reception of Gower in comparison to Chaucer up to two centuries after his death suggests that Gower was more successful in negotiating a place for his literature, and his image as an author, in these changing circumstances than Chaucer was.[49]

---

[49] Consider the comparative assessment of Chaucer and Gower in Robert Greene's *Greenes Vision* (1592), and the characterization of Gower in Shakespeare's *Pericles*.

5

Renaissance, Reformation and Restoration

Dissolution, Dissociation and Displacement

OVER the 15th and 16th centuries, the ideological party represented by William Thorpe achieved the ascendancy, and the Protestant Reformation was established in England. Politically, the story of its triumph began with Henry VIII, ironically given the title of *Fidei Defensor* (Defender of the Faith) by Pope Leo XI in 1521 in the midst of a series of diplomatic manoeuvres involving the Holy Roman Emperor (Charles V of Spain) with the papacy against France, despite the treaty Henry had concluded with her king at the Field of Cloth of Gold only the previous year. The immediate cause of Henry's break with Rome, which was many years in the making and thus no impromptu reaction, was his wish to annul his marriage to his first wife, Catherine of Aragon, who had failed to bear him a successor other than a daughter, Mary, and to marry the beautiful Anne Boleyn. In 1532, the Convocation of the English clergy at Canterbury submitted to Henry's authority, agreeing neither to meet nor to pass ecclesiastical legislation without his consent – a relationship confirmed by an Act of Supremacy in 1534. Early in 1535 Henry assumed the title of Supreme Head on Earth of the Church. Doctrinally, the church then presided over by Henry, as represented by the Ten Articles of 1536, remained more Catholic than Protestant, and one of the articles cautiously reaffirmed the validity of images.[1] The most immediate material consequence of Henry's seizure of the Church was the Dissolution of the monasteries of England and Wales, beginning with the confiscation of the property and closure of smaller religious houses but moving rapidly on to the major ones (1536–40). Virtually concurrently, an attack on fraudulent relics throughout the churches led to the despoliation of richly adorned shrines and works of art, including that of St Thomas à Becket in Canterbury as early as September 1538. Twenty-six cartloads of gold and silver were reportedly taken from the cathedral.

An antiquarian desire to collect ancient (Classical) works of art can be traced in Italy back to the 15th century, and a comparable appreciation of texts and manuscripts made available by the suppression of the monasteries appeared

---

[1] C. H. Williams (ed.), *English Historical Documents. Vol. V, 1485–1558* (London: Eyre & Spottiswoode, 1967), 795–805: Article VI.

almost immediately in England. However the attitude to the medieval artefacts and art of the Church was quite different. Through the remainder of the 16th century and on to the mid-17th, this expressed itself in waves of increasing hostility and methodical destruction. Defaced images – especially sculpted figures of saints or Biblical characters with their faces literally struck off – are still to be seen in many churches and cathedrals. They were not removed or annihilated, but left in this disfigured state as emblems of both iconoclasm and the idolatry it perceived itself as battling against. The break with pre-Reformation practices was, however, gradual. Chantries, for instance, were not effectively suppressed until the beginning of the reign of the boy-king Edward VI in 1547, and a period of reversion towards Roman Catholicism in the reign of Mary (1553–8) even allowed a new chantry chapel to be built for Stephen Gardiner, Bishop of Winchester, between 1556 and 1558. Secular tomb monuments continued to evolve, steadily reflecting changes in fashion and in the public representation of piety that, with the emergence of a popular Puritanism in the second half of the 16th century, were interlinked factors.[2]

Under the long reign of Queen Elizabeth (1558–1603), Protestantism consolidated its hold on the Church of England. Through parliamentary legislation of 1559 known as the Elizabethan Settlement, she assumed the role of Supreme Governor, rather than Head, of the Church. Her first Archbishop of Canterbury was Matthew Parker, *inter alia* a collector and editor of medieval manuscripts with a particular interest in the Anglo-Saxon period. The doctrinal position of the Anglican church was defined by the Thirty-Nine Articles produced between 1563 and 1571.[3] By then, however, major battle lines were already drawn between a conservative Anglicanism and the growing force of Puritanism, inspired in no small practical measure by the success of John Knox's Calvinist church in Scotland. As with most such movements, Puritanism was something one could adhere to more or less, and its ideals were therefore able to seep through society and into the church. When we look at developments in the artefactual repertoire of this period, especially within churches, particularly striking is the switch to a textual culture, venerating scripture – the Word and the Book: for instance by placing conspicuous inscribed or painted tablets of text where images would formerly have stood.[4] By the end of the 16th century, an opposition between the material world and the realm of language and ideas that had been an extreme and radical position for William Thorpe two hundred years earlier had moved to the very heart of English cultural life. With that came a diversion of material production into new channels, and a new scheme of values concerning inanimate objects.

The changes in the inventory of artefacts with which people lived their lives

[2]   Eamon Duffy, *The Stripping of the Altars: Traditional Religion in England 1400–1580* (New Haven: Yale University Press, 1992); J. Phillips, *The Reformation of Images: Destruction of Art in England, 1535–1660* (Berkeley: University of California Press, 1973); Phillip Lindley, 'Innovations, tradition and disruption in tomb-sculpture', in Gaimster and Stamper (eds.), *op. cit.* in Chapter 4, note 33, 77–92; K. A. Esdaile, *English Church Monuments 1510–1840* (London: Batsford, 1946); M. Whinney (rev. J. Physick), *Sculpture in Britain 1530 to 1830*, 2nd ed. (Harmondsworth: Penguin, 1988), 27–85.

[3]   A reduction from Forty-Two Articles of Edward VI.

[4]   Moreland, *op. cit.* in Chapter 1, note 21, esp. 54–61.

through the 15th and 16th centuries were considerable. Productive techniques and skills saw marked advances. The stocking frame for machine-knitting, for instance, was invented in 1589, and threatened to disrupt the established way of life so much that it was virtually outlawed by Elizabeth's government.[5] Even more intricate mechanisms produced in this period are represented by instruments such as clocks and watches, or the fascinating globes so conspicuous in Holbein's famous painting of French ambassadors to Henry VIII's court in 1533. A new ability to construct sufficiently powerful furnaces allowed large, cast-iron stove-backs to be introduced in the 15th century – a change that both reflected and encouraged the desire to shift the fireplace from a central hearth to one side of a room, in a stove or a grate beneath a chimney. The ceramic range came to include large quantities of especially hard, siliceous, stoneware imported from the Rhineland area, often in the form of bulbous tankards that came to be known satirically as *bellarmines*, mocking a portly Roman Catholic theologican and cardinal of that name. The growth in the range and level of international trade is clearly visible. Splendid, usually tin-glazed 'maiolica' pottery was imported from the late 15th century onwards, and growing contacts with the Far East eventually saw a taste for porcelain supersede this, imitated by Delftware, production of which was established in the London area in the 17th century. The new connexions across the Atlantic introduced novelties such as the well-known potato and tobacco. The way the use of the latter was conceptually assimilated to familiar forms of ingestion is nicely shown by one of the earliest English references to it, in John Donne's *Satyre I* of the earlier 1590s, where the term used is 'drinking' rather than 'smoking'.[6]

These changes hardly constitute a cultural revolution.[7] The most significant change lay covert, not in the range and form of artefacts available but in the way they were regarded. Such a change could take place all the more easily and thoroughly for being insinuous rather than obvious. At a practical level, people still had essentially the same range of artefacts to do essentially the same things as had been done in the previous generation, and the generations before that. Such continuity disguised a deep rupture between practical and symbolic life. Fundamental to the incoming order was an absolute distinction between utility and art. Objects could be of value in pragmatic *or* in aesthetic terms. A single artefact could still be critically appreciated according to both schemes, but that meant complexity – even incongruity. Practical use and artistic merit had been dissociated.

A description of a house, the home of Kalander, early in Sir Philip Sidney's prose romance known as *The Countesse of Pembrokes Arcadia* (1593) might initially seem to have gone the further step to a utilitarian aesthetic, the attribution of beauty being totally subsumed within an evaluation of practicality and convenience:

---

5   43 Elizabeth 10: *Statutes of the Realm, ed. cit.* in Chapter 4, note 12, vol. IV, 975–7.
6   The verb *smoke* in this sense is first recorded in the Oxford English Dictionary from 1617. It actually derives from an existing verb meaning to emit smoke (as in 'a smoking chimney') rather than to inhale it.
7   Frans Verhaege, 'The archaeology of transition: a Continental view', in Gaimster and Stamper (eds.), *op. cit.* in Chapter 4, note 33, 25–44.

> The house itself was built of fair and strong stone, not affecting so much any extraordinary kind of fineness as an honourable representing of a firm stateliness. The lights, doors and stairs rather directed to the use of the guest than to the eye of the artificer; and yet as the one chiefly heeded, so the other not neglected; each place handsome without curiosity, and homely without loathsomeness; not so dainty as not to be trod upon, nor yet slubbered up with good fellowship; all more lasting than beautiful but that the consideration of the exceeding lastingness made the eye believe it was exceeding beautiful.[8]

Yet it is not quite so: 'the use of the guest' and 'the eye [of the artificer]' remain distinct critical perspectives. Beauty is not just a narcissistic pleasure of the artist, admiring his own talents, but also lies crucially in the 'eye' of the beholder. It thus resides in the realm of sensation, albeit a sensibility that can be influenced – in the man of good reason – in an interestingly mechanical way by the mind, in its 'consideration' of the well-made character of the house.

Consciousness of the presence of material culture within an ordered and whole scheme of worldly things, and the increasing anxiety about its place there that characterized the end of the Middle Ages and early modern period, could lead either to a perception of artefacts as solely and entirely functional, or to attempts to establish new schemes that would confer acceptable meanings upon them. Sidney's explicit critique of the house is a clear example of this. Donne, the most innovative English poet from the Elizabethan period, also explored these issues in elaborate detail. A characteristic of his poetry (and indeed his sermons) is his use of imagery which embraces the new material experiences that the opening of the world to exploration and trade in the 16th century had brought, and his frequent references to maps and globes. He contributed substantially to the development of the technique of referring diverse experiences to mechanical contrivances of his world in emphatically surprising similes, or 'conceits': the practice that stimulated Samuel Johnson's famous characterization of the wit of what he called this school of 'metaphysical' poets:

> The most heterogeneous ideas are yoked by violence together; nature and art are ransacked for illustrations, comparisons, and allusions . . .[9]

Dr Johnson's criticism is exaggerated and parodic. He could well have had in mind Donne's image of the relationship between a pair of lovers' souls:

> If they be two, they are two so
>   As stiffe twin compasses are two,
> Thy soule, the fixt foot, makes no show
>   To move, but doth, if the'other doe.
>   (A Valediction: forbidding mourning. 1611?)

---

[8]   Sir Philip Sidney, *The Countess of Pembroke's Arcadia*, ed. Maurice Evans (Harmondsworth: Penguin, 1977), Book I, chapter 2.
[9]   Samuel Johnson, 'Life of Cowley', from *idem, Lives of the English Poets*. Note that 'art' here still refers to the realm of artefacts generally.

Donne did not ransack the world of contemporary experience for similes: on the contrary he used a consistent and selective range, reflecting a sense of fitness and decorum – referring primarily to precious commodities, or to laudable advances in human knowledge and skill. An ability to relate diverse experiences to one another was conceptually crucial for Donne, but he was certainly not given to construe love as a mechanical, physio-chemical experience (although far from uninterested in the physical, mechanical, act of sexual love!). Applying a philosophical perception in the Neo-Platonic tradition, he conceived of a scale of inter-related experiences, running from the material, earthly and mortal ('sublunary') to the spiritual, ideal and eternal. Thus in 'Aire and Angels', he justifies the physical preoccupation of his otherwise sublime love with a woman's body by likening it to angels, pure spirit, who could supposedly appear to earthly mortals by condensing bodies of air like clouds. As with Sidney, though, such a system of linkage fundamentally assumes the essential – which at some levels means material – distinctness of its parts: not a confusion, or seamless continuum, between them.

Initially, it can seem puzzling that the positive and constructive aspects of an archaeology of Protestantism are so limited. But a crucial point may be to understand that the new order did not wish to replace the old material culture with some purer equivalent of it: it sought rather to displace it, to embody a quite new attitude to the material world. This point is illustrated by ceramic stove-tiles and stoneware pots of the late 16th century that do have positive, Protestant decoration on them in the form of illustrations copied from woodcuts in printed Lutheran Bibles (Fig. 12).[10] Such ethically charged art was now blatant and unambiguous. The surface of the object was a practical advertising space upon which value-laden symbolism could sit. That symbolism was no longer presumed to reside, latent, within the artefact.

This change in attitude towards the material world can be argued to have been as profound and as consequential as any intellectual shift of what we call the Renaissance. In Roman Catholic and Protestant Europe alike, the intellectual culture of the period of the Reformation and Counter-Reformation was characterized by a liberation of the powers of mental conception and reason at the expense of the dissociation between thought and the material and social worlds. Thus, while the world of ideas might no longer be constrained by those phenomena, it was no longer under any obligation to moderate itself according to its material and social consequences. Philosophies and theories were free to tyrannize and destroy more widely and creatively than ever.

In the field of letters, however, Classical literary scholarship flourished, and the Elizabethan period saw an extraordinary blossoming of English literature.

---

[10] A particularly rich collection is from Witzenhausen, Lower Saxony, Germany: H.-G. Stephan, *Kacheln aus dem Werraland: Die Entwicklung der Ofenkacheln vom 13. bis 17. Jahrhundert im unteren Werra-Raum*, Schriften des Werratalvereins Witzenhausen, 23 (1991); David R. M. Gaimster, 'The Continental tile stove at Camber Castle', in M. Biddle *et al.*, *Henry VIII's Coastal Artillery Fort at Camber Castle, Rye, East Sussex* (English Heritage and Oxford Archaeol. Unit, 2001), 149–64; *idem*, 'Pots, prints and protestantism: changing mentalities in the urban domestic sphere, *c.* 1480–1580', forthcoming in Roberta Gilchrist and David Gaimster (eds.), *The Archaeology of Reformation*, Soc. Post-Medieval Archaeol. Monographs, 1 (Leeds: Maney).

FIG. 12. Stove-tile showing the Temptation of Adam: Witzenhausen, Lower Saxony, Germany. Fragments of a similar tile were found at Camber Castle, East Sussex. After Stephan, *op. cit.* in note 10.

There are elements of Classical influence in Renaissance English literature, such as George Chapman's poetry and his translation from Homer's *Iliad* of the 1590s. The greatest single source of difference between the vocabulary of our own English and that of Chaucer is the profusion of Latinisms introduced in this period. Yet while we can cite distinctly 'Renaissance'-character texts from England, such as Sir Thomas More's *Utopia*, published in Latin in 1516–17 and in an English translation in 1551, or Francis Bacon's *Essays*, a collection expanded between 1597 and 1625, Classicism and lofty humanism characterize only a minor part of the diverse range of English literature from this period. The strength and character of the innovatory processes at work in literature is nicely represented by the contrastive development of what emerged as the three principal modes of literature: poetry, prose and drama. Where tradition was deepest and most robust, innovation was slowest.

Poetic output was high, yet it was a more conservative mode of expression than any other. After a lean period of writing in the 15th century, a number of highly talented, noble courtier poets emerged in the 16th, writing lyrics and the newly popular form of the sonnet modelled on the 14th-century Italian writer Petrarch. Broadly in line with other authors from the 16th century, most notably Lodovico Ariosto in Italy and Miguel de Cervantes in Spain, but still in his own peculiar way, Edmund Spenser adapted the traditions of medieval romance to write a commentary on his contemporary political world in the *Faerie Queene* (1590–6).

Vernacular prose narrative and fiction, meanwhile, went through an earlier process of diversification and growth. Relatively little of this, however, could be described as artistically meritorious or creative. From the late 16th century, *The Countesse of Pembrokes Arcadia* can properly be regarded as a direct ancestor of the English novel, but it was still to be several generations before what we would recognize as an English novel tradition established itself.[11] Equally representative of the mongrel and dubiously respectable origins of English prose fiction are the small jest-books and collections of 'Merry Tales' of which many are known from the 16th and 17th centuries. The production of these collections, which are mostly of vulgar jokes, was due in large measure to the commercial opportunities provided by the introduction of the printing press: appealing to low tastes has always been a secure way of making sufficient sales for a profit. No special explanation is required for the fact that a taste for such *facetiae*, to give them their Latin term, is apparent in learned circles too. Nonetheless, it does not strain mundane good sense too far to suggest that the popularity of this genre can also be perceived as a minor, carnivalesque outcome of the fragmentation of literary culture that accompanied the rupturing of the doctrinal and textual authority of the medieval church. This not only created scope for the expansion of textual culture in some new directions, but also a desire to exercise that freedom, especially in forms that allowed it to be done safely.[12]

---

[11]   Until the mid-18th century, *romance* remained the usual English term for what we would now call a novel, and *novel* denoted something more like a short story. *Romance*, however, also implied a plot of agglutinative structure and fanciful character, and was habitually contrasted with *epic*.

[12]   Governmental control and censorship of published matter was in force for much of this period. From

The most prominent new departure in English literary culture of this period was the growth of the theatre and flourishing of Elizabethan and Jacobean drama. The 16th century began with a dramatic repertoire effectively confined to the Biblical cycles and morality plays or interludes. Most of the cycle plays are preserved for us in late 15th-century and 16th-century copies, and continued to be produced well into the 16th century. The morality plays are generally short dramas involving personified abstractions such as 'Everyman' or 'Conscience'. An innovation that spread from French drama into English in the earlier 16th century but which never quite took root was the farce, another short form of play, exhibiting some absurd case of stupidity for the audience's laughter. By the end of the 16th century, by contrast, as well the works of now lesser known dramatists such as George Peele and Thomas Kyd, the stage had been graced by works of Christopher Marlowe and William Shakespeare, and yet more still frequently performed playwrights emerged in the Jacobean Period: John Webster, Thomas Middleton, Francis Beaumont and Richard Fletcher, Ben Jonson. Even more than the growth of prose fiction, this was a revolution in the history of English literature that was subtly but crucially inter-connected with changes in material culture.

The restricted development of English dramatic writing before the Elizabethan period is surprising in light of the fact that the importance of drama as a means of training and education had long been recognized.[13] It was a practical complement to the rhetorical training in dialectics through which medieval students had to develop their argumentative and analytical skills, taking a given part or position in a staged debate. Renaissance scholarship made an increasing range of Classical dramatic texts, both Greek and Latin, available for schools and colleges to perform. They offered roles for the students to assume that they might variously be expected to emulate or to avoid in their subsequent real lives, or which they might simply empathize with. Such experiences also contributed substantially to the linguistic training of the students, practising grammar and idioms, and providing wider experience in actually speaking the Classical languages.

The history of dramatic production in England for most of the 16th century is consequently strongly marked by records of theatrical performances in schools such as Eton, and at the colleges of the Universities of Oxford and Cambridge or the Inns of Court. At those places of study for older students, organized and rehearsed interludes gradually came to form a substantial part of seasonal revels and entertainments. Boy companies from the ecclesiastical schools of St Pauls, London, the Chapel Royal of the Court, based at Blackfriars from 1576, and the Chapel at Windsor, performed regularly at court. There are also records of theatrical companies of men kept or sponsored by both Queen Elizabeth herself and a

---

1556, the requirement to record publications in the *Stationers' Register* provides invaluable detail of publishing history. Donald Thomas, *A Long Time Burning: The History of Literary Censorship in England* (London: Routledge & Kegan Paul, 1969), 8–33.

[13] There is lost drama – plays referred to of which no copies survive. This does not significantly affect the overall picture. See F. P. Wilson, *English Drama 1485–1585* (Oxford: Clarendon Press, 1968), esp. 1–11.

number of her earls, performing both in halls for select audiences and at inns, even occasionally in churches and churchyards, for a more general public.[14]

The construction of purpose-built public theatres was a London – strictly a *suburban* – phenomenon of the late 1560s onwards. It has been illuminated by archaeological work on these sites in recent years, catalysed primarily by excavations on the site of the Rose theatre, Southwark, in 1989, which coincided closely with the reconstruction of a version of the Globe theatre that stood close by on the south bank of the Thames from 1599 to 1613 and of which Shakespeare was part-owner in a mature period of his career. These theatres had their own direct predecessors in rings and arenas constructed for the ungentle spectacles of animal fights and baiting involving bulls, bears, dogs and cocks. Supplementing diary evidence, our knowledge of the form and location of those enclosures relies for detail upon early maps and panoramas of London. Most of them were located in the modern Bankside area of Southwark, across the river and opposite to the Cities of London and Westminster. This was, pragmatically, an accessible area where space was available both for the arenas and for keeping the animals before the performances. But the entertainments staged here were also quite different from, and alternative to, the commercial, administrative and spiritual business of the Cities. The diary evidence of spectators here records the recourse of the common public to these entertainments, but also, inevitably, is biassed towards recording the visits of more notable dignitaries: men in the service of foreign dukes, and even, in 1592, Frederick Duke of Württemberg himself. Here, then, were places where a greater level of uncontrolled social mixing was able to take place than at any other fixed and frequently visted site.[15]

Visual depictions also provide evidence for the actual form of Elizabethan and Jacobean theatres. Most of these are small-scale, exterior views found in panoramas, but there is a famous, larger-scale, interior view of the Swan theatre, also in Southwark, in an early copy of a drawing made by a Dutch visitor in 1592 (Fig. 13). Since 1989 this has been supplemented by the results of limited archaeological excavations on the sites of the Rose theatre (two phases: 1587–92; 1592–c. 1605), the Globe (two phases: 1599–1613; 1613–42), and the Hope (1614–42), all in Southwark.[16] Each type of source, written, pictorial and

14 Norman Sanders *et al.*, *The* Revels *History of Drama in England: Vol. II, 1500–1576* (London: Methuen, 1980; repr. London: Routledge, 1996), esp. 101–39; Michael Shapiro, *Children of the Revels: The Boy Companies of Shakespeare's Time and their Plays* (New York: Columbia University Press, 1977); Rowley Gair, *The Children of Paul's: The Story of a Theatre Company, 1553–1608* (Cambridge University Press, 1982).

15 Simon Blatherwick, 'The archaeology of entertainment: London's Tudor and Stuart playhouses', in Ian Haynes *et al.* (eds.), *London Under Ground: The Archaeology of a City* (Oxford: Oxbow, 2000), 252–71; Andrew Gurr, *Playgoing in Shakespeare's London* (Cambridge University Press, 1987), esp. 49–79 on the social composition of audiences; Muriel C. Bradbrook, *The Living Monument: Shakespeare and the Theatre of his Time* (Cambridge University Press: 1975), esp. 13–34.

16 Rather more has been published so far on the politics and administration of public archaeology relating to these sites than on the details of what has been found there. For a general survey, see Jean Wilson, *The Archaeology of Shakespeare: The Material Legacy of Shakespeare's Theatre* (Stroud: Sutton, 1995), 159–83. On the archaeology of the theatres: Julian Bowsher, *The Rose Theatre: An Archaeological Discovery* (Museum of London, 1998); Simon Blatherwick and Andrew Gurr, 'Shakespeare's factory: archaeological evaluations on the site of the Globe Theatre at 1/15 Anchor Terrace, Southwark Bridge

physical, has its own particular information to impart, and these sources complement one another productively. The excavated form of all three theatres, and many of the depictions, show high-sided, usually three-storey, roofed polygonal galleries enclosing an open arena. The polygonal ground plan represents a practical, timber-framed building around an open arena. The playing area includes the different levels provided by the galleries above the tiring house and a stage projecting into the central area. The Rose excavations confirmed that the stage could be trapezoidal in plan rather than rectangular, as it tends to be shown in early drawings. The stage of the second phase of the theatre apparently had a covering superstructure supported by columns represented by bases at the very front of the stage. This is a feature that would interfere surprisingly with sight-lines, but the supported 'heavens' were used to lower objects on to the stage, while trap-doors could also give access from below. One public theatre that was probably of somewhat different form was the Red Bull in Clerkenwell, north of the walls of the City of London. As its name suggests, this was a court-yard inn adapted for use as a permanent theatre and in use from 1604 – remarkably continuing to be used across the Civil War and Commonwealth periods (1642–1660) for some sort of public show.[17]

It is important to appreciate that none of the theatre sites has been excavated fully; at the Globe and the Hope archaeological work has scarcely exceeded uncovering ground plans, leaving floor layers and sealed deposits undisturbed. The most substantial find-bearing deposits found and excavated at the Rose are make-up layers relating to the construction, reconstruction, and abandonment of the theatre. The artefactual finds consequently provide few if any insights into activities within the theatre. In general, what was found at the Rose site was day-to-day objects from the contemporary world. The considerable numbers of small, lost or discarded dress pins found, for instance, are typical of London sites of this period. Considerable efforts were made to dress players both elaborately and appropriately for their parts,[18] but we cannot associate these pins in any special way with actors' costumes. However, the fact that the pins, coins, potsherds, etc. found here represent a random sample of what one would expect to find at any London occupation site of this date does not render the assemblage meaningless; on the contrary it physically reflects the embedding of the theatres within regular metropolitan life. The most profitable archaeological perspective to take on the theatre sites is not, in fact, to look at them in isolation – to worry about what special and new information the excavation of a specific theatre site might provide, and thus to peculiarize theatrical history – but rather to locate them within as complete a cultural townscape as we can. They were

Road, Southwark', *Antiquity*, 66 (1992), 315–33; (Hope theatre) Tony Mackinder, 'Riverside House, Bear Gardens SE1: An Archaeological Post-Excavation Assessment' (unpub. report, Museum of London Archaeol. Service, Nov. 2001).

[17] For theatre history independent of the archaeological observations, see further Glynne Wickham, *Shakespeare's Dramatic Heritage: Collected Studies in Medieval, Tudor and Shakespearean Drama* (London: Routledge & Kegan Paul, 1969); Andrew Gurr, *The Shakespearean Stage 1574–1642*, 2nd ed. (Cambridge University Press, 1980); *idem* and Mariko Ichikawa, *Staging in Shakespeare's Theatres* (Oxford University Press, 2000).

[18] Wilson, *op. cit.* in note 12, 104–32.

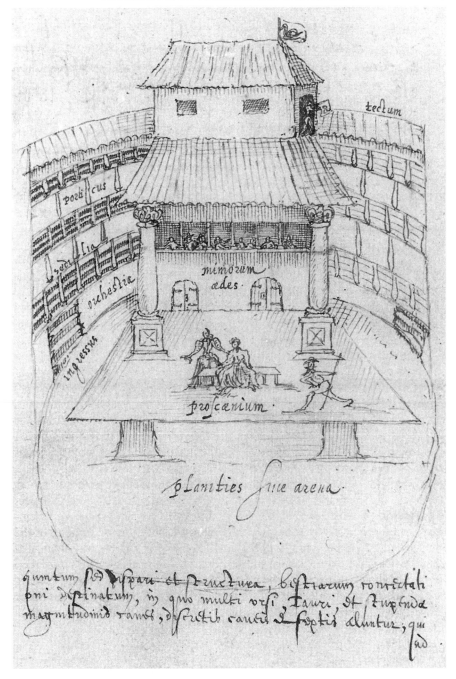

FIG. 13. The Swan theatre, Southwark. Arnout van Buchell's copy of a drawing by Johannes de Witt. Copyright: Bibliotheek der Rijksuniversiteit, Utrecht.

major, if short-lived, public buildings in a period when much was changing: much lost; much constructed new.

If 'displacement' can be suggested as a key concept for understanding changes in material culture in the early modern period at the artefactual level, it was writ much larger and considerably more evident in the archaeology of buildings and the use of space. The assault upon the traditional structures and roles of the Church that was involved in the Reformation forced major social and material phenomena to continue in new locations, and new guises. Amongst such phenomena we can count the construction and maintenance of monumental buildings and public meeting spaces, providing centres for rituals, art and learning. The influential landscape historian W. G. Hoskins was to talk of a 'Great Rebuilding' of English housing of this period, and while his view is now regarded as historically outmoded, there is no doubt that significant reconstruction of the housing stock was the consequence of the occupation of former monastic sites, both urban and rural, predominantly by the 'gentry' classes.[19] In respect of their buildings, cathedrals and churches now entered into a long period of neglect – a neglect that was, to be honest, more benign than eventual Victorian 'restoration' in some cases. New temples of learning benefited from investment in their stead. While much of the distinctive architecture of the Oxford and Cambridge colleges belongs to the later 17th and 18th centuries rather than the Renaissance period, one of the earliest institutions to benefit was the Oxford university library, enlarged between 1610 and 1612 under the patronage of Sir Thomas Bodley, after whom it has been named.

Although involved in the same wave of reconstruction, the theatres were anything but in the mainstream of this tide of pomp and show, or built with Sidney's quality of 'lastingness'. They were carefully but more lightly and quickly built structures, and emphatically marginally located. In all the cases we can look at in detail we find bases of stone, chalk, brick and/or rubble provided for a timber superstructure to frame walls of lath-and-plaster. This was still the most common style of construction for simpler, ordinary houses in both towns and countryside in the Elizabethan and Jacobean periods. The specific history of the known theatres encourages us even more to perceive them as intrinsically temporary, even mutable, structures. The first Globe theatre was rather hastily constructed in 1598–9 using timbers brought from an earlier playhouse, 'The Theatre', that had been built in 1576 just north of the City of London in the former grounds of Holywell Priory, Shoreditch. Although conscious of Puritan hostility to the theatre, the Elizabethan and Jacobean dramatists could not have foreseen the closure of the playhouses by Parliament in 1642. It was nevertheless essential that they were both peripheral in location and transitory in character. They literally pretended to transport their visitors to different times and places.

---

[19] W. G. Hoskins, 'The rebuilding of rural England, 1570–1640', *Past & Present*, 4 (1953), 44–59. The predominance of architectural studies in archaeological approaches to this period is reflected by the articles and chapters in Gaimster and Stamper (eds.), *op. cit.* in Chapter 4, note 33, 93–155, and Richard Newman *et al.*, *The Historical Archaeology of Britain, c. 1540–1900* (Stroud: Sutton, 2001), 10–99.

'All the world's a stage' is a well-known quotation from Shakespeare encapsulating a key theme and characteristic of both his own drama and that of his contemporaries. Inside the high-sided and inwardly focused theatres, spectators of the plays were offered vicarious experiences of other worlds. The theatrical arena could stand as an ironic counterpart to the rebuilt, and often elaborately redecorated, stages and stagecraft of the official and secular world outside. Its structure allowed the playwright, actors and audience to shut out the exterior world both materially and sensibly, and to focus upon the alternative world on and above the stage before them. Herein lay a subversive potential that was feared by contemporary authorities.[20]

The Winter's Tale in the Theatre

A play of the Jacobean period of which we can locate a performance precisely in both place and time, is Shakespeare's *The Winter's Tale*. This was watched in the Globe theatre on 15 May 1611 by Simon Forman, who had begun to compile a booklet of notes on plays he saw.[21] The scripts of Shakespeare's plays were subject to variation and modification. In the case of *The Winter's Tale* we depend upon the posthumous First Folio edition of 1623 for our only version, and this bears clear traces of scribal interference. Shakespeare appears to have composed this play during the year or two before Forman saw it. In addition to the performance in the Globe, there is a record of it being staged in the Banqueting House at Whitehall during festivities to mark the marriage of King James's daughter, Princess Elizabeth, to Prince Frederick the Elector Palatinate during the winter of 1612–13. The plot of this play is largely concerned with the behaviour of a king, Leontes of Sicily, in his court, and other royal events that may be associated with it include the investiture of the Prince of Wales in June 1610 and the unveiling of a statue of Mary Queen of Scots in Westminster Abbey some time between 1609 and 1612. Thematically, the play is highly relevant in the context of a royal marriage, although by no means simply or comfortably so.

Shakespeare's principal source for *The Winter's Tale* was a short prose tale (*novella*), *Pandosto*, by his part-contemporary Robert Greene (ob. 1592). This is an explicitly moral story, on the subject of marital jealousy.[22] Like the play, the novella can be described as a tragi-comedy, with a series of potentially catastrophic situations eventually converted to a happy ending – despite which, the jealous husband responsible for the whole chain of events finally punishes himself by committing suicide. Shakespeare made major changes to this source, some of which seem so capricious they appear to be due to a desire to create an oppositional distance between the two versions more than anything else. All of

---

[20] Explored in detail by Steven Mullaney, *The Place of the Stage: License, Play, and Power in Renaissance England* (Ann Arbor: University of Michigan Press, 1988).

[21] Simon Forman, The Book of Plaies and Notes thereof per formans for Common Pollicie, Oxford, Bodleian Library, MS Ashmole 208, fols. 200r–207v: fols. 201v–202r. Forman's account is printed in Stephen Orgel (ed.), *The Winter's Tale*, The Oxford Shakespeare (Oxford University Press, 1996), 233.

[22] Also printed, as edited by Stanley Wells, in Orgel (ed.), *op. cit.* in note 2, 234–74.

the characters' names are changed, and the events in the two kingdoms concerned, Sicily and Bohemia, are completely transposed. Many of the changes, however, enhance and deepen the artistic sophistication of the stage version. Whereas Greene has a jailor bring the jealous king news that his wife is pregnant again, in the hope that it will mollify him, Shakespeare introduces a lady-in-waiting, Paulina, to bear the new-born baby daughter herself to the Leontes. Paulina's courtier husband, Antigonus, is then made to carry the baby off to abandon her (rather than her being cast adrift, alone) and is punished for his compliance by immediately being chased off stage by a bear and eaten. The following pastoral section where the unidentified princess grows up in a rustic, shepherd's household, is very different in the two versions. Greene pairs the shepherd with a jealous but mercenary wife, Shakespeare with a bumpkin son, known only as the Clown (= fool). There is much greater emphasis in *Pandosto* on the power of love over the local king's son, who falls for the supposed shepherd's daughter; Shakespeare has a long scene portraying a pastoral feast where the prince woos the girl, himself dressed as a shepherd. This scene is further embellished by a new character, Autolycus, whose Greek name means 'lone wolf'. He appears in Classical literature, but only in allusions to a wily, deceptive and musical character, precisely as he features in *The Winter's Tale*. The greatest difference, however, is that the wrongly accused queen, Hermione in *The Winter's Tale*, does not die in suffering from her injustices in the play but is hidden away, having merely appeared to have died. She is then dramatically resurrected and brought back into social life from what is purportedly a memorial statue of her in the play's powerful final scene.

Amongst the precepts of ideal Classical drama are the unities of time and place: that for verisimilitude the action of the play should be set in a single location, and not exceed the length of the drama in time. *The Winter's Tale* could not turn these more emphatically upside down. The action is set in two locations, Sicily and Bohemia. That Bohemia, in central Europe, is supposed to have a sea-coast might seem only to add to the grotesque anti-realism of the play, but this was in fact a familiar fictional motif, also a feature of Greene's *Pandosto*. Bohemia, however, was no exotic and mysterious land for 16th-century Englishmen. On the contrary it was well known as a haven for early Protestants, while Sicily remained firmly in the Roman Catholic fold. The passage of time, meanwhile, is strongly emphasized as a theme of the play, not least in the 16-year jump in the action of the play (from the princess, Perdita's, infancy to her maturity) announced to the audience by a chorus identified as Time personified at the beginning of Act IV.

Structurally, the play immediately appears as a typical tragi-comedy. The temporarily disastrous consequences of Leontes' jealousy are not only his rejection of Hermione and Perdita, but also the disruption of his friendship with Polixenes, King of Bohemia, whom he suspects of being Hermione's lover. The healing of Leontes' jealousy actually occurs in the middle of the play (Act III, scene 2), just too late to recall Antigonus and his daughter, during a trial scene in which a report from the oracle of Delphi is revealed. Leontes had assumed this would confirm his wife's guilt. In fact it declares:

'*Hermione* is chast, *Polixenes* blamelesse . . .'   (1143 [**III.2**])[23]

Leontes immediately rejects this statement, but is instantly brought news of the death of his son from sheer anxiety over his mother's fate − and so acknowledges and repents his unjust jealousy at the very moment when Hermione collapses, apparently dying of grief herself. More tragedy is threatened when Perdita and Florizel, Polixenes' son, flee Bohemia for Sicily to escape the wrath of Polixenes at his son's infatuation with a girl he (wrongly) takes to be a humble shepherdess. The momentary threat here is that Florizel will be arrested, while Leontes might incestuously take his own daughter to replace the queen, of whom she (rightly) reminds him. But their real identities and history are revealed, not in a scene we see on the stage but as we hear of reported in a conversation between Autolycus and three gentlemen. The final resolution of a tragic situation comes with the restoration of Hermione in the last scene. This may be regarded as a comic ending in the technical sense of the averting of the destructive catharsis that the events and situations appear to be heading for, rather than for being a conclusion that implies real optimism for the future and for the state of human affairs.

There are many more facets to the plot of *The Winter's Tale* than appear in this skeletal summary, none of which makes the story *per se* any less preposterous. Where the play is a sublime work of literary art is in its exploration of profoundly serious themes. It is a drama that asks its thinking audience to contemplate a series of insights into the human condition. One of these involves the basic biological fact of human society: the existence of sexual difference, and the power of sexual desire. When the latter takes the form of Leontes' jealousy, it can be lethally destructive. We can regard jealousy as a corruption of passionate love, and the intensity of Leontes' feelings is most positively expressed in his remorse when he eventually recognizes his error, and in his joy at Hermione's ultimate restoration − although the latter is admittedly somewhat cursorily represented:

LEONTES: Oh, she's warme!
            If this be Magick, let it be an Art
            Lawfull as Eating!
                        (2971–3 [**V.3**]. Exclamation marks my own)

We simply do not encounter any very positive portrayal of the power of conventional love in this play. The good relationship between Leontes and Hermione seen at the start of the play takes the form of a dignified and respectful marriage. Paulina's relationship with Antigonus seems much the same, and while her attempt to compose a final image and role for herself in the play is to say that she will:

---

23 In keeping with the policy of quoting primary literary sources in as close to the original form as possible, quotations and line references to the play are taken from Stanley Wells *et al.* (eds.), *William Shakespeare: The Complete Works. Original-Spelling Edition* (Oxford: Clarendon Press, 1986). This text numbers the scenes, but not Acts, in the play. Act and scene references as in Orgel (ed.), *op. cit.* in note 21, are given in bold.

> . . . wing me to some wither'd bough, and there
> My mate (that's neuer to be found againe)
> Lament, till I am lost.   (2996–8 [**V.3**])

she is in fact directed in the following, concluding, speech by Leontes to marry the courtier Camillo and then lead them all from the stage. There is noticeably more passion underlying the same-sex friendships between Leontes and Polixenes – which is disrupted by an equally powerful same-sex rivalry – and between Paulina and Hermione.

The Bohemian Prince Florizel's relationship with the princess-shepherdess Perdita hardly emerges as a model of innocent and worthy passion, and thus as a positive endorsement of romantic love, either. Polixenes' objections to it may be worldly-wise and deeply unsympathetic, but the part of Florizel does plenty to validate his view that this is merely a stubborn and immature infatuation. Florizel's pursuit of his desires, deceiving all but Perdita, shows little if any concern for her predicament in the relationship, while his use of pagan myth to justify his disguise – referring to Classical gods who metamorphosed themselves, usually to rape gorgeous nymphs – only disgraces him. Particularly unworthy is his pledge to Perdita's stepfather, the Old Shepherd, of the wealth he will command when he inherits his father's estate:

> One being dead,
> I shall haue more then you can dreame of yet . . .   (1992–3 [**IV.4**])

Perdita shows some greater delicacy of feeling, but not too much to prevent her overcoming conventional maidenly modesty for this time and accompanying Florizel to Sicily playing the part – an ambiguous commitment – of Florizel's wife.

This drama seeks neither to endorse nor to reject a romantic view of love. It is infused rather with a consciousness of a wide difference between the sexes, and as a result it offers a more philosophical view of love and heterosexual relationships as the means to yoke the intrinsically divergent forces of masculinity and feminity in a productive way. Paulina in particular embodies constructive feminity: a point symbolically reinforced when she attempts to use the baby daughter as a token, on behalf of the wronged wife and mother, to instruct and heal Leontes (**II.2–3**). At this juncture Paulina's feminine strategy manifestly fails, although it will succeed eventually – albeit at the cost of her husband's life, and less directly that of Hermione and Leontes' son Mamillius. But just how fully does she succeed? The final scene (**V.3**) is dominated by female action and male passivity, bringing about the happy resolution of the potential tragedy. It is in an exclusively female zone that the life of Hermione has been preserved and through which it is eventually restored. Complementing Paulina's role in producing the Hermione-statue are Perdita's actions. Paulina could vivify the statue herself, but then she would stand open to the charge of witchcraft, a sexual stereotype:

> If you can behold it,
> Ile make the Statue moue indeed; descend,
> And take you by the hand: but then you'le thinke

(Which I protest against) I am assisted
By wicked Powers.   (2949–53 [**V.3**])

Ultimately Perdita's prayer is required to bring Hermione fully back to life: when, at Paulina's direction, she kneels before Hermione, the latter finally recovers her voice to ask Perdita (ironically) where she has been living. Yet at this point, rather than expressing the astonishment one might expect, let alone his thanks, or welcoming his wife, the male King Leontes finally steps in to reimpose conventional order by betrothing Paulina to Camillo and Florizel to Perdita. Of course we can see this as a form of general reconciliation, implying that they should all now live happy ever after, but it is hardly accentuated as such. We have no time to contemplate this joyful state of affairs: 'Hastily lead away,' says Leontes, to end his speech and the play (3018 [**V.3**]). Such is the closure that it appears is as neat and satisfactory as one is going to get.

The female as mother has a larger role than the male to play in producing life, and in this play also a predominant role in preserving it. If the play is life-affirming, though, it is so in a stoical rather than a joyous way. The human desire for life is explicitly commented on both at the very beginning of the play and in the central trial scene. The opening scene, between Camillo and a Bohemian courtier Archidamus, ends with a remarkable compliment from Camillo to the Prince Mamillius:

CAMILLO: . . . they that went on Crutches ere he was borne, desire yet their life, to see him a Man.

ARCHIDAMUS: Would they else be content to die?

CAMILLO: Yes; if there were no other excuse, why they should desire to liue.

ARCHIDAMUS: If the King had no Sonne, they would desire to liue on Crutches till he had one.

(40–7 [**I.1**])

Archidamus rejects Camillo's strange suggestion that people need a particular reason to want to live, but only by implying that they must then live in hope rather than in a state of satisfaction. Anyone who has puzzled over the implications of this exchange in the opening dialogue will be able to hear an echo of it in Hermione's words at her trial:

Now (my Liege)
Tell me what blessings I haue here aliue,
That I should feare to die?   (1116–18 [**III.2**])

The political and religious orders of Shakespeare's contemporary world are extensively represented within the play. It does not take up definite public positions on controversial issues but is rather a critique of those phenomena as facets of human experience. They are forcefully examined as cultural and social institutions that surround and interfere with the essential biological concerns of the reproduction and preservation of life itself. Generally, the setting of the play is a Classical pagan one rather than Christian and contemporary. Florizel may have cited the Classical myths purely as a literary allusion, but Leontes consults

Apollo as a trustworthy oracle, and invokes the 'blessed Gods' (e.g. 2620 [**V.1**]).
However the directions at the end of Act III, scene 2 for Hermione and
Mamillius to be entombed in a *chapell*, which Leontes will visit and weep in
daily, sound distinctly Christian – even Catholic, as a form of chantry. Barely
covert versions of Catholic ritual are recalled time and again, especially in the
final Act, where Perdita is described as one who might found a sect, a sort of
sainthood of beauty (2559–62 [**V.1**]), while her worship of and prayer to the
statue is required for the process of bringing Hermione fully back into life. This
cannot be separated from the accusations of heresy and witchcraft in the
women's world either. Just as those are extreme interpretations and false accusations relating to what women do, so too is the superstition that Perdita carefully
denies she is guilty of when kneeling before the statue and uttering her prayer to
the 'Lady, deere Queene' (2904–8 [**V.3**]). It is presumably most realistic to characterize Shakespeare's sympathetic use of these motifs here as an understanding
and tolerant dramatization of what such actions can represent rather than as
covert Catholic propaganda. However controversial in contemporary public life,
the external details are *in*essential to the central conflicts and dramas of life
informing *The Winter's Tale*.

Shakespeare was thus acutely conscious that the Catholic church had been –
still was, in much of Europe   –   a place where liturgies and rituals were
performed, and acted out as a form of drama. In England, and above all in
London, such dramatic performances had by his time been displaced, partly into
the theatre, and partly too into the political arena. *The Winter's Tale* is full of
conspicuous and reflexive allusions to play-acting, performance, reality and
illusion, and to the theatre itself, that thus constitute a sharp political commentary. And there is no shying away from the recognition that theatrical experiences can be deceptive and therefore dangerous. In the opening scene once
more, the 'entertainment' (8) that Archidamus anticipates providing for the
Sicilian court in Bohemia soon resolves itself into 'sleepie Drinkes' (13) as,
ironically, Archidamus's 'honestie puts it to vtterance' (20). What is here
presented in the abstract immediately takes a concrete and serious form in the
second scene, portraying a disastrous confusion of playful and courteous
pretence, misrepresentation and misinterpretation. The elaborate protestations
of Polixenes, Leontes and Hermione give rise and give way to Leontes' jealousy:

> . . . oh, that is entertainment
> My Bosome likes not . . .   (167–8 [**I.2**])

In the same scene, the word *play* is used emphatically:

> Goe play (Boy) play: thy Mother playes, and I
> Play too; but so disgrac'd a part, whose issue
> Will hisse me to my Graue . . .   (265–7 [**I.2**]; cf. also 296–8)

The term 'honesty' itself appears in a significantly ambiguous light in the words
of Antigonus in Act II, scene 1 (668–71), asserting that if Leontes' suspicions
are true there's no honesty left in the world: *honesty* here could mean either the
factual truth, or the socially vital convention of fidelity.

The theatrical framing of this reflexive drama becomes increasingly complicated and confusing from the middle of the play onwards. Hermione, on trial, declares that her sufferings are beyond what could appear even in a play (1045–7 [**III.2**]). But it is in the long pastoral scene set in Bohemia (**IV.3–4**) that we are faced most persistently with characters playing out roles even within the play: Autolycus, Florizel, Perdita, Polixenes and Camillo all appear in guises and roles that are not 'properly' their own, and thus as other than their 'real' selves. Despite this, much of the play-acting here reflects the truth of the play in a manifest and significant way. Art, as Polixenes declares in a thematically heavily laden speech that ostensibly, but with obvious allegory, refers to gardening and the cultivation of flowers, is itself a product of nature and can 'mend Nature' (1657–1704 [**IV.4**]). Art can therefore transform a shepherdess into a princess; as Florizel says to Perdita:

> . . . all your Actes, are Queenes   (1751 [**IV.4**])

Multiplying the irony, Perdita is, of course, royal-born after all; but the point here is not so much that such an important truth will out in the end as that the artificial contrivances of culture nonetheless originate in nature, with the implication that cultural interference with the course of human life cannot be discounted as 'unnatural'.[24] The role of this intense theatricality upon the stage in *The Winter's Tale* can therefore be seen as to draw attention to the theatricality of life outside the theatre. Consequently the scene shifts again in Act V, back to Sicily, where we immediately hear a courtier telling Leontes that he has 'perform'd' his sorrow and repentance perfectly (2454–7 [**V.1**]).

It is in this light that it may be easiest to explain and understand Shakespeare's introduction of the character of Autolycus to the tale as something much more than the creation of an engaging and amusing rogue, dramatizing the kind of witty anti-hero who featured in contemporary jest-books and coney-catching tales. Autolycus acts out a series of different parts: the first, ironically, being as the victim of a footpad whom he can describe in convincing detail since he uses himself as the model. At the pastoral feast he exchanges costumes with Florizel to disguise the latter as he flees to Sicily; re-dressed in this way Autolycus then assumes the mien of a courtier to the Old Shepherd and his son in order to rob them of a share of the knowledge they have concerning Perdita's background:

OLD SHEPHERD: Are you a Courtier, and't like you Sir?
AUTOLYCUS: Whether it like me or no, I am a Courtier. Seest thou not the ayre of the Court, in these enfoldings? Hath not my gate in it, the measure of the Court? Receiues not thy Nose Court-Odour from me? Reflect I not on the Basenesse, Court-Contempt? Thinkst thou, for that I insinuate, to toaze from thee thy Businesse, I am therefore no Courtier?
(2337–44 [**IV.4**])

and't like you: if it please you; *enfoldings*: garments; *toaze*: tease

---

24 Eagleton, *op. cit.* in Chapter 1, note 2, 1–4 and 87–111.

As, we have learnt, a former servant of Prince Florizel, Autolycus is here resuming a former role, though we might also note that he can disguise himself sufficiently that Florizel entirely fails to recognize him. The courtier's guise, in fact, is that in which Autolycus is left in his last appearance on the stage (**V.2**), although, lest we be led to imagine he has here found or reverted to some lasting or even true role, his final exchanges are comic courtesies with the Old Shepherd and Clown, themselves now reconstructed as gentlemen as a result of their good fortune and the favour of the kings, with new clothing, and assuming preposterous behaviour they suppose to be in character:

> CLOWN: Giue me the Lye: doe: and try whether I am not now a Gentle-
>   man borne.
> AUTOLYCUS: I know you are now (Sir) a Gentleman borne.
> CLOWN: I, and haue been so any time these four houres.
>
>   (2821–4 [**V.2**])

I (2824) = aye, yes.

Here we have also seen the Old Shepherd and his son discussing precisely how they should *act*, now they are gentlemen.

If there is any character or role that we could consider as that of an Autolycus in his natural state it must be that of the travelling pedlar, a 'snapper-vp of vnconsidered trifles' (1502 [**IV.3**]) like his father before him, and a trader. In this role, he brings a variety of wares to sell at the feast: music and songs, ribbons, jewellery, pins and perfume (1787–1928 [**IV.4**]). As casually as he picks the Clown's pocket on their first encounter he steals the truth about Perdita from him and his father, in order to profit from it as the freely adaptable entrepreneur he represents. Autolycus is neither a simple villain nor simply a lovable rascal. What makes him such a perdurably intriguing character for theatre audiences and scholarly critics alike is the utter ambivalence of his deceitful performances. While he may declare that he could not be honest if he tried (2441–2 [**IV.4**]), he equally ends up doing good despite himself: not only bringing pleasure, however ephemeral, to the consumers at the feast and in the theatre audience, but also assisting in the restoration of Florizel and Perdita. Both for better and for worse, Autolycus embodies the culture of the class-free and amoral commercial realities of his time.

Not least amongst the incongruities of scene and setting in *The Winter's Tale* is the fact that it is the supposedly unsophisticated rural wastes of Bohemia that are full of goods and products. Here, as we see, even the peasant Clown could be on his way to town or market to buy spices and other luxurious commodities for the feast (**IV.3**). The other kingdom, Sicily, with its constant court setting, offers a troubling contrast in that there the counterpart of this material culture takes the form of the commodification of people. Leontes' children are perceived as copies of him: Mamillius seems to be Leontes 23 years younger (202–5 [**I.2**]), and Paulina claims exactly this mechanical reproduction of the father as proof of Leontes' paternity of Perdita, and so of Hermione's fidelity (878–89 [**II.3**]). The astonishing final scene with the statue proceeds from the conceit that a perfect woman might be constructed. Paulina prepares for the ultimate denouement by chiding Leontes:

If one by one, you wedded all the World,
Or from the All that are, tooke something good,
To make a perfect Woman; she you kill'd
Would be vnparallel'd.   (2466–9 [**V.1**])

Subsequently she elicits a promise from him to re-marry only with one 'As like *Hermione*, as is her Picture' (2527 [**V.1**]). Yet the optimistic final revelation of *The Winter's Tale* is not that Renaissance court culture is turning people into impersonal objects, but rather that the apparently lifeless material of the statue can indeed be given life: Perdita's return, her emotional involvement, and Leontes' repentance allow Hermione to come back from her immobile and closeted state. How crucial a part the arts play in this! Paulina's command on which Hermione finally moves is:

Musick; awake her . . .   (2960 [**V.3**])

Paulina acts here, however, as scriptwriter and director of the final scene. Amongst artists, it is pre-eminently the dramatist's achievement to recreate and create new life in such a rounded way as here.

Without compromising its literary status, the Jacobean play of *The Winter's Tale* involves a movement away from and beyond the textual culture that otherwise seems so dominant in the Renaissance and Reformation period. The baby Perdita is left in Bohemia with a scroll, telling her story, and a box – both of which items the Clown and the Old Shepherd are unable to read or interpret fully. They fail even to link the gold in the box with Perdita's special social status, but see it either as fairy gold, identifying her as a changeling, or mere treasure, fortunately acquired. The proper identification and reading of these tokens and the text is reported in the dialogue between Autolycus and the three gentlemen in Act V, scene 2. This scene itself can be interpreted as a deliberate disruption of the dramatic mode expected, demonstrating how easily the author can switch to a different narrative genre – while the whole is still acted out on the stage. The scroll and the box are crucial factors for Perdita's survival and ultimate redemption. The Old Shepherd and the Clown fail to understand them fully, but where their knowledge is deficient their intuitive sense of the significance of these two objects plays a vital role.

Altogether, then, it is difficult to come away from *The Winter's Tale* reassured that there is some absolute contrast in terms of solid reality between the fictions performed within the theatre and the facts acted out in the world outside. The major change of location within the play, beween Sicily and Bohemia, is presented in the script in such a way as to draw attention to and exploit two different ways the physical form of the theatre could be sensed, and so to underline the uncertain character of its peculiarity. The enclosed court of Sicily is framed by the high, encircling walls of the theatre and their galleries. The desert wastes of Bohemia belong rather to the open, unroofed arena. Shakespeare had to use the words spoken by his actors to signal changes of scene, but he does so here in a way that emphatically invokes precisely this change of perspective and a self-consciousness in the audience, leading their eyes to look upwards when Antigonus and a sailor land in Bohemia:

ANTIGONUS: Thou art perfect then, our ship hath toucht vpon
              The Desarts of *Bohemia*.
MARINER: I (my Lord) and feare
              We haue Landed in ill time; the skies looke grimly,
              And threaten present blusters.

                                                    (1254–7 [**III.3**])

Like the modern television set, the Elizabethan and Jacobean theatre – not just
the plays, nor merely the plays and the stage, but the whole material structure of
Shakespeare's 'Woodden O'[25] – enabled audiences to experience a virtual
reality: a created reality that was different from the reality outside the theatre but
which challenged the contrast between inside the theatre and the outside,
between fiction and fact, and thus brought into question the necessary reality of
the public and conventional world. This power of the theatre was not used by
Shakespeare, nor any of his successful fellow playwrights, in any attempt to
bring about a revolutionary distrust of and thus change to the public order whose
contrivances they could lay bare in such a way. He exploited it rather for his
drama to validate itself. To enter a theatre such as the Globe and be part of a
critical audience of *The Winter's Tale* need not merely be to be entertained, or to
escape into some fantasy world for a few hours, but rather to step into an analytical and educational forum. Perhaps most constructively of all in the perspective
of cultural history, after generations of anxiety and conflict between materiality
and textuality, the Renaissance English theatre tried to bring literature and the
physical world back into association with one another.

1666, *Annus Mirabilis*

        That thence the *Royal Actor* born
        The *Tragick Scaffold* might adorn:
                While round the armed Bands
                Did clap their bloody hands.
        He nothing common did or mean
        Upon that memorable Scene:
                But with his keener Eye
                The Axes edge did try.   (from: Andrew Marvell, 'An *Horatian*
                                          Ode upon *Cromwel's* Return from Ireland' [1650])

In the decades immediately following the reign of James I and VI and Shakespeare's life-time, the friction caused by political and religious divisions, reinforced by complex economic, social and regional differences in England and
Wales, flared into the conflagration of the English Civil War. Victory fell to the
Parliamentarians, who were closely allied to the widely supported and ideologically resolute Puritan party in religion. King Charles I, as recounted by Andrew
Marvell using imagery from the now closed theatres, was beheaded in January

---

[25] *King Henry V,* Prologue, line 13.

1649. A state that had styled itself as the united kingdoms of Britain and Ireland was replaced by the government of the Commonwealth of England from 1649 to 1660.

As is often the case, this revolution served to entrench cultural conservatism in many respects rather than being the occasion for widespread change. By 1653 Cromwell had dismissed Parliament. More than once he refused to accept the Crown and adopt the title of King, ruling instead in the style of Lord Protector until his death in 1658. The monarchy was 'restored' in late May 1660, in the person of King Charles II. A vital problem for Charles I had been his lack of a regular army – not so much to fight the Civil War with, but for campaigns earlier in his reign, which he endlessly struggled with Parliament to obtain money for. Correspondingly, the formation of the New Model Army was a crucial element in Cromwell's success. The diary of Samuel Pepys begins on 1 January 1660 and gives us an invaluable insight into the perceptions of the events of the Restoration of a relatively ordinary citizen. His entries for the first few months of 1660 clearly reveal that England was then under what we would now describe as a military government, the crucial decisions residing with the army commander, General Monck. The Civil War and Restoration did not, of course, make civil strife a thing of the past in Britain, but the outcome of this process was a constitutional monarchy together with an authoritative and regular parliament, permanent armed forces under government control, and a considerable measure of religious toleration. Under the guise of Restoration, these amounted to a striking set of innovations.[26]

John Dryden is the foremost of the English poets associated directly with the Restoration period. He was born in August 1631, and thus was seventeen when Charles I was executed. He entered Trinity College, Cambridge, in 1650, from where he graduated in 1654. He had been working for the government by 1657, and also forming literary connexions and a reputation for himself during the 1650s, as a result of which he walked in Cromwell's funeral procession in November 1658 alongside John Milton and Andrew Marvell. He wrote a funerary eulogy for Cromwell, *Heroic Stanzas: Consecrated to the Glorious Memory of his most Serene and Renowned Highness Oliver, Late Lord Protector of this Commonwealth, etc.*, and also a poem celebrating Charles II's return, *Astraea Redux: A Poem on the Happy Restoration and Return of His Sacred Majesty Charles the Second*, which was ready for publication by mid-June 1660. Not unlike Samuel Pepys, it is reasonable to regard Dryden as a pragmatic professional rather than a sycophantic crony in all of this.

Dryden was certainly a cipher of his times; nowhere, we may suggest, more clearly so than in the poem he composed to mark the events of 1666, *Annus Mirabilis: The Year of Wonder, MDCLXVI*. According to the date of a prefatory epistle to his poem addressed to his brother-in-law and patron, Sir Robert Howard, this poem was completed by 10 November 1666 and it had been

---

[26] The term *Restoration* was used in this context in the records of the House of Commons for 30 May 1660.

published by 1 January 1667. Dryden had left London in the early summer of 1665 to escape the Great Plague and reside on the estate of the family he had married into in Wiltshire. With the number 666 identified as the Mark of the Beast in the Biblical Book of Revelation, apocalyptic expectations and views of the year 1666 were very much in the air. It is therefore likely that the idea of writing a poem about the year had been in Dryden's mind for some time, and that *Annus Mirabilis* is no mere reaction to major events.

It was first composed as a panegyric on British naval successes (hailed in a considerably more triumphant spirit than was actually justified) against the Dutch in that year. The Dutch were Britain's principal maritime rivals at a time when command of the seas also meant dominance in the highly lucrative trade in precious commodities (principally gold, gems and spices) brought from Africa and the East Indies. The poem was then adapted and extended to respond to the Great Fire of London, of the first week of September of that year. It appears that Dryden relied on gazettes and pamphlets for rapid information and accounts of the events that he could use in his verses.[27] In itself, this is testimony to the extent to which cultural reliance upon literacy, and the production and dissemination of textual materials, had now grown.

If Shakespeare emerges as a philosophical author from his reflections upon the relationship between his art and his contemporary, material situation, Dryden was a great deal more worldly. He has a clear sense of the vital importance of trade, and reveals it in the very first stanza of *Annus Mirabilis*:

> In thriving arts long time had Holland grown,
>   Crouching at home, and cruel when abroad:
> Scarce leaving us the means to claim our own;
>   Our King they courted, and our merchants awed.   (1–4)

The poem also concludes with a vision of Britain, through a rebuilt London, dominating world trade (sts. 297–304):

> The venturous merchant who designed more far
>   And touches on our hospitable shore,
> Charmed with the splendour of this northern star
>   Shall here unlade him and depart no more.   (1196–1200)

In an important passage near the middle of the poem, Dryden inserted an 'Apostrophe' to the Royal Society, a scholarly and scientific body, which suggests that the ultimate goal of expanding horizons through navigation and exploration is not simply material profit but cosmic knowledge (sts. 164–6):

> This I foretell from your auspicious care,
>   Who great in search of God and nature grow;

---

27 For an informative annotated edition of Dryden's works, see Paul Hammond (ed.), *The Poems of John Dryden*, 2 vols., Longman Annotated English Poets (London: Longman, 1995). All quotations, and stanza and line references here are from vol. I of this collection.

> Who best your wise Creator's praise declare,
> > Since best to praise his works is best to know.   (657–660)

Yet the use immediately afterwards of the alchemical image of the limbeck, a distillation glass, for producing 'rich ideas' (663) serves only to reinforce the sense that these sentiments are facile piety. For a fuller view of Dryden's religious attitude, we must also consider his irreligious reference to a capricious, 'unseen Fate', that followed the naval victories with the disastrous Fire (841–4).

This worldliness is not in any way disguised in *Annus Mirabilis*. Dryden sees it as morally problematic primarily in terms of the challenge he faces in making battles fought for the dominance of trade appear heroic rather than mercenary. Remarkably, part of his solution is a metrical one, rejecting the 'heroic couplet' for the stanzaic form used here:

> I have chosen to write my poem in quatrains, or stanzas of four in alternate rhyme, because I have ever judged them more noble, and of greater dignity, both for sound and number, than any other verse in use amongst us . . .,

he writes in the epistle to Sir Robert Howard. Dryden would in fact have been most familiar with quatrain stanzas used in this way in ballads, a popular mode of commemorating great deeds. He was certainly aware of, and willing to face, the incongruity of extolling trade, a cooperative relationship within human society, alongside prowess in war, which is destructive conflict:

> These fought like husbands, but like lovers those:
> > These fain would keep, and those more fain enjoy;
> And to such height their frantic passion grows
> > That what both love, both hazard to destroy.
>
> Amidst whole heaps of spices lights a ball,
> > And now their odours armed against them fly:
> Some preciously by shattered porcelain fall,
> > And some by aromatic splinters die.   (109–16)

Trade, Dryden saw, should be reciprocal exchange; it should involve a circulation of material commodities like the natural flow of blood around the living human body (5). Ultimately, Dryden envisages the redundancy of the fleet in the British-dominated free-trading world:

> The beauty of this town, without a fleet,
> > From all the world shall vindicate her trade.   (1203–4)
>
> *vindicate*: protect

We have already noted how Donne drew on the new experiences provided by exploration and trade as a source of images for the conceits of his poetry.[28] This practice remained strong in *Annus Mirabilis*, although in fact, despite the diversity and persistence of Dryden's references to the goods being imported and

---

[28] Above, pp. 140–1.

exported, none of these is used metaphorically, or as a simile for something else, except in the single case of Charles II learning by experience from naval engagements with the Dutch how to improve his navy:

> As those who unripe veins in mines explore,
>   On the rich bed again the warm turf lay,
> Till time digests the yet imperfect ore,
>   And know it will be gold another day . . .   (553–6)

Dryden's preferred source for conceits in this poem is the field of scientific exploration, with references, for instance, to the distillation process using limbecks (51, 663), the properties of the glass lens in projecting images (209–12), and the revelations of human anatomical investigations and surgery (5–6, 567–8).

The latter image is one of 'brawny carpenters' working on the British fleet 'as the surgeons of maimed ships', when it was being repaired during the June and July of 1666. With navigation for trade, and naval warfare, now recognized as vital to British interests, Dryden reveals a strong concern not only to possess a detailed knowledge of ships and relevant technical details but also to display it. The prefatory epistle refers to his determination to learn about the sea, of which he previously had but little knowledge. Two extended passages in the poem contain the fruits of Dryden's efforts: from stanzas 56–60 (lines 221–40) there is an account offering details of strategy in a naval battle (cf. also lines 325–6), while the repairing of the fleet is described in considerable detail in stanzas 142–8 (565–92). Shortly after this, in stanzas 155–8 (617–32), advances in ship-construction are placed within a scheme of technical evolution, implying a gradual progress towards mastery over materials and the elements of the sea-currents and winds. Again, this continuous material-cultural improvement is associated directly with trade. Saturn used the sail to voyage from Greece to Italy:

> And with the golden age to Tiber steered,
>   Where coin and first commerce he did invent.   (631–2)

The sequence had begun with imitation of the natural world:

> Thus fishes first to shipping did impart
>   Their tail the rudder, and their head the prow.   (619–20)

One of the most remarkable features of the conceptual scheme of *Annus Mirabilis* is the persistency with which Dryden uses animal similes for ships and their movement in battle (lines 235–6, 263–4, 358, 445–6, 491–2, 521–8, 717–24 and 780: astonishingly, no simile is repeated). This is a clear and illuminating reflection of how deeply ingrained a sense of the categorial difference between animate and inanimate was in a 17th-century mind like Dryden's. Where poets of the period so frequently turned to the physical sciences and material world for similes to present and explore mental and emotional experiences, when the subject matter is specialized artefacts of the material world the semantic field selected for the similes is that of zoology.

The question of how conscious Dryden may or may not have been of such aspects of his style is an interesting one, not least when the prose preface to *Annus Mirabilis* provides a critical introduction of a kind to the poem. This includes substantial indications of how Dryden himself viewed his poem, although there is no reason to suppose that those comprise everything the author consciously thought about his work. A crucial element in this preface, however, is to evaluate the poem in comparison with other major works of verse, and in particular to seek to explain and validate its devices by association with the Classical master, Virgil. In this context, Dryden appears to regard the historically specific character of his own range of reference, and its difference from Virgil, as a matter of *idiom*:

> . . . I have never yet seen the description of a naval fight in the proper terms which are used at sea; and if there be any such in another language, such as that of Lucan in the third of his *Pharsalia*, yet I could not prevail myself of it in the English, the terms of arts in every tongue bearing more of the idiom of it than any other words.

In other words, the words for the 'arts' (still meaning practical and technical skills) are more idiomatic than other domains of vocabulary. In the term 'idiom', Dryden would have understood connotations of 'vernacular', or 'colloquial', as opposed to formal and classical diction, rather than of esoteric figures of speech. It is not so much the case, therefore, that Dryden was naively unaware of the fact that he belonged in specific material circumstances, and that those had a major impact on his composition, as that the incipient modern supremacy of a textual and linguistic view of culture led him to perceive the difference between himself and Virgil in terms of the fitness of their languages to their particular periods, and so to see these linguistic differences as the fundamental issue for the critic to explain. The poetic use of language was the common factor between them, not their inescapable fixity in a material world.

Thematically, it was not difficult for Dryden to accommodate the Great Fire of London within the poem: the link is of a simple and familiar type – fortune swings in her fickle way, and triumph is followed by tragedy. Looking for a positive potential in the disaster to accentuate, the destruction of the heart of London provided another challenge for Charles II and his nation to rise to and overcome. Physically, it confirmed the point that the Restoration was more a matter of the culmination of change than the reversal of events in order to retrieve some better, older order of things. Now the Reformation could be completed:

> The fugitive flames, chastised, went forth to prey
> On pious structures by our fathers reared,
> By which to heaven they did affect their way,
> Ere faith in churchmen without works was heard.   (1089–92)

The destruction of St Paul's Cathedral similarly burned away the stains of the Civil War, when it had been used as a stable:

> The daring flames peeped in, and saw from far
>   The awful beauties of the sacred choir;
> But since it was profaned by civil war
>   Heaven thought it fit to have it purged by fire.   (1101–4)

In a wishful vision, Dryden (who in fact was later to convert to Catholicism) consigns destructive political and religious dissenters into the flames along with witches (889–92). The city can now be rebuilt, as described in the final vision: the metropolitan heart of a new order of trade and material consumption.

Despite The Great Fire's fitness to be laid hold of and interpreted in such a way, a noticeably large part of the section of *Annus Mirabilis* on this event – nearly one-third of the whole poem – is taken up with a sequential, narrative account of the progress of the fire over five days (865–1128). Given Dryden's sources, and the speed at which he was composing, it is easy to see the influence of journalistic writing here. The account is nonetheless, unsurprisingly, embellished in various literary ways. Epic and literary similes are used profusely to ballast the account:

> Old father Thames raised up his reverend head,
>   But feared the fate of Simois would return;
> Deep in his ooze he sought his sedgy bed,
>   And shrunk his waters back into his urn.   (925–8)

Dryden treated the city itself as an emblem: an emblem of a civilized universe 'Where some may gain, and all may be supplied' (651–2). In the Classical world of Virgil, Rome served in the same way as the archetypal image of the good order and civilization that was supposedly distended throughout the Roman Empire, and this had been superseded in post-Classical Christian thought by the symbol of the holy and eternal city of Jerusalem. Dryden's City of London, however, even rebuilt as a New Augusta –

> More great than human, now, and more August,
> New deified she from her fires does rise   (1177–8)

– cannot rise to such admirable heights of virtue, so thoroughly and irredeemably materialistic is she (see especially lines 1185–1200). Cromwell had legalized the presence of a Jewish – business – community in London for the first time since the expulsion of all Jews from England under Edward I in 1290, and Dryden's comfortable use of the Jewish reconstruction of Jerusalem after the Babylonian captivity as an analogue for the rebuilding of London (1157–60) reveals a new indifference to formerly sensitive religious issues. Shortly after this he is equally easy about presenting the rebirth of London as the product of a successful alchemical transmutation (1169–72). The demise of superstition and prejudice here may be laudable, but that has to be recognized as having been inseparable from the rise of self-centred materialism and imperialism.

Behind his rhetoric, then, and behind what really was a façade of literary Classicism, Dryden can be perceived as being intensely, even honestly, secular. No less characteristic of that period, but deeply contrastive in almost every perceptible way, was an even more influential English author, John Bunyan. In

1666 Bunyan published the first version of his spiritual biography and confession, *Grace Abounding to the Chief of Sinners*, which he revised five further times before his death in 1688. Few copies of the first edition survive; it is suspected, in fact, that many perished with the stock of a London nonconformist bookseller in the Great Fire. From the end of Parliamentary rule until his death, Bunyan's life was a continuing struggle with his times, and a story of repeated endeavours to overcome attempts to hinder and thwart him. Despite Charles II's declaration, upon his accession, of 'liberty to tender consciences', the more zealous Protestants – Puritans, nonconformists, dissenters etc., some of whom had indeed been guilty of fanatical excesses in the previous decades – were subject to legal harassment. As early as November 1660 Bunyan was committed to Bedford county jail under an Elizabethan Act of the early 1590s against nonconformity. He remained a prisoner until 1672. While the actions of the authorities were repressive, his treatment in fact partially represents their desire to compromise: something which Bunyan absolutely could not and would not do. The local magistrates' behaviour was pragmatic, in that they did not 'throw the book' at him and follow the letter of the law, according to which he was liable to transportation for his disobedience. Bunyan had one further, shorter spell in jail, in the first half of 1677, at the end of which year the first part of his best known work, *The Pilgrim's Progress*, was published.

There are several reasons for the enduring fame and popularity of *The Pilgrim's Progress*. The resolute and sincere Christian seriousness of the work is one of these, and would have made the work a particular comfort to some in the following period of the Enlightenment, when a sceptical and philosophical approach to natural science and theology increased the pressure on the individual to take responsibility for his or her own Christian ideology. But there were many equally devout texts available: why, then, was this one so successful? The dramatic structure of the work – the allegorical dream-vision of Christian's journey to Heaven (the Celestial City, or Jerusalem), followed in the Second Part by the same pilgrimage undertaken by his wife, Christiana, and their children – is certainly palatable and comprehensible in a way that more abstract theological and spiritual treatises rarely are. Bunyan also wrote in a robust and forceful English. From this, it would be easy to form the impression that Bunyan, a tinker's son, succeeded as a man of the people, speaking directly to a large readership in their own idiom, with a down-to-earth, familiar range of allegorical reference. That, however, would be a complete misrepresentation.

Bunyan thought of his style as plain and direct. He refers to this in the Preface to *Grace Abounding*:

> I could also have stepped into a stile much higher then this in which I have here discoursed, and could have adorned all this more then I have seemed to do: but I dare not:[29]

Bunyan's style is in fact intensely scriptural. His grammar, vocabulary and idioms were pervasively influenced by the language of the English Authorized

---

[29] *Grace Abounding*, 1st ed. (London: 1666), ed. Roger Sharrock (Oxford: Clarendon Press, 1962).

Version of the Bible, published in 1611 but drawing substantially on and therefore echoing earlier translations, particularly that of William Tyndale in the
earlier 16th century and behind him John Wycliffe in the late 14th. Its diction
was dignified and old-fashioned. As examples one can cite Bunyan's extensive
use of the *do* periphrasis with verbs; his fondness for the preposition *unto* where
to could perfectly well be used; a habit of opening sentences emphatically and
rhetorically with *Yea*; use of an archaic relative pronoun *the which* . . . etc. This
is a form of influence of which Bunyan himself may have been largely unconscious; quite different is the persistent and frequent use of scriptural quotations
and references throughout these texts, highlighted in the printed versions by
inserted or marginal notes citing Biblical chapter and verse for these. As
Bunyan discusses directly in an account of his committal to prison in 1660 that
was not published until 1765,[30] the Biblical scriptures were absolutely his ideological touchstone, and he was fully confident in the validity of his use of the
English version. In the prefatory verses to the Second Part of *The Pilgrim's
Progress*, Bunyan discusses the question of how the authenticity – both textual
and spiritual – of the text can be verified for doubters:

> If such thou meetst with, then thine only way
> Before them all, is, *to say out thy say,*
> In thine own native Language, which no man
> Now useth, nor with ease dissemble can.[31]

In the mouths of the elect and devout, the anachronistic Biblical idiom is a
native language.

Bunyan therefore represents in a very intense form that text-centred culture
that we have seen to be characteristic of the Protestant Reformation. His allegorical style, meanwhile, does involve references to and imagery from the contemporary and material world, but not in a way that could really be considered a
counterweight to this essential textuality. The great majority of his allegorical
figures are simple, general and non-detailed: topographical features like steep
hills and deep mires; roads, paths and stiles; castles, prison-cages and dungeons.
One of the more interesting and richly constructed settings is the stately home,
or 'palace', called Beautiful which Christian lodges in early on his pilgrimage.
This is the home of a family of three virtuous women, Prudence, Piety and
Charity. Christian is not allowed to depart after a night's rest until he has been
shown this great house's collection of antiquities, rarities and records. The first
of these to be examined, characteristically, are textual records; these are
followed by an armoury of spiritual weapons and armour:

---

[30] *A Relation of the Imprisonment of Mr. John Bunyan, Minister of the Gospel at Bedford, in November
1660* (London, 1765), ed. John Brown: John Bunyan, *Grace Abounding and The Pilgrim's Progress*
(Cambridge University Press, 1907), 103–32, p. 111. See also Sharrock, *ed. cit.* in note 29, xxiii–xxv.
[31] Quoted from the second edition of this Part, 1687. Brown, *ed. cit.* in note 30. Brown printed the
version of *Grace Abounding* and both Parts of *The Pilgrim's Progress* that had received the author's latest
modifications.

. . . they showed him all manner of Furniture, which their Lord had provided for his Pilgrims, as Sword, Shield, Helmet, Brest-plate, *All Prayer*, and Shoes that would not wear out.

Finally there is a remarkable collection of religious relics: all, after Moses' rod, weapons used in the Old Testament by God's champions. When Christiana reaches the same house on her pilgrimage there is a comparable flash of detail when Mr Skill cures her sick child with a purge:

. . . made *ex Carne & Sanguine Christi*. (You know Physicians give strange Medicines to their Patients) and it was made up into Pills with a Promise or two, and a proportionable quantity of Salt. Now he was to take them three at a time fasting in half a quarter of a Pint of Tears of Repentance.

This kind of direct appeal to specific contemporary experience and knowledge ('You know . . .') is the exception rather than the norm in *The Pilgrim's Progress*.

Christian's journey is from the City of Destruction to the Celestial City. Little is portrayed of life in the City of Destruction – which, as Bunyan explains in a note at the very beginning of the book, represents 'This World' rather than urban life – and which Christian learns, from reading 'the Book', will be burned with fire from Heaven. At the start of both Christian and Christiana's pilgrimages this City provides scoffing neighbours who seek to dissuade them from their journeys, but that is all. A more specifically focussed examination of urban life appears when Christian, at this point accompanied by a fellow-pilgrim Faithful, reaches the Town of Vanity, with its market of Vanity-Fair, the features of which are listed in profuse and nakedly disapproving detail:

This Fair is no new erected business, but a thing of ancient standing: I will shew you the original of it.

Almost five thousand years agone, there were Pilgrims walking to the Celestial City, as these two honest persons are; and *Belzebub, Apollyon* and *Legion*, with their Companions, perceiving by the Path that the Pilgrims made, that their way to the City lay through this *Town of Vanity*, they contrived here to set up a Fair; a Fair wherein should be sold all sorts of *Vanity*, and that it should last all year long. Therefore at this Fair are all such Merchandize sold, as Houses, Lands, Trades, Places, Honours, Preferments, Titles, Countries, Kingdoms, Lusts, Pleasures, and Delights of all sorts, as Whores, Bawds, Wives, Husbands, Children, Masters, Servants, Lives, Blood, Bodies, Souls, Silver, Gold, Pearls, precious Stones, and what not?

And moreover, at this Fair there is at all times to be seen Jugglings, Cheats, Games, Plaies, Fools, Apes, Knaves, and Rogues, and that of every kind.

Here are to be seen too, and that for nothing, Thefts, Murders, Adulteries, False Swearers, and that of a blood red colour.

And as in other Fairs of less moment, there are several Rows and Streets under their proper Names where such Wares are vended; So here likewise, you have the proper Places, Rows, Streets, (*viz.* Countries and Kingdoms) where the Wares of this Fair are soonest to be found: Here is the *Brittan* Row, the *French* Row, the *Italian* Row, the *Spanish* Row, the *German* Row, where several sorts of Vanities are to be sold. But as in other *Fairs*, some one Commodity is as the chief of all the Fair, so the Ware of *Rome* and her

> Merchandize is greatly promoted in this Fair: only our *English* Nation, with
> some others, have taken a dislike thereat.

This place, which apart from the implication of public, dominant Roman Catholicism is manifestly modelled on the metropolis of London, is truly full of
corruption. Religion here is merely another commodity in the trading that is the
only life and activity of the place. Christian and Faithful are put on trial as
enemies to and disturbers of trade, and Faithful is martyred by being whipped,
beaten, cut, stoned and finally burned at the stake as a heretic against the reli- ·
gion of trade. Christian, like Bunyan, is left in prison – but escapes rather
easily.

When Christian finally reaches the Celestial City, Bunyan is faced with the
problem of how to conceive and portray a virtuous and holy city. This could
partly be done by drawing on the Biblical visions of Isaiah and St John the
Divine in the Book of Revelation: for instance a city built of pearls and precious
stones, and with streets paved with gold. It is also a form of church, in which
hymns of praise are continually sung. Other that that, Bunyan represents the
City through an interestingly pastoral vision, emphasizing the orchards, vine-
yards and gardens that surround it to provide material sustenance for the inhab-
itants and travellers. As Christiana and her growing family and entourage
approach the Celestial City they come into a meadow, where a charitable institution (hospital and orphanage) has been established 'at the Charge of the King':
again the actual supplies there come, wishfully, from a variety of trees, 'such as
bear *wholsom Fruit*'. This sort of practical, charitable patronage by the rich and
powerful was a substantial feature in developing market townscapes in the 17th
to the 18th century: as in the sequence of almshouses and schools, dating from
1697 onwards, leading away from the parish church of St Alkmund at
Whitchurch, Shropshire, itself rebuilt in 1712–13 (Fig. 14). Bedford itself flourished in the Georgian period to a degree that little of the historical architecture
of the town pre-dates the mid-18th century. There are records of one Thomas
Hawes leaving money to buy land that would be rented out to provide support
for the poor in the year of Bunyan's death (1688), and a Thomas Christie
funding almshouses in his will of May 1697. It was the 18th century before
Bunyan's nonconformist followers were in a position to emulate these local
Anglican benefactors.[32] The charitable King Bunyan referred to in the Second
Part of *The Pilgrim's Progress* is God, but by including this image he made a
brief but telling gesture of acceptance towards elements of the hierarchical
world and the real society in which he lived.

Even in this case, though, it is plain that Bunyan did not use the allegorical
method as a means of making religious instruction easier. Allegory did not
demystify the things of God through familiar images and examples; on the
contrary allegory in Bunyan's hands meant the spiritualization of every single
facet of worldly experience. No building, street, feature of the landscape, object

---

[32] Violet Rickard, 'Bedford borough', in William Page (ed.), *The Victoria History of the County of
Bedford. Vol. III* (London: Constable & Co., 1912), 1–33, at pp. 31–3.

FIG. 14. Whitchurch, Shropshire. To the left from the point of view, a series of
public buildings along the road leading away from the parish church of St Alkmund
(rebuilt 1712–13). From the top of the hill: the almshouses of Samuel Higginson
(1697); the school founded by Jane Higginson (1708); the Grammar School (1848),
in Elizabethan style. The Higginsons' almshouses and school buildings were
modified in the 18th and early 19th centuries.

or action was exempt from Christian evaluation; nothing too banal to be relevant
to the overall scheme of salvation in the view that informed *The Pilgrim's Progress* and was promulgated by it.

Bunyan was not quite three years older than Dryden. Their circumstances and
lives, however, were vastly different. Bunyan served as a teenage soldier during
the Civil War, probably in the Parliamentary garrison at Newport Pagnell
(Beds.) from 1644–7. He had been baptised in the parish church of Elstow near
Bedford. He represents his own early life as irreligious and sinful, and his religious awakening as a form of conversion he underwent in the early 1650s. Two
to three years before Bunyan's death, Dryden joined the Roman Catholic church.
It is easy to see how the circumstances of their lives allowed Bunyan and Dryden
to develop in the way that they did. Yet in no way can we use their biographies
and practical circumstances as determinative explanations of their hugely
contrastive characters as authors. The difference between them was not that
between the working class and an upper middle class. It was that between ideological worldliness and otherworldliness in culture. To compare the two in this
way is also to confirm that Dryden's text has to be read with reference to the
whole contemporary context in order to comprehend its materialist economic
and social ideology fully. It is likewise to dispel the illusion that he wrote in

some rarefied, unrealistic mode, inspired by and validating itself only in terms literary and Classical standards.[33]

The works of both Bunyan and Dryden discussed here are therefore fully understood and appreciated both in their literary/textual and their material context – even if the relationship with the physical context was very different. Bunyan sought not to reject, but to transcend the real world: to put it into its proper place in relation to the Scriptural revelation that showed the true way to the eternal bliss of salvation in the Celestial City. Those Biblical directions are unambiguous – and therefore not a matter over which compromises could be made – although they are also difficult both to understand and to follow. By writing, Bunyan sought to share and clarify the necessary insights he had gained. He was consequently quite explicit on the subject of both his aims and the message he had to convey. That is precisely the reason why his allegory becomes almost entirely detached from the profuse and diverse realities of the contemporary material life it is superficially rooted in.

Dryden and Bunyan may thus be perceived as a stark embodiment of the dissociation of the material and the spiritual that can be seen as one of the crucial developments dividing the medieval and modern eras. They corroborate the difference in relations with the archaeological context in literature of, respectively, implicit and explicit moral function.[34] Despite the sharp differences between them, they are complementary in more than just confirming this special proposition. It is significant that both treat artefacts as a relatively trivial feature of the material world, and are inspired most intensely by opportunities to imagine the re-ordering of place: a rebuilt London, at the hub of the world's trade routes for Dryden; a more diverse and provincial landscape for Bunyan. Reassuringly, they together reveal that the dissociation of mind and matter in this period was a matter of divergency and never quite the opening up of an unbridgeable gulf. Bunyan could still concede that the social elite might and should do acts of true charity, and Dryden acknowledge religious values.

Both zones of experience remained firmly embedded in the living world. In the same year as *The Pilgrim's Progress* was first published, 1677, Sir Christopher Wren's Monument to the Great Fire of London was completed and work commenced on his even better known new building project following the fire, St Paul's Cathedral. For most people at that time, as still now, the division between the tangible world and the realm of ideas was accepted as an essential difference in nature between the two, that could be managed by compartmentalizing the behaviour and responses appropriate to both relationships. It remains open to evaluation whether this has meant a greater diversity of available experience, or an obligation (rather than a 'freedom') to make unnecessary choices between worldliness and unworldliness. This indeed is a critical issue that is a

---

[33] E.g. '*Annus Mirabilis* is a great and serious poem. That does not mean, however, that it is any more "realistic" than the other poems of the period.' William Myers, *Dryden* (London: Hutchinson, 1973), 26.
[34] Above, p. 70.

disconcertingly still a live one today. Constructively, it enables us to appreciate all the more how the most outstanding art of this period stood above the division of experience. This is why Shakespeare is a great and serious author, and why his seriousness is culturally still so important.

6

Household Words and the Victorian Experience

The Great Exhibition

THE Great Exhibition of the Works of Industry of All Nations was held in the specially built Crystal Palace, in Hyde Park, London, through the summer of 1851. It is a seductively obvious landmark for anyone seeking some emblem of mid-19th-century England, not least as far as material life is concerned. The Exhibition was a project blessed both by the political power of the state, which set up a Royal Commission, chaired by Queen Victoria's consort, Prince Albert, to manage it, and by the Church of England. The Archbishop of Canterbury presided over the opening ceremony on 1 May, while the closing ceremony on 15 October concluded with prayers led by the Bishop of London. It was also a great popular success. The number of visitors over the 24 weeks it ran was counted at six million, and was accelerating up to the closing date. All this has made it very easy for those with particular views of the Victorian Age to find them made concrete in the Great Exhibition. Karl Marx anticipated that it would be a bourgeois pantheon of commercial idols.[1] To the fastidious Nikolaus Pevsner, commenting after half a century's conventional anti-Victorianism amongst the 20th-century intelligentsia, it was simply 'æsthetically distressing'.[2] More recent assessments have been more sympathetic in seeking to understand and evaluate the aspirations and achievement of this remarkable project, which most decidedly had a real and extensive impact on subsequent English cultural life and consciousness.[3]

The planning and organization of the Great Exhibition was actually characterized by self-doubt and a sense of inadequacy rather than bouyant imperial

---

[1] 'Die Bourgeoisie der Welt errichtet durch diese Ausstellung im modernen Rom ihr Pantheon, worin sie ihre Götter, die sie selbst gemacht hat, mit stolzer Selbstzufriedenheit ausstellt': Karl Marx and Friedriech Engels, 'Revue. Mai–Oktober', *Neue Rheinische Zeitung: Politisch-ökonomische Revue*, 5–6 (1850). Trans. in K. Marx and F. Engels, *Collected Works. Vol. 10: 1849–51* (London: Lawrence & Wishart, 1978), 490–532, at pp. 499–500.

[2] Nikolaus Pevsner, *High Victorian Design: A Study of the Exhibits of 1851* (London: Architectural Press, 1951), 116.

[3] Recommended introductions and discussions of the Great Exhibition are Jeffrey A. Auerbach, *The Great Exhibition: A Nation on Display* (New Haven: Yale University Press, 1999); John R. Davis, *The Great Exhibition* (Stroud: Sutton, 1999); Louise Purbrick (ed.), *The Great Exhibition of 1851: New Interdisciplinary Essays* (Manchester University Press, 2001).

self-confidence. The germ of the idea lay with the [Royal] Society of Arts, which had mounted a number of increasingly ambitious exhibitions in London prior to 1849, when the Great Exhibition project was launched. The principal model for the Great Exhibition, however, was the series of exhibitions that had been held in post-Revolutionary Paris. For Henry Cole, a leading advocate and promoter of the plan within the Society of Arts, British manufacturers faced a crisis for being unable to compete with French products in terms of artistic quality, and the Exhibition, along with recently founded institutions such as Schools of Design, was intended to educate British manufacturers, artisans and consumers in good taste in order to remedy this deficiency.

At the heart of such a perception lay a particular conceptualization of that shifting relationship between art and artefact we have encountered on a series of occasions, particularly in considering late-medieval and early-modern material culture.[4] For Cole and his associates, the two categories had been conclusively divided, not only in cognitive terms but also in practice. Fine art worthy of the name had to be re-introduced to material production. The key strategy for achieving this – and thus also the terms in which success was to be measured – was education in 'taste'. In the evolving range of categories presented at the Exhibition, Fine Arts retained its position at the culmination of the scheme. However, it stood on its own as the thirtieth of thirty classes into which the exhibits were divided, principally for the purposes of comparing and judging them and awarding of prizes. Classes I–IV were grouped together as Raw Materials, V–X Machines, XI–XXIX Manufactures and XXX Fine Arts (Table 1). There was also a distinct emphasis in the Fine Arts section on new techniques and materials.

In face of initial misgivings and caution, Cole succeeded in persuading the new Liberal government of Lord John Russell, and public figures such as Prince Albert and Sir Robert Peel, a former Conservative Prime Minister, to associate themselves with the project, and eventually to support it very actively. The proposal had much to recommend it to a government eager to promote the virtues of the still deeply controversial idea of international free trade. The Royal Commission entrusted with the running of the Exhibition was established in January 1850 after about half a year's lobbying and preparations. Yet a crucial factor of the scope and substance that was eventually to form the Exhibition was the fact that British exhibits were primarily chosen by a series of local committees. Local public meetings were held around the country to launch and explain the scheme, stimulating reactions from hostility to enthusiasm but generally succeeding in advertising and promoting the plans. The planning of the Exhibition was by no means taken over by the public, but a relatively wide spectrum of the community could feel that it had some local stake in the show: it thus became an exhibition by them, not just an attempt to educate them by those who believed in the superiority of their own vision.

British products, with Ireland included within the United Kingdom at this time, nevertheless were shown by fewer than half the 17,000 exhibitors who

---

4   Above, esp. pp. 113–16, 135–6 and 138–42.

Table 1 The Classes of Exhibits at the Great Exhibition, 1851

I.   Mining, quarrying, metallurgical operations, and mineral products

II.   Chemical and pharmaceutical processes and products generally

III.   Substances used as food

IV.   Animal and vegetable substances chiefly used in manufactures, as implements, or for ornaments

V.   Machines for direct use, including carriages, and railway and naval mechanism

VI.   Manufacturing machines and tools

VII.   Civil engineering, architecture, and building contrivances

VIII.   Naval architecture and military engineering; ordnance, armour, and accoutrements

IX.   Agricultural implements

X.   Philosophical instruments and processes depending upon their use

XI.   Cotton manufactures

XII.   Woollen and worsted manufactures

XIII.   Manufactures in silk and velvet

XIV.   Manufactures from flax and hemp

XV.   Mixed fabrics, including shawls, but exclusive of worsted goods

XVI.   Leather, including saddlery and harness, skins, furs, feathers, and hair

XVII.   Paper and stationery, printing and bookbinding

XVIII.   Woven, spun, felted, and laid fabrics, when shown as specimens of printing or dyeing

XIX.   Tapestry, including carpets, floor-cloths, &c., lace, fancy embroidery, and industrial works

XX.   Articles of clothing for immediate personal or domestic use

XXI.   Cutlery and edge tools

XXII.   Iron and general hardware

XXIII.   Works in precious metals, jewellery, articles of virtu, &c.

XXIV.   Glass

XXV.   Ceramic manufactures

XXVI.   Decorative furniture and upholstery, including paper-hangings, papier maché, and japanned goods

XXVII.   Manufactures in mineral substances, used for building or decorations; as – in marble, slate, porphyries, cements, artificial stones, clay, &c.

XXVIII.   Manufactures from animal and vegetable substances, not being woven, felted, or included in other sections

XXIX.   Miscellaneous manufactures and small wares

XXX.   Sculpture, models, and plastic art

contributed a total of over a million items to the display. Overseas representation was therefore substantial, although somewhat haphazard, reflecting complex political and diplomatic relationships within and between Britain and the countries concerned – as well as widely varying attitudes to international trade and competition ranging from the fiercely protectionist to avidly liberal free-traders. The importance attached to the foreign exhibits, however, is reflected in the distribution of awards (Council Medals as the highest accolades, and Prize Medals as a lower but still distinguished tier) by juries appointed for each class. All the juries included overseas representatives. The success-rate of French exhibitors in winning medals was three times that of their British rivals.

In relation to one major aspect of social division within Britain, however, the Great Exhibition emphatically reiterated the power and interests of the governing and propertied classes, and the conservative order of the realm, rather than passively mirroring the real spectrum of the whole community. 1848 is known as the year of revolutions in Europe, and in London had seen a rally by the embryonic democratic and socialist Chartist movement on Kennington Common sufficiently alarming to see the aged Duke of Wellington entrusted with the defence of the capital. In a highly class-conscious and now extensively industrialized culture, there was a practically ubiquitous perception of the existence of a working class; the political representation of this class, however, was fragmented, and the politicians and intellectuals of the more affluent classes were equally at odds over how they should regard this large body of less-privileged, often suffering and politically threatening fellow-countrymen. Even though it was led by and largely constituted of liberal-minded individuals with a paternalistic vision of the dignity of labour, a Central Working Classes Committee recognized but not established by the Royal Commission voted itself out of existence after only a few weeks because it could not reconcile reactionary fears with any significant representation of working-class interests in the Exhibition, for instance in a dedicated section. Nevertheless, as an experience, the success of the Great Exhibition depended on mass popular support. A graded admission-price system, from season-ticket-holder-only to shilling days encouraged both the genteel and the common people to see the Exhibition at times specially designated for them and their like, while special initiatives to arrange cheap transport to see the show, especially by rail, were also a major element in encouraging this form of participation. In the same tentative way as the Exhibition itself came together, but, again, ultimately on a comparably massive scale, as a social experience the Great Exhibition succeeded in demonstrating the value of mass popular endorsement of a national enterprise; that the working classes could assemble in huge crowds and behave themselves; and for them, that they too could be admitted to a great national display, and be crucial to its success with their numbers and their shillings – an optional poll tax, for which they got something in return.

The greatest single item to be marvelled at by the crowds drawn to the Great Exhibition was the wondrous Crystal Palace building in which it was held. This was radically innovative in design and construction: the building itself a modular iron frame skinned with huge panels of glass. The conception of this structure was put forward as a late entry in the design competition for an

Exhibition building by Joseph Paxton, the Duke of Devonshire's head gardener, whose relevant previous experience had been designing an advanced glasshouse for his employer. Once more, his success represented the contribution a man of humble origins could make to a national project. It also nicely represented both advances in industrial techniques, in the production of the building's components, and political and economic liberalization, as Sir Robert Peel had only a few years previously abolished a duty on glass that had made this material an expensive luxury. In starting out as a structure and eschewing any primary selection of some existing architectural style, the Crystal Palace also offered a conspicuous specimen of the aesthetic potential of pure engineering. To the people of the mid-19th century, and indeed to cultural historians specializing principally in such relatively recent times, this could well appear as a new phenomenon in the history of art, one appropriate to an industrialized and utilitarian context. In producing his solution to the Exhibition building problem, Paxton in fact seized an opportunity to bridge the cleft between art and artefact, style and object, that had dominated considered perceptions of material culture and art since the end of the Middle Ages.

Without even starting to look at the products of the industry of all nations that were supposedly the substance of the exhibition, it can be seen that the very organization of the project, and the thrill of a visit to its venue itself, were major communal experiences of considerable cultural historical significance. Meanwhile, the presence of the huge range and quantity of items on display within or immediately around the Crystal Palace posed a massive problem for the organizers of how they should be located systematically, and extended the number of ways in which the Exhibition could be experienced by a visitor to a practically infinite level. Those most responsible for how the display was ordered, Henry Cole, Lyon Playfair – a scientist, and at the time a Victorian version of a government special advisor – and Prince Albert himself, decidedly had their own agenda to promote. The key means for achieving that was the evaluation and reporting process that went on alongside the Exhibition and which produced the *Reports by the Juries* to accompany the *Official Descriptive and Illustrated Catalogue* of the Great Exhibition, both published by the Royal Commission.[5]

At heart these men had common objectives founded upon a reflective approach to material culture characteristic of the period. At one end of the spectrum this involved a classificatory and analytical approach to the objects, something that from this time onwards could be called a 'scientific' perspective upon them, with classes recognizing the sequence of material-cultural production from raw materials, through tools, to finished products. Correspondingly, the discussions by the juries sought to exemplify a properly scholarly approach that was pre-eminently methodical and objective. At the other end of the spectrum their agenda was determined by the value-laden and ethically charged concern with taste, a quality perceived both as a necessity for maintaining the prosperity

---

5   *Great Exhibition of the Works of Industry of All Nations, 1851: Official Descriptive and Illustrated Catalogue*, 3 vols. (London: The Royal Commission, 1851); *Exhibition of the Works of Industry of All Nations, 1851: Reports by the Juries on the Subjects in the Thirty Classes into which the Exhibition was Divided* (London: The Royal Commission, 1852).

of the nation and as an integral element of a virtue of civilization and good social order that could be spread not only across the social spectrum in Britain but between and through all the nations in the world. For many liberal idealists, free trade and a broad internationalism were the greatest values promoted by the Great Exhibition. The multinational character of the Exhibition was emphasized by organizing the displays from the foreign nations that took part into their own discrete sections, while the class system deliberately compared items between nations.

As well as being a logical starting-point, the special interest in raw materials is particularly pertinent to this historical context. One of the most characteristic features of material production in the modern period has been the ingenious and creative exploitation of special properties of basic materials. The range is very broad, including new dye-stuffs affecting the range of colours used in dress, the manufacturing of specialized ceramic fabrics, the use of exotic woods, ivory and semi-precious stones from the tropics and other colonized areas in furniture and ornaments, and the transformation of heavy industry. In the mid-19th century industrial chemistry was beginning to expand the range of available basic materials significantly. The process of making rubber, a naturally occurring polymer, stable and durable by vulcanization (heating with sulphur) was patented in 1846, and a number of applications of what was then known as india-rubber appeared in the Exhibition. The first synthetic polymer – what we know of as plastics – appeared in the 1850s. Chemical and pharmaceutical processes and products formed the second class of Raw Materials, and the goods on display included a new form of phosphorous well-suited to the newly developing match industry,[6] and early samples of paraffin and bitumen products used as fuels or in construction. But the majority of items on display in this class represented decorative processes: especially dyes, but also paints and electro-plating processes. We should bear in mind that through the mid-19th century over half of Britain's lucrative export trade was accounted for by textile products.[7] Textile fabrics and clothing also accounted for nine of the thirty classes (ten with the somewhat anomalous inclusion of stationery and book-binding).

The displays classified as exhibits of machinery show a fundamental ambiguity over whether the items were to be admired as productive implements, turning raw materials into finished products, or as products in themselves. Coal-fired steam engines were then utterly predominant as the most powerful equipment converting energy resources into movement. Correspondingly, two enormous blocks of coal were on display as raw material just outside the western entrance to the Crystal Palace – the British half of the building, and perhaps just coincidentally the end towards provincial England and Wales, not the City. There was a diversity of machinery for specialized purposes: much from the textile industry or for manufacturing other machines, and a rather novel section on mass food-processing to complement the various machines for

6 Asa Briggs, *Victorian Things* (London: Batsford, 1988), 69 and 179–205.
7 François Crouzet, *The Victorian Economy* (London: Methuen, 1982), 185–228 and 350.

arable agriculture, some of them steam-powered but many of them seeking to apply manual or animal power with greatest efficiency. More to be marvelled at for their size and power were Leviathans like Nasmyth's steam hammer from Manchester, of which the *Official Catalogue* noted laconically, in brackets:

> This steam hammer is capable of adjustment of power in a degree highly remarkable. While it is possible to obtain enormous impulsive force by its means, it can be so graduated as to descend with power only sufficient to break an egg-shell.[8]

Class VII, devoted to civil engineering, architecture and building contrivances, was characterized particularly by models of bridges and other structures associated with travel and communications, such as lighthouses. These were somewhat curiously thus linked with useful domestic appliances, and model houses, including one innovative concept involving prefabricated structures of corrugated iron sheets for the use of 'emigrants'. Echoing the charmingly naïve delight in the range of control over Nasmyth's steam hammer – you would never need a machine such as that to deliver the power required to break an egg! – the final class in the machinery section celebrated the degree of precision and delicacy that could now be achieved for precision instruments, and included a particularly large number of clocks. As relative novelties, this introduced early electrically driven instruments, such as clocks and telegraphs, a section on photography, and a particularly well-stocked display of musical instruments many of which were exotic experimental derivatives of more familiar types.

The machinery displays also reflected new developments in technology that were directly affecting the lives of many people through the emphasis on modes of land transport. Shipping was represented, but as much by ships' furniture and individual pieces of equipment as by new types of ship – with the exception of what must have been an alarmingly large selection of experimental life-boat designs. A considerable number of chic horse-drawn carriages could not honestly be regarded as much more than a shop-window display aimed at the smart and fast set of the day. In 1851, meanwhile, Britain was in the middle of a railway-building boom, and a stretch of track was laid within the building with static displays of the latest and most powerful locomotives, as well as of coaches. This mode of fast, long-distance transport, which required passengers to be conveyed in large groups together to be economical, far out-stripped the rival possibilities of private transport by road. Steam-driven road transport was represented only by a model of an engine built in 1785, a historical curiosity, and plans for a carriage from a Welsh inventor.[9]

At once acknowledging and endorsing the fact that productive ingenuity and technical skills allowed a limited range of raw materials to be converted into a profusion of special, useful or valued products, the section of Manufactures comprised twice as many classes as Raw Materials and Machinery put together: twenty against ten, if Section IV, Fine Arts, be counted with the Manufactures.

---

[8]   *Official Catalogue*, vol. I, 295.
[9]   Cf. *Reports by the Juries*, 192–3, where the absence of development in this field is bemoaned.

CUT CRYSTAL FOUNTAIN.   MESSRS. OSLER.

FIG. 15. The Crystal Fountain at the Great Exhibition, as illustrated in the *Official Descriptive and Illustrated Catalogue*, vol. II.

The number and order of these classes is a reflection of the relative importance of fields of manufacture in mid-19th-century Britain: dominated by the textile industry, followed by iron- and steelworking. Studying the range of displays and the attitudes expressed in the *Official Catalogue* and *Reports* on the glass section is particularly interesting. The range of applications of this newly emancipated material, as it seemed, was remarkably wide, from highly utilitarian structural uses to sheer ostentatious display in the form of the massive crystal fountain at one of the crossing points of the Crystal Palace (Fig. 15).[10] There was a considerable amount of domestic tableware, but this did not dominate the class. The report of the relevant jury (XXIV) showed a marked consciousness of the politically constrained history of glass, and of many opportunities opening up for use of the commodity; the jury mimicked the same sort of enterprise that it eagerly anticipated by freely appropriating to itself the right to comment on the lighthouse equipment that properly belonged to another class and jury. And it was equally forthright in pointing out how fundamental glass was to the whole Great Exhibition experience:

> The magnitude and brilliant effect of the Building itself, which have obtained for it the denomination of the Crystal Palace, render it the first and principal object of admiration.[11]

A considerably different impression of the Great Exhibition from the Royal Commission's own *Catalogue* and *Reports* is given by an alternative, and conveniently portable, catalogue published by a popular journal, the *Art-Journal*.[12] This offered illustrations and comments on objects selected from the range of items on display. The special nature of its principal interests and endorsements is unmistakable. In its Preface, it specifically declares its primary purpose to be to educate manufacturers and artisans, to draw their attention to the qualities of design they ought to be emulating. But it was intended to educate the consumer public to be more discerning and discriminating as well, as it subsequently acknowledges. Its concluding item is a prize-winning essay discussing the Great Exhibition by Ralph Wornum, which itself ends by emphasizing precisely that link:

> . . . we have undertaken to analyse the various ornamental expressions, in this unexampled collection of the world's industry, to place them distinctly before our manufacturers, in order that they may make their own uses of them, towards the cultivation of pure and rational individualities of design, which will not only add to their own material prosperity, but will also largely contribute towards the general elevation of the social standard.

The introduction to the volume is ostensibly a 'History of the Great Exhibition', but this involves idealistic pictures of international collaboration and characteristically recognizes the French lead both in enterprises of the kind and in design.

---

10 *Official Catalogue*, vol. II, 700–1.
11 *Reports by the Juries*, 532.
12 *The Art-Journal Illustrated Catalogue: The Industry of All Nations 1851*, repr. as *The Crystal Palace Exhibition Illustrated Catalogue, London 1851* (New York: Dover, 1970).

There is the usual excitement and pride in the building itself, describing how the visitor is first struck, on entering and looking around to orientate him or herself, by purely ornamental details: the colours and the sculptures. On moving in, the imaginary visitor is shown where displays from the Empire and the Mediaeval Court are:

> To these succeed Birmingham, the great British Furniture Court, Sheffield, and its hardware, the woollen and mixed fabrics, shawls, flax, and linens, and printing and dyeing.

The focus thus moves rapidly to British manufactures and the familiar principal consumer and export goods, textiles and hardware.

Like the *Official Catalogue*, this too is a catalogue that cannot be read from beginning to end. It has to be browsed; yet, in comparison with the *Official Catalogue*, even leafing through it and gaining a general impression or allowing individual entries or pages haphazardly to catch the eye, it is striking what a high degree of attention is paid to domestic ornaments and furniture in this selection from the exhibits. The Raw Materials and Machinery that offer a sternly instructive introduction to the *Official Catalogue* are barely in evidence, and the emphasis falls far more heavily on furniture and artistically elaborated appliances. Partly because of their size, but also because of the number of them illustrated throughout the volume, the chimney-pieces and other fireside equipment make a particularly marked impression. The comfortable concept of the hearth as the heart of the home is directly alluded to in comments such as:

> The great improvements made of late in all the appointments of "an Englishman's fireside" are visible to the least observant.[13]

The *Art-Journal Illustrated Catalogue* was thus especially concerned to underline the point that the innovations displayed at the Great Exhibition were capable of direct translation into English homes.

Along with this, it is hard to detect any particularly sharp sense of a distinction between utility and decoration in the *Art-Journal Illustrated Catalogue*'s judgments. It took a less strict line than the report of the jury of class XXVI (furniture etc), which complained that there was not enough 'practical' furniture on display, a point repeated by Richard Redgrave in a 'Supplementary report on design' that formed an appendix to the *Reports by the Juries*. Redgrave was bold enough to discuss the discrepancy between the ornate and the practical explicitly in terms of international comparisons, noting – not without justification – that the Austrian furniture on display showed elaborate skill but was deficient in respect of practicality, while again praising France for the degree to which 'art-knowledge' there was diffused amongst the relevant workmen.[14] The *Art-Journal*, by contrast, was unwilling to suggest so fundamental a division between utility and ornament, which in turn might imply that one had to choose one or the other. There are echoes of Redgrave on the Austrian furniture, for

---

13 *Op. cit.* in note 12, 77.
14 Richard Redgrave, 'Supplementary report on design', *Reports by the Juries*, 708–49, esp. p. 724.

instance on pages 262–3 where it is coyly noted that in some of M. Leistler's work, from Vienna, 'parts are better than the whole', and the items are juxtaposed in what may have been a gently satirical manner with a particularly baroque chair from Dublin with details such as arms in the form of wolf-hounds 'intended to illustrate Irish history and antiquities'. A similar attitude seems to lurk in the comment on a grand canopy bedstead by Smee & Sons of London:

> There is sufficient ornament in this object to constitute it an elegant article of domestic furniture, but the manufacturers have not aimed at producing an elaborate work of industrial art. (p. 164)

A grotesque-looking iron bedstead from Madrid likewise seems to tax the commentator's resources of diplomatic evasiveness to the utmost:

> The IRON BEDSTEAD is a Spanish contribution, and is the work of TOMAS DE MEGNE, of Madrid. It presents some peculiar features of a graceful character, besides being well designed for its use. The great improvement in articles of this class, both at home and abroad, cannot fail to attract the notice of the most unreflective, the Crystal Palace alone contains a great and striking variety, both in construction and ornament. (p. 208 [sic])

Far more directly, we do find lightness in furniture, practicality and a tasteful balance of utility and decoration consistently praised. This is especially noticeable in relation to chairs. A light and graceful 'Légère chair' by Bell of London is explicitly praised, and commended in terms of 'popularity'. There was enthusiasm for the 'light and elegant material' of papier-mâché used for chairs, other furniture and household articles such as trays by McCullum & Hodgson of Birmingham and Clay of London, and explicit praise of an innovative tubular drawn iron four-poster bed involving delicate wrought ornament and frames emphasized by much openwork, by Winfield of Birmingham.[15] An informative comment is that on a chair by Gillow of London:

> It presents a solidity of construction that would have appeared too massive, if not lightened by the character of the ornament with which it is judiciously relieved. (p. 253)

In other words practical construction and an ornamental finish collude to produce a well-balanced and tasteful article. Finally, the unclassified ordering of the items in the *Art-Journal Illustrated Catalogue* – chairs alongside a sideboard and rugs, for instance – shows clearly how nothing stands alone in this survey of options for domestic furnishing and decoration. In the end, all has to form a suite, in a complete home.

The Great Exhibition could hardly have been a major public curiosity and success if it had merely held up a mirror to the material life of its time and shown the public what it was already familiar with. Nevertheless, however much a cliché it may be to say so, the Great Exhibition really does represent the

---

[15] *Op. cit.* in note 12, 66, 156, 190 and 243.

momentum and extent of material developments in mid-19th-century English cultural history extremely well. In their own separate and complementary ways, the evidence of what was available to put into the Exhibition, the fact that it happened and the records of how that proceeded, and finally the diverse reactions of contemporary commentators, are rich sources of information – the more readily comparable for having a common focus. The Great Exhibition represented the dramatic recent growth in productive technology and in the availability of goods, especially for private consumers, although an awareness of what in 1851 were little more than minor new curiosities, and technologies that were yet to be developed such as the internal combustion engine, helps us to assess how much further such 'progress' has gone down to our own time, just over 150 years later at the start of the 21st century.

Crucially, the Great Exhibition also demonstrates for us how extensively and acutely people in mid-19th-century England were conscious of their situation. This is reflected in the many ways in which they – as thinking and, in many cases, sincerely religious and self-consciously spiritual people – sought to understand and define the relationship between themselves and a material world that with the burgeoning of engines and machinery was appearing less and less inanimate. This state of affairs has significant consequences for both the critical reading of contemporary literature and the delineation of a comprehensive archaeology of the Victorian Period, as we shall now see.

'What's home?' The Focus of *Bleak House*

If the ways in which the Great Exhibition could be perceived were so enormously varied, it is hardly suprising that any one individual's reactions might also vacillate, applauding some aspects of it and disappointed by others. Such, indeed, appears to have been the situation of Charles Dickens, the most distinguished English author of the period, who was both directly involved, to a degree, with the preparations for the Exhibition, and who wrote specifically about it. Dickens was one of the sympathetic but non-revolutionary liberals who sat on the abortive Central Committee for the Working Classes in 1850, and in fact it was he who moved the vote for its dissolution. His public utterances on the Exhibition phenomenon appeared in a weekly magazine, *Household Words*, he had launched in March 1850, while further insights into his views can be gleaned from his private letters.

It has proved tempting to make rather more of the vague 'instinctive feeling against the Exhibition [I have always had]' that Dickens admitted to in a letter to his sub-editor and partner on *Household Words*, W. H. Wills, of 27 July 1851, and his decision to leave London during that summer than is probably justified.[16] Admittedly, the journal's first essay on the plans, published in July 1850,

16 Graham Storey *et al.* (eds.), *The Letters of Charles Dickens: Volume Six 1850–1852* (Oxford University Press, 1988), xii and 447–50; Philip Landon, 'Great Exhibitions: representations of the Crystal Palace in Mayhew, Dickens, and Dostoyevsky', *Nineteenth-Century Contexts*, 20 (1997), 27–59, esp. 37–43.

shows an irritation with the organizing process that would accord with a frustration at the failure of the Central Committee on the Working Classes on his part. Interestingly, though, he points his ire by focusing on the probable form the building was to take, suggesting that the Commissioners and their committees:

> . . . seem likely to produce an interminable range of cast-iron cow-sheds, having (as a specimen of the present high state of constructive genius) an enormous slop-basin, of iron frame-work, inverted in the centre.[17]

This must have been written just as Paxton's design was being considered, and was published four days after the Royal Commission accepted it. Subsequently articles in *Household Words* extolled the design, and indeed the slightly irregular but successful way in which Paxton presented it.[18] Dickens seems to have followed a consistently positive line about the potential of such an exhibition, emphasizing its educative and liberalizing qualities, and showing an enthusiasm for the degree of international contact and cooperation it could entail.[19] In connexion with the latter aspect, however, he characteristically identified an opportunity to contrast the ideals of the Great Exhibition with the realities of international travel to produce satirical articles on its inconveniences, especially the institutional obstacles imposed by the Customs and Excise.[20] Before the Exhibition opened his journal had likewise contrasted the achievement of bringing the idea to fruition with the authorities' failure to clear London of the problem of pestilential, overcrowded and rank burial grounds, a pet topic of his at this time.[21]

The great novel that Dickens began work on in the immediate aftermath of the Great Exhibition was *Bleak House*, which he started to write in November 1851. It was published in nineteen monthly instalments from March 1852 to September 1853, and on completion was available in bound form as a single book. It is a long novel even by mid-19th-century standards, and while it would be facile to describe it as as multi-threaded as the Great Exhibition itself, the analogy is not entirely specious. The central character in the novel is Esther Summerson. In 33 of its 67 chapters she tells her own story in the form of a first-person narrative, using the past tense. This starts with relatively brief recollections of her harsh upbringing as a child by a dogmatic, moralizing, religious fanatic of an aunt – who identifies herself only as Esther's godmother – from which it is easy to surmise that Esther is illegitimate. In the course of the novel it emerges that she is the daughter of a woman who had since married Sir Leicester Dedlock to become Lady Dedlock and a father of whom we see little,

[17] 'The wonders of 1851', *Household Words*, 20 July 1850, 388–92 at p. 391. All contributions to *Household Words* were anonymous.
[18] E.g. 'The private history of the palace of glass', *Household Words*, 18 January 1851, 385–91.
[19] See 'A shilling's worth of science' – an enthusiastic review of the educational benefits of an exhibition at the Royal Polytechnic Institute, London – *Household Words*, 24 August 1850, 507–10; 'Three May-days in London', *Household Words*, 3 May 1851, 121–4.
[20] 'A pilgrimage to the Great Exhibition from abroad', *Household Words*, 28 June 1851, 321–4; 'The foreign invasion', *Household Words*, 11 October 1851, 60–4.
[21] 'A time for all things', *Household Words*, 22 March 1851, 615–17; cf. 'Heathen and Christian burial', *Household Words*, 6 April 1850, 43–8.

Captain Hawdon. Just before Esther's fourteenth birthday her aunt dies, and Esther starts to receive the benevolence of John Jarndyce, firstly sending her to school, and subsequently employing and housing her as a companion to a young ward of his of a similar age, Ada Clare, and as his own housekeeper. Eventually we learn that John Jarndyce had known Esther's mother and aunt, but not the secret of Esther's birth, and had become involved in response to an application from the aunt. Despite a great inequality in age, it appears for much of the novel that Esther is destined to marry Mr Jarndyce, from whom she certainly believes she has accepted a proposal of marriage. Yet in a remarkable twist in the final instalment of the novel, he effectively presents her in marriage to the worthy, and in conventional ways more equally matched, doctor, Allan Woodcourt. The story ends with Esther as a contented wife and mother.

Through her association with John Jarndyce, Esther's story becomes connected to that of the case of Jarndyce and Jarndyce and the iniquities of the Court of Chancery. This is an apparently interminable civil suit over the inheritance of property, dragged out by the court and lawyers to the detriment of all the parties involved except for John Jarndyce, who has the wisdom to decide to have as little as possible to do with it. The case finally collapses when the entire property has been consumed in legal costs. As a strand of the story it is introduced and almost entirely told in the alternative narrative to Esther's: a third-person, or authorial, narrative, also distinguished by being written in the present tense. The opening chapter of the novel is a *tour de force* of Dickens's prose, moving from a description of London in November, cold, wet, muddy, disease-ridden, and in the grip of a pea-souper fog, to the equivalent obfuscation inside the Court of Chancery. Where the very environment is so polluted, culture and nature at their worst are indistinguishable, and the novel appears already to be searching for a cultural cure to the whole:

> If all the injustice it [the Court of Chancery] has committed, and all the misery it has caused, could only be locked up with it, and the whole burnt away in a great funeral pyre – why, so much the better for other parties than the parties in Jarndyce and Jarndyce!   (Chapter I: In Chancery)[22]

The reference to the pyre recalls one of the earliest articles in *Household Words*, which had surveyed different burial practices and shown an interest in cremation as a form of funeral rite that would relieve the pressure on the city burial grounds. This was still a scandalous proposition for most mid-19th-century Victorians.[23]

In the second chapter of the novel we are introduced to Sir Leicester and Lady Dedlock, and learn that they too have a small interest in Jarndyce and Jarndyce. This also introduces their lawyer, Mr Tulkinghorn, who is ultimately to pry into and discover Lady Dedlock's secret, and significantly is the first development of a huge network of coincidences and connexions between characters and experiences that faces us, in *Bleak House*, with a world in which

---

[22] All quotations follow the 1853 edition, where the chapter titles are also found.
[23] 'Heathen and Christian burial', *op. cit.* in note 21.

nearly all facts intertwine, and there is an all-embracing cultural and social interdependency.

Bleak House is manifestly a novel concerned with issues, even scandals, of public concern, which call for political solutions. Yet, while Dickens – as shown by his involvement in the Great Exhibition planning – moved in politically influential circles and was certainly not averse to appealing directly to the authorities to act, *Bleak House* should not properly be regarded as a enlightened political lobbying. In so far as it was designed to enlist wide public support for specific reforms, Dickens's principal strategy and objective was to inform, awaken and influence the moral attitudes of the large literate public who read his novels. This is shown particularly well by the satirical assault on perverted religion and charity that runs insistently alongside the searing denunciation of the Court of Chancery, particularly in the earlier parts of the novel. That evil manifests itself in the merciless judgmentalism of Esther's godmother/aunt, associated with her neighbour, Mrs Rachael, who is to reappear subsequently as the new wife of the hypocritical and sanctimonious preacher, Mr Chadband. It is manifest too in the destructive charity, or 'telescopic philanthropy', of Mrs Jellyby and Mrs Pardiggle, obsessed with ostensibly virtuous committees and campaigns, in the African territory of Borrioboola-Gha for Mrs Jellyby, and totally failing to appreciate the need for love, understanding and support of those literally under their noses. Esther tests her instinctive reaction to Mrs Jellyby on Mr Jarndyce:

> 'We thought that, perhaps,' said I, hesitantly, 'it is right to begin with the obligations of home . . .' (Chapter VI: 'Quite at Home')

Her observation appears banal, and the words tentative, but in such an understated way a vital theme of *Bleak House* emerges.

An abiding fear of the unconfidently charitable is that of being taken for a ride: deceived into subsidizing and even confirming in their vice the undeserving and unneedy. It is not, however, the poor and destitute who are presented as parasites upon the benevolent: even the thuggishly drink-sodden brickmaker who appears repeatedly in the novel, and whose behaviour can be held substantially responsible for the continuing privations of his family, asks for no charity and scorns the insulting ministrations of Mrs Pardiggle. The worst parasite is the effete dilettante Harold Skimpole, who deceives John Jarndyce into believing him a totally innocent and thus refreshingly childlike and playful creature; until his mercenary betrayal of Jo the crossing-sweeper and Richard Carstone, John Jarndyce's second ward, who *does* get sucked into the Jarndyce and Jarndyce case, are exposed. A more ambivalent character is the preposterously self-regarding and selfish Mr Turveydrop, the 'Model of Deportment', living off his exhausted son, the master in a school that teaches 'joyless dancing'.[24] Yet some latent good potential in Mr Turveydrop starts to emerge after Mrs Jellyby's daughter Caddy has married the son, and brings her younger brother Peepy into the newly constructed household, stimulating a grandfatherly care in the portly old dandy.

---

[24] Chapter XXXVIII: 'A Struggle'.

The positive inverse of selfish, exploitative indifference is the real love and charity found above all in Esther and John Jarndyce, although represented also by several further characters: the upright Allan Woodcourt, and George Rouncewell, the old soldier; and the less stereotypical hero in the caring but timid and harrassed law-stationer Mr Snagsby, repeatedly reaching into his pocket for half-crown coins as a palliative for characters and situations that move his sympathy. Mr Snagsby is paired with an intensely suspicious and jealous wife, who is directly linked to the appalling religiosity of the Chadbands, and whose jealously is partly responsible for truly disastrous consequences when her suspicions drive their epileptic maid Guster (Augusta) into a seizure, just when Esther, the police detective Inspector Bucket and Mr Woodcourt are desperate to retrieve a letter from her that should give them information on the fleeing Lady Dedlock's intentions in time to save her life. They are too late.

Mrs Snagsby's jealousy is associated directly with another central and tragic character within the novel, the truly destitute boy Jo, the crossing sweeper. Jo lodges in the foul and ruinous slum of Tom-All-Alone's. He earns a small amount of money as a road-crossing sweeper. He first appears in the novel as a rejected witness at the inquest on Captain Hawdon, who has been found dead of an opium overdose in his own poor lodging above Krook's rag-and-bottle shop in Chancery Lane:

> O! Here's the boy, gentlemen!
> Here he is, very muddy, very hoarse, very ragged. Now, boy! – But stop a minute. Caution. This boy must be put through a few preliminary paces.
> Name, Jo. Nothing else that he knows on. Don't know that everybody has two names. Never heerd of sich a think. Don't know that Jo is short for a longer name. Thinks it long enough for *him*. *He* don't find no fault with it. Spell it? No. *He* can't spell it. No father, no mother, no friends. Never been to school. What's home? Knows a broom's a broom, and knows it's wicked to tell a lie. Don't recollect who told him about the broom, or about the lie, but knows both. Can't exactly say what'll be done to him arter he's dead if he tells a lie to the gentlemen here, but believes it'll be something wery bad to punish him, and serve him right – and so he'll tell the truth.
> 'This won't do, gentlemen!' says the Coroner, with a melancholy shake of the head.
> 'Don't you think you can receive his evidence, sir?' asks an attentive Juryman.
> 'Out of the question,' says the Coroner. 'You have heard the boy. "Can't exactly say" won't do, you know. We can't take *that*, in a Court of Justice, gentlemen. It's terrible depravity. Put the boy aside.'
> Boy put aside; to the great edification of the audience –
>
> (Chapter XI: 'Our Dear Brother')

Mrs Snagsby conceives, wrongly, that Jo is her husband's illegitimate son, and Mr Tulkinghorn's inquisitiveness, having detected Lady Dedlock's interest in the dead man, with further interference by other vultures and parasites on the fringes of the Jarndyce and Jarndyce suit, serves only to feed her misconception. But Jo is far more than a bit-player in this strand of the narrative: he is made literally to embody the spiritually and physically lethal failings of provision for the needy in mid-19th-century Britain. And his (innocent) ignorance is a crucial factor within that. With no sense of risk or consequences he visits Hawdon's grave in the infected burial-ground, muttering:

'He wos wery good to me, he wos!' (Chapter XI)

When Lady Dedlock has discovered that her former lover lies there, she gets Jo to take her, disguised, to the place. No one can know, at this stage, that he is thus instrumental in the sequence of events that leads to her own untimely death, and is even directing her to the place of her death. With cruel irony, Lady Dedlock only compounds Jo's problems by paying him a sovereign (£1): he is mercilessly robbed by the low-life characters who are the only ones he can turn to to change the coin, and then comes to the attention of the police, the lawyers in Chancery Lane, and Mrs Snagsby when taken into custody for having more money on him than he could be expected to earn. Forced by the police to 'move on', he carries disease (smallpox) to Bleak House in St Albans, Hertfordshire, where Esther contracts and is disfigured by the disease. In one of Dickens's classically melodramatic but painfully emotional scenes, he dies, taken under George Rouncewell's roof, with Allan Woodcourt ministering to him the spiritual medicine of the opening lines of the Lord's Prayer.[25]

While Jo falls totally below the recognition and care of the State, and even the newly formed upholders of its laws, the Metropolitan Police, can do nothing more formal with him than to harass him to move on, neither he nor anything else is so mean as to be beneath the notice of the self-seeking band of profiteering lawyers: principally the naïve Mr Guppy and the sinister Tulkinghorn. The corruption of the law into a parasitical profession serving only its own ends – however modestly expressed, as by the sepulchral Mr Vholes, a widower supporting three daughters and an aged father – rather than an instrument serving the common good is the most obvious public theme of the novel. The civil Chancery suits suck the sanity and often the life out of those who become enmeshed in them; and even proximity to the Court sucks the moral life out of practically everybody except the good-hearted Mr Snagsby. As Jo embodies the evil caused by lack of domestic charity and social welfare, the rag-and-bone man Krook, who so nauseatingly dies by spontaneous combustion from his essential, gin-sodden corruption, and who is mockingly but tellingly known by the nickname of the Lord Chancellor, embodies the dehumanized depravity at the heart of this crucial element of the British state. The perverting character of demands of strict, mindless and conscienceless law is illuminated by a brief vignette of the real Lord Chancellor, who presides in Chancery, at the beginning of the novel, when Esther, Ada and Richard appear before him to approve of John Jarndyce's wardship:

He gave us a searching look as we entered, but his manner was both courtly and kind.   (Chapter III: 'A Progress')

---

[25] Chapter XLVII: 'Jo's Will'.

This man retains a degree of his native humanity. But, as Esther very soon remarks:

> The Lord High Chancellor, at his best, appeared so poor a substitute for the love and pride of parents.

A moral theme of equal pervasiveness and importance, though far less obvious than that of the failure of Civil Law, is the vicious consequences of family ruptures, and its corollary, the lauding of stable family life. The absence of family order thwarts and corrupts the relationship between Esther, her mother and her natural father. Sir Leicester Dedlock has immense ancestral pride in his family, but no true family of his own except a flock of more or less idiotic, sponging cousins. Esther knows no father-figure until John Jarndyce steps into this role, and it is an uncomfortable prospect for the majority of readers when it appears he will cross over from here into the role of Esther's paternalistic husband – not despite, but indeed because of the characteristically Victorian asexual portrayal of marriage, and consequent tolerance of (for us) ill-matched unions.[26] Esther's aunt had rejected a Mr Boythorn as a fiancé, in order to bring up her sister's child – and to vent her frustration on Esther, with whom she would admit no blood relationship – leaving Boythorn a pleasingly comical but impotent and frustrated bombast. A more optimistic story is provided by the reconciliation of Mrs Rouncewell, the Dedlocks' housekeeper at Chesney Wold, their place in Lincolnshire, and her (prodigal) son George who had left to join the army, as also between George and his unnamed elder brother, who became a successful and upright industrialist.

Jo has no family. He has no concept of a family name. 'No father, no mother, no friends'. The nearest he gets to redressing this pitiful state is the degree of adoption Mr Snagsby sympathetically affords him – but only at the cost of Mrs Snagsby suspecting he is in fact her husband's natural son. (They have no children of their own.) Perhaps, though, the most poignant expression of Jo's abandoned state is the simple question with which he answers his preliminary interrogator at the inquest:

> What's home?

Fundamental to an appreciation of the positive role of contemporary material culture in the composition of *Bleak House* is an appreciation of the essential link between family and home, and of the essential physicality of the latter. Home is not an abstract concept; not, sentimentally, just where the heart is, nor merely a

---

[26] A coherent analysis and explanation of the Victorian view can be offered in psychological terms. The mature male took a younger wife who was regarded as still child-like and made a woman of her through marriage. This preceded a reversal of roles, as the aging husband became increasingly child-like and dependent upon his wife, now a mother-figure as much to himself as to their own children. This may in turn be linked to the lauding of home in Victorian culture, as the expression of a subconscious desire to return to the carefree security of a sentimentally recalled childhood. Frances Armstrong, *Dickens and the Concept of Home* (Ann Arbor: UMI Research Press, 1990), esp. 13–16.

state of mind. It was something to be realized in concrete form, and something that could be constructed, or misconstructed, in many different ways.[27]

The reader of *Bleak House* is conducted by its two narrators into a wide range of homes. The range visited contrasts the wealth and comfort of Chesney Wold and John Jarndyce's Bleak House in St Albans with the squalor and privation of a brickmaker's cottage, also in St Albans, and Tom-All-Alone's in London. Cutting across the material scale of wealth, however, is another moral and comparative scale of orderliness in the household: an orderliness that is to be understood in terms of a wholesome organization of the material furnishings and possessions of the home and thus a model relationship between the characters and their material culture. Again, Bleak House (despite its name) is close to the virtuous ideal in this respect, precisely, indeed, as it is excitedly described and introduced to us by Esther in Chapter 6, entitled 'Quite at Home'. An equivalent example as the home of a family of much humbler means is that of George Rouncewell's friends, the Bagnets. Disorderliness too presents itself right across the social spectrum, from the brickmaker's cottage and Krook's rag-and-bottle shop to the chaotic room in which Richard finally expires, or Mr Skimpole's home, visited by Esther, Ada and John Jarndyce in an attempt to impress a moral message upon him: '. . . dingy enough, and not at all clean; but furnished with an odd kind of shabby luxury' (Chapter 43) – and where Esther subsequently notes most of the chair-legs are broken. Certainly, the way people (in so far as they have a choice) live at home is always expressive of their personality. Perhaps the most extreme example is Tulkinghorn's sitting room, with an apparently meaningless Painted Allegory of a Pointing Roman on the ceiling, which ends up still saying nothing but pointing to Tulkinghorn as himself, finally, a victim of the web of intrigue and exploitation he had sought to control:

> . . . Mr Tulkinghorn's time is over for evermore; and the Roman pointed at the murderous hand uplifted against his life, and pointed helplessly at him, from night to morning, lying face downward on the floor, shot through the heart.
>
> (Chapter XLVIII: 'Closing In')

Where the allegory of the inanimate domestic furniture and ornament ultimately finds real meaning is in the dramatic events that are acted out in the context they provide.

The marriage between Esther and Allan Woodcourt is organized by John Jarndyce, by him taking Esther – still believing she is shortly to marry her guardian – to Yorkshire, to lend her womanly and housekeeperly final touch to ensure that 'things were all as they should be' in a house that Mr Jarndyce is providing for Mr Woodcourt. Esther discovers that house to be a sentimentally exquisite rustic cottage with flower-garden and orchard – a 'cottage of doll's rooms', she calls it: momentarily recalling the doll with whom she found such happiness and comfort (her 'solitary friend') as a child. Here she saw:

---

[27] Armstrong, *op. cit.* in note 26, esp. 93–103; Alison Milbank, *Daughters of the House: Modes of the Gothic in Victorian Fiction* (Basingstoke: Macmillan, 1992), esp. 80–101.

. . . in the papering on the walls, in the colors of the furniture, in the arrange-
ment of all the pretty objects, *my* little tastes and fancies, *my* little methods
and inventions which they used to laugh at while they praised them, my odd
ways everywhere. (Chapter LXIV: 'Esther's Narrative')

Soon afterwards she is shown that this house is called Bleak House too; and
John Jarndyce's proposal to her was couched in the form of asking her if she
would consent to be mistress of Bleak House. The only sense, then, in which
Esther is absolutely needed to make Esther's home for her is to be present and
live there: her choice and way of arranging things can be fully reproduced.

This significantly echoes the situation in the original Bleak House, where
Esther is installed as housekeeper – and disconcertingly is characterized as and
called 'little woman', Dame Trot and Dame Durden. She repeatedly refers to
herself going about her business with her housekeeper's keys but we do not see
her changing or reorganizing materially the form of the household in any way.
The house itself has a microcosm in Richard's room, which appears as 'a
comfortable compound of many rooms'; its furniture is 'old-fashioned rather
than old, like the house . . . pleasantly irregular':

All the moveables, from the wardrobes to the chairs and tables, hangings,
glasses, even to the pincushions and scent-bottles on the dressing-tables,
displayed the same quaint variety. They agreed in nothing but their perfect
neatness . . . (Chapter VI: 'Quite at Home')

The objects do indeed make the house, but it only becomes a virtuous and
morally uplifting home if it is lived in in the proper manner. That involves the
correct attitude to and use of the material objects available; and a liberal choice
of and command over a range of goods on offer is not essential.

Shortly after Esther has arrived at the original Bleak House – as the narrative
is ordered, at least – she and Ada accompany the insensitively missionizing Mrs
Pardiggle on a visit to the brickmaker's cottage. Most of the negative details of
the description of the place that accompanies this reflect the poverty of these
representatives of the labouring class: the cottage is a 'wretched hovel' in a wet
and filthy place. Esther notes that pigs are kept there: an ironic allusion to a lost
rural background, but also a realistic detail as pig-keeping in towns and suburbs
was a practical matter and long-standing custom. It also suggests that the brick-
makers and their family are forced to live with and like the swine, with an echo
in the parable of the Prodigal Son again. Inside the room, the fire is the warming
and illuminating focus, and this is where a woman, Jenny, sits attempting to
nurse her dying child. The brickmaker himself – a brutalized and brutal
drunkard – is lying on the floor in front of the fire. The significance of this is
not to demonstrate his lack of polish in failing to rise when the ladies come in –
an absurd possibility – but rather to point the fact that there is no direct reference
to any use of furniture in the household until Mrs Pardiggle sits on a stool,
'knocking down another' that had been standing there unused (Fig. 16). There is
much to excuse the brickmaker's offensive attitude, and a glimpse of latent
conscience is even seen in him when Esther and Ada leave. But the detail of how
he deports himself in his house importantly represents a stubborn, not heroic,

The visit at the Brickmaker's.

FIG. 16. *The visit at the Brickmaker's*. Engraving by Hablôt K. Brown from the original instalments and first edition of Dickens's *Bleak House* (1852–53).

refusal to engage with the material goods available and to attempt to construct a happier and better-ordered house. Even of the few things available to him, there are opportunities he neglects to take advantage of.

The inverse of such a failure to use material goods at all is portrayed by various examples of people whose character or humanity is effectively lost when the objects with which they are most closely associated – particularly within their homes – swallow them up. The home and specifically the fireside of the Smallweeds, a viciously predatory family, is dominated by two 'black horse-hair porter's chairs', beside one of which Grandfather Smallweed keeps a spare cushion, to throw repeatedly at his deranged wife. This usurious old man is constantly seen being carried in or between chairs: his malignancy contrasts powerfully with his dependency, emblematized by his inseparability from his chair. The Dedlocks' country seat, Chesney Wold, is sumptuous, but dominated by portraits and mementos of the family past. It has a Ghost's Walk outside, and after the death of Lady Dedlock ends up little more than a mausoleum. In the original, serialized publication of *Bleak House* the final illustration is of Lady Dedlock's Mausoleum at Chesney Wold, and the two previous views of the house have been of the Ghost's Walk, and a melancholy view of sunset in the empty drawing room. Krook, an obsessive compulsive, crazed old man, is swamped in his 'shop' by the rubbish he collects – which does, as the

Smallweeds eventually discover, include the document which is the key to Jarndyce and Jarndyce that he wants but is unable to find, let alone read. In the end he burns, like an oily object, by spontaneous combustion in his filth.

Do these observations coalesce into some sort of consistent moralized material culture propounded in *Bleak House*? There is certainly here an axiom that people must control objects, not objects people, and that taste, relative simplicity, and a contentedness with no more than is really needed are the desiderata. So far, so simple: however an anti-materialist ethic is neither possible nor desirable. The world is revealed to be unalterably material and constituted of an ever wider variety of products in the form of houses and consumer goods. The moral target has to be to create and attain the correct form of materialism to live rightly in these circumstances. Inseparable from the campaigning, public and political satire of *Bleak House* is thus also a profound concern to set up the model of an ideal family household: constituted equally of stable social relations and stable material-cultural relations. Most of the alternative titles we know Dickens considered for this work – *Tom-All-Alone's*; *The Solitary House*; *The Ruined Building/House* – point to this primary recognition of the central place of the house and home in his mind as he planned it. We miss a fundamental part of *Bleak House* if we do not follow the material clues in a full cultural historicist reading to the domestic theme that also constructively informs the novel.[28]

This involves a dichotomy between the public and the personal/domestic that is closely related to the twin narratives of *Bleak House*. Esther's narrative is concerned primarily with the stories of individuals and their relationships. Superficially, it is concerned primarily with the tragic but anaemic story of the insipid young couple, Ada and Richard. In a covert way, meanwhile, it tells Esther's own, more intriguing story – intriguing not least for the problems posed by the portrayal of her sexuality: apparently deeply suppressed until restored to her by the paternalistic John Jarndyce, and even troublingly misdirected in her references to her 'love', 'pet' and 'darling' Ada. Her story is in the past tense, as indeed the stories of individual people are subject to the remorseless progress of time, aging and mortality. To risk a clichéd metaphor, the leading characters and relationships of one time become memories and part of the furniture in the next, like the portraits at Chesney Wold. The public story of the scandal of the Court of Chancery, and of the failure to tackle urban pollution, poverty, deprivation and blight, moves on a different timescale: seeming ever-present in the present tense.

Despite his concern for concrete, structural and tractable problems of contemporary London, such as adequate sewerage and hygienic graveyards, Dickens associated the material world much more subtly and diversely with an individualist and spiritual ethic than with the liberal-interventionist social programme he was also passionate about. His blueprint for a proper human-material relationship was rooted in the home – where, as Esther had

---

[28] For further and alternative approaches to the material context in mid-Victorian novels see Andrew H. Miller, *Novels Behind Glass: Commodity Culture and Victorian Narrative* (Cambridge University Press, 1995); Thad Logan, *The Victorian Parlour* (Cambridge University Press, 2001), 202–18.

said, charity, and virtue, begin. Just as he distanced himself, literally, from London in the summer of 1851, he stood back from the Great Exhibition experience. That event placed materialism, commodification, spending power (or lack of it) and taste at the centre of cultural life and high on the list of critical concerns for thinking men and women. *Bleak House* is as fundamentally informed by these concerns as it is by the public scandals – the failure to deal with which Dickens elsewhere pointedly contrasted with the successful staging of the Great Exhibition.[29] This novel is not merely the product of Dickens's journalistic responses to the Exhibition carried over into novel form. He seems almost to mock, or at least to cancel out, his own satirical analysis of the material foibles of Chinese culture represented by a junk moored in London in 1851, which he contrasted with the substance and dynamism of western industrial culture, by allowing a picture 'of the whole process of preparing tea in China, as depicted by Chinese artists' into the original Bleak House.[30] Whatever his shifting attitude, he nonetheless continued to take account of the fact that the Great Exhibition *happened*: something that he, like other commentators of the time, referred to in *Household Words*, not mockingly, as the key to 'the moral power of the Exhibition'.[31]

Charity may begin at home but it does not end there. Dickens's enthusiasm for the benefits of domestic good order thus did not mean that he advocated the restrictive enclosure of 'the angel in the house'. Esther reaches out of the domestic setting to do good to others such as Caddy and Charley: as Alison Milbank says, John Jarndyce needs her 'to turn his benevolent intentions into efficacious actions'[32] – although one may just as well stress the complete interdependency of the couple. Correspondingly, Esther's ultimate domestic happiness, with Allan Woodcourt, is as much a reward for her social virtue as a precondition for it. In *Bleak House*, the hearth and home are the foci of a comprehensive moral vision, satirising and criticising what is wrong, but just as determinedly identifying and extolling what is good. An essential part of such a comprehensive vision had to be a full engagement with the materiality of the real world. Dickens dealt with this facet of his time every bit as much as Marx did; but did so with a liberal optimism that offers a very different alternative to Marx's illiberal materialism. For ourselves, at the further remove of a century and a half, this also points the way towards a more critical and comprehensive approach to the archaeology of Victorian England.

[29] 'A time for all things', *op. cit.* in note 21.
[30] 'The Great Exhibition and the little one', *Household Words*, 5 July 1851, 356–60; *Bleak House*, Ch. VI: 'Quite at Home'.
[31] 'What is not clear about the Crystal Palace', *Household Words*, 19 July 1851, 400–2, at p. 402.
[32] *Op. cit.* in note 27, 90.

A Contribution to an Archaeology of Victorian England

While it is tempting in considering Victorian things to treat them entirely archaeologically, as if they were the only evidence available to the historian, and to approach the 'material culture' of Victorian England like the study of ancient or medieval pottery, solely through a study of materials, design of products and their spatial distribution, such an approach would have been too restrictive. *Pace* the great French historian Marc Bloch, who suggested misleadingly that with objects 'there is no need to appeal to any other human mind as an interpreter', an examination of the contemporary publicity surrounding things – much of it rhetorical – is a necessary and enriching part of my subject. It puts the psychology as well as the economics into the archaeology. So, too, do surviving ephemera such as undertakers' bills which must be considered along with lavish cemetery art. So, too, do solidly bound volumes of sermons, designed, like gravestones but unlike bills, to last.

(Asa Briggs, *Victorian Things*,[33] 16)

Despite the range and thoroughness of the primary research that underlies Asa Briggs's potentially groundbreaking but actually largely neglected study *Victorian Things*, he must have neglected to consult an up-to-date archaeologist when writing the paragraph above. He makes a familiar, naïve supposition that archaeology does not raise its eyes above simply material, technical and quantitative facts, and his words show no awareness of the excitement and debate caused by ambitions to write an 'archaeology of the mind' from the beginning of the 1980s.[34]

Briggs's misconception is, however, more excusable in relation to the archaeology of a recent period than in relation to what he says about the study of ancient and medieval pottery. As it approaches the present day, the discipline of archaeology grows increasingly fragmented and unsure of its role, less confident that it can be an essential part of any comprehensive presentation and interpretation of the recent past. These difficulties are partly a reflection of the profusion of production and surviving material from what we can call modern times – although it is obviously an odd situation where a field of study is tempted to complain of there being too much evidence! A subtler, but perhaps therefore more significant factor is the changing nature of the forms of evidence. The material remains themselves seem to include vast amounts of ephemera: cheap items of little material or symbolic value in any Victorian household, like a match-box. The range of goods produced and available is also copiously illustrated in catalogues and photographs, and thus better described in documentary sources than from the haphazardly collected and preserved, and often decaying, objects themselves. Copious statistical records from this period tell us much about its material life. What role is left, then, for the hands-on archaeologist, working directly with the objects?

[33] *Op. cit.* in note 6.
[34] E.g. Colin Renfrew, *Towards an Archaeology of Mind: an inaugural lecture delivered before the University of Cambridge on 30 November 1982* (Cambridge University Press, 1982).

The question is a distorted one: the hands-on excavator or finds specialist is not the only sort of archaeologist. Archaeology is the study of the material culture of the past, and that domain can be approached through a multiplicity of sources.[35] There is still a difference between archaeology and economic history – albeit not a major one, nor a radical divide. The complementary roles of the pair that are worth emphasizing most are the ability of the archaeology to engage in detail with the specificity of individual cases while the economic history leans towards generalization and mass statistics.

The material culture of England, like that of virtually the whole of Europe and elsewhere, changed dramatically in the 19th century in ways already outlined in this chapter. This brought with it a degree of disorientation in re-lations with the material world, mid-19th-century attempts to overcome which we have considered, and which equally requires present-day would-be archaeol-ogists of the Victorian Age to be open to a substantial re-orientation of their discipline in comparison with the practical archaeology of other periods. The situation can be illustrated by considering the phenomenon of the new technique of photography itself. This emerged in the mid-19th century as the product of a familiar combination, for the time, of mechanical skill, to design the appropriate apparatus, and material science, controlling the properties of particular chem-ical compounds as they react to light. Photography underwent a rapid develop-ment over the span of a generation from the 1830s to the 1860s. It was, as we have noted, represented in the Great Exhibition, albeit as a novelty, and we do have a photographic record of the Exhibition.[36]

An early, popular and, as we know, continuing application of this new 'art' was in portraiture. Studios sprang up, especially in London and Paris, to cater for the demand for individual and family portraits. The images were rapidly adopted for further social purposes on visiting cards, and photographic post-cards were available in profusion by the end of the century. Suddenly a relatively inexpensive and quick alternative to the painted or sketched portrait or landscape was available – and one that appeared almost brutally objective and accurate. Of course, photographic compositions and images can be arranged and manipulated: the real distinction between the art-forms is that where painters start with the subjective impression of the artist, and may progress from that to convey some measure of realism to the viewer, photography essentially involves an objective image of what is exposed to the plate or film through the lens, which may initially be arranged or subsequently processed and presented in a selective and expressive way.

It is a highly familiar image of an eminent Victorian produced by this new technology, but Robert Howlett's photograph of the engineer and designer Isambard Kingdom Brunel standing in front of the anchor chains of his last and biggest ship, the *Great Eastern*, built on the Isle of Dogs east of London, in 1857, illustrates the complex factors beautifully (Fig. 17). Brunel stands in the centre of the composition: we see what he looks like; we see him dressed and

[35] See Logan, *op. cit.* in note 28, 105–201.
[36] Briggs, *op. cit.* in note 6, 103–41.

FIG. 17. Isambard Kingdom Brunel. Photographic portrait by Robert Howlett at the construction site of the *Great Eastern* (1857). Copyright: National Portrait Gallery.

posing rather jauntily in the fashion of the day: a large cigar, and watch-and-chain, form part of his self-presentation, as does the mud on his trouser-legs and boots. Yet in this shot the backdrop of the colossal chain-links is intriguing. From records associated with the image, although not a title of the work as such, we know what these are. The picture does not tell us that. It does not tell us how high they stretch up over the engineer's head or how far the backdrop continues to either side. We do have other photographic images of the construction site that yield this information, and, most significantly, a second – one suspects preceding – photograph by Howlett at the same spot which includes the end of the huge drum around which the chain was wound, on Brunel's left.[37] Unbounded, the objects are all the more awe-inspiring tributes to Victorian engineering. A single link looks more than any individual could lift or move without difficulty, yet the whole mighty chainwork is clearly designed by Man and produced by Man: not for its own sake, but in order to control some even more colossal machine. By no means all of his contemporaries had complete confidence in Brunel's ambitious schemes, and the *Great Eastern* project encountered major practical problems. The photograph, however, superbly encapsulates Brunel's vision not only of himself but also of his engineering project.

To suppose that all of these ideas were consciously in the photographer's mind as he arranged the shot, or Brunel's as he agreed to it, is manifestly over-imaginative, although the existence of two photographs from the same spot implies a certain amount of conscious editing of the composition in this direction. Brunel's watch-chain and satchel were in fact conspicuously adjusted between the two shots. It would be similarly fallacious to suggest that the new technique of photography was entirely under human control, and a slave to the objectives of those who used it. It had its own deep impact on human perceptions of the world and cognition. By the end of the 19th century family photograph albums were not unusual possessions, providing a new basis for internal family history and memories of the past – at the risk of reducing such repositories of memory and affection to the cheap, the two-dimensional, and the objective. The objectivity of photography was embraced across a range of analytical and scholarly disciplines. It found applications in medical research and teaching, principally to provide clear records of the visible manifestations of physical and psychological abnormalities. It soon started to form part of the historical record: there is a photograph of the Chartist rally on Kennington Common in 1848, for instance, and a number of photographs from the Crimean War (1854–6); along with that, it could be used in sociological analysis and for political campaigns. Where Dickens used his pen, Thomas Allen used the camera to depict Glaswegian slums for the City Improvement Trust. Photographic records also became an important element in police work.[38]

Photographers therefore did not just record people and settings: they affected

---

[37] National Portrait Gallery, London, P662.

[38] Richard W. Ireland, 'The felon and the angel copier: criminal identity and the promise of photography in Victorian England and Wales', in L. A. Knafla (ed.), *Policing and War in Europe*, Criminal Justice History, 16 (Westport CT, 2002), 53–86.

them, more or less directly; people adjusted psychologically to the availability of objective visual records, and both people and locations began to be adapted for the camera. Although it does afford a record of material culture, photography has always at the same time been a part of that whole material culture, not separate from it. The enthusiasm with which it was adopted as part of Victorian material life reflects less of an obsession with committing images to record as the same desire either to see something new, or to see the familiar in a novel way, that was essential to the success of the Great Exhibition. The same impulse can be detected in the prurient fascination with sensuous, sculpted nude female figures at the Exhibition,[39] and the success of freak shows quite unacceptable to present public taste and ethics. This also means that the illustration of novels such as *Bleak House*, with printed engravings, was more than just a childish prop, helping the reader to visualize the story. It was a more expressive extension of the narrative, rounding out the experience of reading by re-embedding it within a familiar material culture.

The slight and permeable boundary between the mundane material culture of the day and the concerns of a literary work such as *Bleak House* is evident in a striking way in the form of the instalments in which the novel was originally published. Here the publishers were selling advertising space on the end-papers, and the range and relative saliency of different goods and services offered there provides us with a direct insight into contemporary material and business life. The advertisements usually started with large quantities of books, paper and maps, followed by toiletries (especially for gentlemen's hair grooming, one notes!), but also a diversity of drugs and remedies, clothing, spectacles, watches, umbrellas, needles, cutlery, all sorts of household goods and furniture, insurance, beer – and as the Crimean War grew imminent military gear and tents. Some of these advertisements soon began to make explicit references to the novel they were appearing alongside, and by the sixth instalment an advertisement by Dakin & Co., Ironmongers, imitated the front cover of the fascicules, which carried a series of engravings of street scenes, with a set of views of interior comfort in the same layout. The technique used for the illustrations was that of engraving: essentially the same as that of much earlier woodcuts, but of finer quality with technical improvements and the introduction of metal plates. Although the manual art of engraving offered obvious scope for greater creativity, engravings, in publications such as the *Illustrated London News* for instance, sought to resemble photographs more and more.[40] Ultimately, photography made visual realism seem mechanical and trite, and the visual arts developed in a variety of ways, through impressionism and expressionism to the abstractionism and surrealism of the 20th century.

Although the parameters of the material cultural record thus move in confusing ways for the 19th and 20th centuries in particular, it remains a valid criticism that small and simple, day-to-day objects and goods are particularly neglected in comparison with their place in the material life of the Victorian

---

[39] Davis, *op. cit.* in note 2, 160–1.
[40] Horace Harral produced an engraved copy of the photograph in Figure 17 for the *Illustrated Times*, 16 January 1858: National Portrait Gallery, D1127.

Period. There is a huge body of expert knowledge of material Victoriana, but, in what we might claim to be the victory of the *Art-Journal* approach to the Great Exhibition, this has overwhelmingly been left in the hands of highly specialized connoisseurs and the antiques trade, who have less interest in the whole contextualization of specific items in their contemporary material culture and history and more interest in their financial value than academic archaeologists should have. It is both ironic and frustrating that nonetheless the high levels of specialist knowledge required in these capacities in the antiques business largely concern craftmanship within what is essentially industrial-scale and -style production. The famous Thomas Chippendale was the first to publish a commercial catalogue and pattern-book of furniture designs.[41] A distinct type of connoisseur is the specialist collector. Again, this practice tends to isolate and insulate areas of interest. It is consequently hard for us to think of, say, a major collection of Victorian post-cards or postage stamps as a necessary part of the archaeological record of the period. But we ought to do so.

As in post-medieval archaeology generally, archaeological studies of this recent period currently pay most attention to the built environment: to the large numbers of surviving or otherwise well-attested buildings, public, industrial, and for housing; and to their layout, and townscapes generally. Given the massive growth of industrial and metropolitan conurbations in the 19th century this can hardly be thought unjustified. It is also an aspect of the material history of the period within which the archaeologist can still look directly at the physical evidence for significant details of form that may be overlooked in contemporary accounts and records, and are unlikely to attract the attention of social and economic historians.[42]

It is temptingly easy, in such circumstances, to conceive of an archaeology of the Victorian Period, when urban expansion was a massive phenomenon, as one in which it is appropriate for urban archaeology to dominate the archaeological agenda. However for this period, as for virtually all preceding periods, the concept of a fundamental separation between town and country remains false. Industrial settlements – factories, mines, quarries, and their associated housing – could be on a small scale and in the midst of farming areas. The Great Exhibition was certainly dominated by aspects of industrial production, but agricultural implements still formed one of the largest single classes. The mechanization of agriculture proceeded in a steady way through the 19th century. The Exhibition included a number of portable steam-engines to drive agricultural machinery in the field, and a few items such as a steam-driven plough, but the majority of exhibits in this class were especially finely crafted or efficient manual or animal-powered tools for tillage, sowing, reaping and processing crops. Several horse-carts and even a novelty pea-stick made it into the display. The practical importance of this kind of equipment is rarely effectively conveyed to the visitor by the collections of discarded, slightly

---

[41] Thomas Chippendale, *The Gentleman and Cabinet-Maker's Director* (1754).

[42] E.g. Newman *et al.*, *op. cit.* in Chapter 5, note 19, 10–99 and 145–67; likewise Sarah Tarlow and Susie West (eds.), *The Familiar Past? Archaeologies of Later Historical Britain* (London: Routledge, 1999).

rusty-looking static tools and equipment one can find in so many 'country life' museums.

The principal features that otherwise fall within the domain of rural archaeology for the Victorian Period are large-scale, landscape matters, again, indeed, reflecting the inseparability of rural matters from the larger context. Economically, farming was revolving around a slow-moving cycle of alternating boom and depression, with particular lows in the period after the end of the Napoleonic Wars in 1815 and from the late 1870s up to the end of the century, and something of a golden period in between, especially for the three decades from the late 1840s – ironically, when the protectionist Corn Laws were repealed. That peak coincided with an expansion of the area under cultivation to a maximum matched neither before nor since. This was the product of a long-term process of land-reclamation from former heath- and moorland and the drainage of wetlands: a process that itself created major new features in the landscape. In the most marginal areas lands were enclosed for grazing purposes, and in some cases land used briefly as arable was given back over to pasture.[43]

The creation of enclosed fields within the open fields characteristic of a much earlier agricultural regime was a process that continued in the earlier 19th century but was virtually complete by 1850. Thus a new pattern of field-boundaries was being produced in some areas, while in others, for instance Kent, hedges were being grubbed up to create larger and more efficient fields. The mid-century prosperity also saw some new, model farm building, particularly on the estates of mighty aristocratic landowners such as the Duke of Bedford, at Woburn, the Earls of Rother and Macclesfield, in Oxfordshire, and the Marquis of Bath, at Longleat.[44] There was, however, nothing going on in this that can really be counted more than the normal life and gradual development of the rural context: no major transformation was taking place. More symptomatic of significant long-term change seems to have been the incipient centralization and effective industrialization of facilities for processing agricultural produce, such as the emergence of large steam-driven mills, usually close to major towns, and from the 1870s using the new roller-milling process, or large-scale maltings reflecting the interests of major industrial brewing companies that emerged in the same circumstances.[45]

Such new features are essentially linked to major changes in the rural landscape in the 19th century as the result of developments in transport. Prior to the railway age, the poor state of roads in England had made the conveyance of agricultural produce in large quantities any further than to local markets impractical. In the 18th and earlier 19th centuries canals had catered for the increasing needs to transport commodities such as coal and iron ore, but they had made little

[43] Tom Williamson, *The Transformation of Rural England: Farming and the Landscape 1700–1870* (University of Exeter Press, 2002); G. E. Mingay (ed.), *The Agrarian History of England and Wales. Vol. VI: 1750–1850* (Cambridge University Press, 1989); E. J. T. Collins, *The Agrarian History of England and Wales. Vol. VII: 1850–1914*, 2 parts (Cambridge University Press, 2000); Newman *et al.*, *op. cit.* in note 42, 127–35.

[44] Roy Brigden, 'Farm buildings', 497–504 in Collins (ed.), *op. cit.* in note 43.

[45] R. Bennett and J. Elton, *History of Corn Milling*, 4 vols. (London: Simpkin, Marsall & Co.; Liverpool: Edward Howell, 1898–1904), vol. III, 283–315.

difference to the distribution of agricultural produce.[46] Steam railway trains made a critical difference. The railway network rapidly outstripped the canal network in extent, introducing a highly visible – and audible – new element into rural landscapes as well as urban ones. The invention of oil-powered internal combustion engines and introduction of private motor-cars, buses and goods vehicles began only at the end of the 19th century, and it was then to be half a century before this technology was used in sufficiently cheap, mass-produced vehicles, and catered for by improvements to the road system, for it to supersede rail as the most common form of land transport beyond the immediately local range.

An interesting detail in *Bleak House* is an excursion that Esther and her maid Charley make from London to Deal, on the Kent coast, by overnight coach:

> It was a night's journey in those coach times . . .   (Chapter XLV: In Trust)

Esther's narrative is in the past tense, as we have noted, and it is placed more palpably in a physically different past by this reference. With all the continuing horrors of earlier 19th-century life Dickens denounces in the novel, placing Esther's narrative in such a recent past can hardly be interpreted as a nostalgic reaching back to happier times on his part. One may, however, suggest that Dickens was intuitively unsure of the status of innovations – of the degree to which newer experiences would command the same general recognition. The personal virtues he wished to commend could therefore be made more universally recognizable by locating them in a securely shared, recent past, *inter alia* materially constituted in just such a way.

Dickens certainly had no illusions about the difficulties of road travel. The two penultimate instalments of *Bleak House* are dominated by Esther's graphic account of the painful and stressful pursuit of her mother up and down the roads north of London. Despite all the advances in technology, and the ingenuity of the new professional class of police detective, Lady Dedlock slips through the net by the simple ruse of changing clothes with the brickmaker's wife, Jenny, and forces those trying to save her back to the most basic of technologies, and constant changes of horses, chasing around after her in a cold and leaky carriage. In such a light, it is all the more striking that 19th-century developments in transportation saw travel develop beyond being a means to an end or a necessary evil into an object in itself. It might remain an adventure, but generally could increasingly be more of a pleasure for those who could indulge in it that a challenge. Where the Grand Tour and seasons in fashionable resorts had been an elite and exclusive privilege, tourism became another commodity for middle-class consumers, and desirable places to visit – pleasurable beaches and resorts, and romantic countryside – developed facilities such as places of amusement and hotels to respond to that.

Although industrialization was the dominant development that moulded 19th-century cultural life, there has to be more to an archaeology of Victorian England than conventional industrial archaeology alone. The principal topics

---

[46] Richard Perren, 'Markets and marketing', 190–274 in Mingay (ed.), *op. cit.* in note 43, at pp. 216–23.

considered by industrial archaeologists include the technology of industry and its accommodation, in factories, workshops, and constructed labour colonies of workers' housing. Considerable attention has also been paid to the mass movement of goods, from mines and quarries, through ports, warehouses and the like; and, to an extent, to the movement of finished products either for export or into shops like the major department stores of which many appeared in the mid-19th century. These intrinsically major issues have the accidental result of tending to monumentalize industrial archaeology – to encourage the same sort of thrill at the sheer scale of some constructions as was expressed in the face of, for instance, the steam press used in the construction of George Stephenson's Britannia tubular Bridge over the Menai Straits in the Great Exhibition.[47] We would miss a vital aspect of material life at this time if we did not also follow the circulation of goods through to the individual consumers, not least back into the homes of workers in the factories, be they 'blue-collar' hands or 'white-collar' managers.[48]

The burgeoning material production of Victorian England caused many contemporary problems. There was social stress in the struggle for the best share of the material prosperity one could get, particularly on behalf of working-class and trades union movements. Anxieties amongst the longer established country-based gentry over connexions with newly rich trading and manufacturing groups are strongly reflected in mid-19th-century novels. In such a context, the Society of Arts' and comparable groups' concerns over the need for a cultivated taste as a directing principle in face of the profusion of choice may seem trivially misdirected. In the following decades, however, deeply serious and influential intellectuals such as Matthew Arnold and John Ruskin argued resolutely for the unity of decent public and private cultural life through the integration of a strong critical aesthetics with a harmonious social order.

In the novels of a witty social commentator and gentle cultural critic like Anthony Trollope one tends to find clear and amusing descriptions of how *not* to comport oneself in various social and material circumstances; for the most direct statements of the reciprocal rules of how one should do such things – and use things – properly we have to look principally to explicit text-books like *Mrs Beeton's Book of Household Management* of 1861. The challenge for the investigative and analytical cultural historian is, therefore, to look into literature, historical documents and archaeology alike in order to make a close examination of the use of objects in Victorian England. On the one hand, we should seek to explore the range and patterns of positive and creative responses to the new opportunities, like photography; on the other, we should recognize the limits

---

[47] *Official Catalogue*, vol. I, 228–30: 'Four such cylinders have been cast at Bank Quay Foundry [Warrington], and they are, perhaps, the most powerful machines ever constructed.'

[48] A rare and laudable study in respect of England undertaking precisely this is Keith Matthews, 'Familiarity and contempt: the archaeology of the "modern"', in Tarlow and West (eds.), *op. cit.* in note 42, 155–79. Such case-studies have understandably been developed more in the context of colonial 'historical' archaeology: Grace Kanskaus, *Inside the Rocks: The Archaeology of a Neighbourhood* (Alexandra NSW: Hale & Iremonger, 1999); Godden Mackay Heritage Consultants, *The Cumberland/Gloucester Street Site, The Rocks: Archaeological Investigation Report Prepared for the Sydney Civic Authority*, 4 vols. + CD-ROM (Redfern NSW: Godden Mackay Logan, 1999).

imposed on such responses by a variety of constraints: not just by wealth and disposable income, but also by varying local availability; by ideologies of abstinence and value-judgments in relation to particular types of item; and by traditions of class-solidarity and group-identification right across the social spectrum. Within this, archaeology has a vital role to play in marrying economic and social history on the one hand with specialist connoisseurship on the other. When philatelists, railway buffs and match-box collectors are properly integrated into the enterprise, we shall be writing a cultural history that is also truly human: not just the materialist account Asa Briggs mistook archaeology to be.

Epilogue: Spelling Progress

FOR a motif to introduce some final reflections upon what this book may claim to have done, and acknowledgement of what it has left undone, we leave English literature of the mid-Victorian period for a contemporary Russian novelist, Ivan Sergeyevich Turgenev. Turgenev was a cosmopolitan character. As for many 19th-century Russians of higher social status or pretensions, French was the language of his immediate family in his childhood, while at the end of his teens he developed a passion for things German and went to study for two years in Berlin. He became infatuated with the Spanish wife of a fellow Russian and followed her around western Europe. He visited London and other parts of England, and it was reportedly during a holiday on the Isle of Wight in 1860 that he conceived the idea of his earliest successful and influential novel, *Fathers and Sons*, which was published in 1862.

The novel is set in a Russia in its own process of 19th-century change, and dramatizes a deep gulf in perception, experience and expectations between generations there. The narrative context is entirely provincial, where the agricultural society is emerging from a system of bond-peasant farming or serfdom. Arkady Nikolayevich Kirsanov, the son of a landowner, has been away to university in St Petersburg and returns home in May 1859: by explicit reference to the date, then, the novel is set directly in the period in which it was written and published. Arkady brings with him a friend, Bazarov, who is a scientist, doctor and ideological nihilist: a type of character that at the most positive can be regarded as advocating a wholesale rejection and erasure of conventional attitudes as the essential preliminary to the reconstruction of a better cultural order; in harsher terms, no more than a habitually negative sceptic. Bazarov's cynical self-assurance is not enough to save him from falling tragically and painfully in love with the clever and attractive Anna Odintsova, a rich widow, or subsequently from contracting an infection, typhoid, from a dead peasant on whom he performed an autopsy, bringing an untimely end to an unfulfilled life. His deliberately contrived emptiness renders him defenceless against the forces of sexual love and family ties, while the dirt and disease of the Russian countryside invade and destroy him.

Early in the novel, Bazarov retires to his bedroom in Arkady's family home, and finds a new washstand – a purpose-built, unplumbed, stand and basin. This provokes the comment alluded to in the title of this section:

Английские рукомойники, то естъ прогрессъ!

'English washstands – that's progress!' (*Fathers and Sons*, Chapter 4)

Even at this introductory stage, contemplating a material instance of the internationalization of cultural life through trade, Bazarov recognizes the existence of a 'progress'. The irony of this situation is absorbed by the incongruity of the presence of this modern item in a room of an old house where the door doesn't fasten properly, obviating any suspicion that Bazarov's comment may be regarded as mere sarcasm. The washstand is one of a series of foreign luxury commodities that appear in the novel, many of them associated with Arkady's uncle, Pavel, who first appears in a suit of English style in that same chapter, who has travelled widely, and who is devotedly cosmopolitan. Pavel is one of the few characters in the novel who proves capable of making a life on his own; but he ends up moving back to Germany. At the level of material culture, the novel poses the question of whether the foreign and the new can really be accommodated in Russia, especially in the vast rural regions. At a personal level it implies that survival and contentment depend upon surrendering some individuality and independence to marriage and family life: the story, eventually, of Arkady, who marries Anna Odintsova's sister, and of Anna herself, who remarries. Those who do make a life on their own, break away and move abroad.

Despite the clear historical and contextual proximity of Turgenev and this novel to the characters, experiences and events of England in the 1850s discussed in the last chapter, the reference in *Fathers and Sons* brings sharply to our attention an entirely new perspective on the complex of literature and material culture considered there. The history and circumstances of Russia provide a completely different context of meaning and effect, as indeed do those of France in a similarly materialistic, contemporary novel set just across the Channel, Gustav Flaubert's *Madame Bovary* of 1856–7. This proves more than a merely nominal representation of the limits to what this study of English literature and archaeology has considered so far, when we recognize how Dickens himself was inspired to move beyond the familiar English and recent-historical frameworks for his novels in *Little Dorrit* (1855–7) and *A Tale of Two Cities* (1859), as, too, George Eliot used early-Renaissance Florence as a figuratively general setting for her *Romola* (1862–3). Those moves seem to embody a recognition by the English novelists of a need to break out of the constraints of the familiar time and place in order to achieve a greater universality of moral comment.

The examples of periods and literature discussed in this book have been selected to emphasize the chronological range over which the integrated study of literature and archaeology can be undertaken. Certain key themes recur throughout the chronological spectrum: how vitally material-cultural allusions or assumptions form the semantic context, and how their recognition thus leads to a fuller comprehension of the text; and how, too, when we perceive the physical setting as a necessary context for the text as speech-act or performance, the literature testifies directly to – indeed is an essential component of – the meaning of the innate, material world. It proves easiest to observe this when the literature can be correlated with substantial changes in historical and material circumstances, although since those are the norm rather than the exception that is not a seriously limiting factor. The artistic use of language in literature, meanwhile, provides many of the richest, most subtle and articulate insights into the meaning of material culture. It shows how the significance of the whole cultural environment is rarely static but was the subject of dramatic negotiation and construction. Altogether, we find literary culture entering into a dialogue with its material circumstances as much as we find it merely rejecting or reflecting them. Through all of this, interdisciplinary cultural historicism should produce genuinely new insights into the past.

It has, one hopes, been so obviously pragmatic an approach to seek to illustrate the case for such interdisciplinarity by following a predictable path through the so-called canon of widely read English literature that that needs no particular apology. We may have deliberately avoided the over-familiar topics of *Beowulf* and Anglo-Saxon royal sites, or medieval romance and medieval castles, but we still have Christian-heroic epic for our Old English examples, and have traced a course through such familiar names as Chaucer, Gower, Shakespeare, Dryden and Dickens. It has not proved possible, consequently, to avoid practically exclusive reference to male authors, and an overwhelmingly London-centred view of English cultural history from the late Middle Ages onwards.

A valid defence of this situation is that it is an accurate reflection of the overall shape of English history across the period from which the selections have been made. To be aware of such biases in the power relations of English history is sufficient, without deliberately challenging the dominance of those interests by seeking out less privileged areas of experience. If there is one potentially misleading point of focus of which acknowledgement really must be made, it may in fact be for the emphasis on the domestic and the mundane in material life that is to be found here: from chapter to chapter, the colonization and settlement of land, architecture, use of space, and household items. This is precisely the domain in which, historically, a female audience and readership, and female characters, are best able to claim an essential place in the cultural history of English literature. Yet there are many other important aspects of material culture, and it is really archaeology that is represented most selectively represented in this book: not the genres of English literature, the fullness of history, or the social spectrum.

If the book does give the impression that we can conceive of English cultural history primarily in terms of the continuing but developing history of households, usually occupied by family units of varying structures, no apology is offered for that in view of the sheer interest of the fact that it can be done. It was not, however, the intention of the book to propose such an idea. It is not intended, for instance, to ignore or belittle the fact that war has impinged directly and seriously on the lives of people in England horribly frequently throughout England's history; and the changing technology of warfare, the history of military organization, and the responses to these experiences would certainly be a valuable area for special consideration. Portraying a difference of geographical context by contrasting England with Russia could also be considered extreme, and even evasive, in light of the scope for looking comparatively at English literature in the non-metropolitan regions of England, in Scotland, Ireland and Wales, where the language has become naturalized at different times and in different circumstances, and across the former British Empire and Commonwealth, in American and 'post-colonial' literatures. Rather than seeking immediately for some kind of ostentatious inclusiveness in those directions, however, one may suggest that a valuable next step would be to redress the urban bias of what has been considered here, and explore an immediately comparable area, by looking at the particular circumstances of rural life. The early-modern pastoral tradition and the cult of the Picturesque, Romanticism, and the novels of Thomas Hardy, exceptional for his desire to explore such experiences in the period of the late 19th-century agricultural depression, offer tempting prospects.

Not that such topics have been entirely omitted, or have passed unnoticed. John Bunyan, not a popular author now with literary scholars and critics, represents a provincial and culturally dissentient voice in later 17th-century literature. By separating the pilgrimage of Christian from that of Christiana and the children, Bunyan also reflects in stark form the issue of gender differentiation and the typically different historical experiences of the two sexes, albeit in a way that few if any modern critics will find at all agreeable. Gender issues have indeed been present throughout this book, from the silent exclusion of the female from the Old English poems discussed, through the sexual dramas at the heart of most of the Middle English literature considered, to the central problematization of the role assigned to the female in *The Winter's Tale* and *Bleak House*. It may be argued that these shifts in the type of attention paid to the issue of sexual difference and gender relations accurately reflect the culturally dependent and therefore historically variable construction of gender. A comparative study of gender experiences and attitudes reflected in literature and archaeology across such a range of periods should therefore be valuable, but it would be a more specialized perspective than this book has set out to present.

It may have been presumptuous to have had such ambitions, but this book has sought to suggest a way of enhancing the experience of reading English literature – perhaps even to bring some new readership to historical English literature – and likewise to introduce or enhance the interest and pleasure of looking at historical buildings and archaeological finds and sites for those who have not hitherto had any particular engagement with them. It has sought to offer specific examples, worked through in as much detail as is feasible here, to show what can be done and how. Much is left untouched. It will be a rewarding endorsement of what has been attempted here if the years to come see an extension of truly interdisciplinary critical studies of culture into those fields, and satisfying enough if the present study serves only to advertise that potential, and can provide a basis for subtler theoretical and methodological approaches to be developed.

Index

representation 7, 93–104, 113, 154
Restoration, The 159, 163
Revard, Carter 78 n.13, 88
Richard II, King 34 n.25, 109–10, 112, 127–8, 129 n.40, 135
Richard's Castle 92
road 45, 166, 178, 202
Roman Period 16, 32, 37–8, 44, 45–50, 67, 69, 81, 164
roman script 41
romance
  medieval and chivalric 44, 71, 95, 98, 103, 117, 125, 143, 207
  prose 78, 139, 143 n.11
Romanticism 31, 202, 208
room 104, 119, 190–1
Round Table, The 105–9, Fig. 10
rubber see polymers
runic script 40–1, 43
rural life and setting 35, 51, 53, 57–8, 80, 83, 85, 92, 128, 148, 156, 191, 200–2, 205–6, 208
  settlement 45, 52, 54, 81, 90, 150
Ruskin, John 203
Russia 205–7
Ruthwell Cross, the 41

salt-making 49, 67
Sapir, Edward, and Benjamin Lee Whorf 33
satire 94–5, 101, 103, 113, 184, 186, 193–4, 203
scholarship 9, 15–17, 22, 135, 144, 148, 156, 160, 176, 198, 208
school 144, 168–9, 185–7, Fig. 14
  of Design 173
science 17, 23, 27–8, 115, 160, 162, 165, 176, 184 n.19, 196, 205
Scotland 10, 41, 42, 138, 207
sculpture 54, 115, 138, 150, 152, 154, 156–7, 174, 181, 199, Table 1
semantics 12–13, 21, 26, 32, 35, 57, 61, 70, 162, 206
semiotics 12
sermon see homily
service block see kitchen
settlement 18, 35, 39, 45–53, 55, 67–8, 81–2, 83, 85, 90–2, 128, 207
  dispersed 52, 81
Shakespeare, William 144–5, 149, 160, 171, 207
  Pericles 136 n.49
  The Winter's Tale 149–58, 208
sheep/goat 49, 90
shield see armour
ship 129, 162, 178, 194
  SS Great Eastern 196–8, Fig. 17
shoes 11–12, 110, 126, 167, 198
shop 11, 124, 165, 178, 187, 192, 203
shrine 112, 125, 137
Shropshire 38, 72, 78, 90, 168–9
Sidney, Sir Philip 139–41, 143, 148
sign 12–13, 19
silkwork 128, Table 1
slum 187, 190–3, 198
social relationship, society 12, 22–3, 31, 33, 34,

36, 40, 50–1, 54, 83, 102, 107, 110, 125, 135, 141, 168, 175, 177, 186, 203–4, 205, 207–8
socialism 4, 30–1, 175
solar 89, 119, 124
song 20, 24, 94, 97, 102, 120, 125, 132–4
Southwark 111, 127, 145–8
  cathedral and priory of St Mary Overie 111–12, 129
  see also inn, theatre
space 2, 4, 90, 113, 117–21, 123–5, 148, 207
spectator see observer
spice 96 n.50, 98, 103–4, 123, 128, 156, 160–1
sport 13–14, 31, 108
stage 118, 146, 149, 151–2, 155, 157–8
statement 11, 13, 113
steam power 177–8, 200–2
steel see iron
Stephenson, George 203
stewe 118, 121
Stokesay Castle 79, 88–91, 101, Fig. 9
stone building 49, 89, 91
stove 139, 141–2
stylus/-i 52, 68
suburb 127, 145, 191
sunken hut 38, 48
Sutton Hoo 29, 51
sword see weaponry
symbolism 11, 12, 19, 32, 106, 109, 139, 141, 195
  see also archaeology, symbolic

taste 173, 176, 182, 191, 193–4, 199, 203
taxation 80, 90, 108, 175, 176, 184
tea 11, 194
technology 4–5, 9, 13, 16, 48, 49, 70, 104, 139, 162–3, 173, 176, 178, 183, 202–3, 207
television 9, 13, 20, 158
temple 38, 47, 118–19, 123, 148
text 6, 20, 23, 27–8, 32–3, 36, 41, 71, 103, 106, 137, 165, 206
  literary 25, 31
  non-literary 25, 33, 41
textile production 68, 86, 91, 109, 133, 174, 177, 180
textuality 33–4, 36, 61, 116, 138, 143, 157–8, 163, 166, 170
theatre 35, 143–9, 154–8
  Globe, the 145–8, 149, 158
  Hope, the 145–6
  Rose, the 145–6
  Swan, the 145–6, Fig. 13
Thomas à Becket, St 86, 112, 137
Thomsen, Christian Jürgen 16
Thorpe, William 114–16, 137–8
tile
  floor 88–9, 91
  roof 90–1
  stove 141, Fig. 12
tile-making 45, 49
timber-frame building 148
time 15, 35, 150, 193, 206